Harlem

A Community in Transition

EDITED BY JOHN HENRIK CLARKE

The Citadel Press/New York

TO MY WIFE EUGENIA

Books by John Henrik Clarke
REBELLION IN RHYME (poetry), 1948

Edited
HARLEM: A COMMUNITY IN TRANSITION, 1964; reprinted 1969
HARLEM U.S.A., 1964
AMERICAN NEGRO SHORT STORIES, 1966
WILLIAM STYRON'S NAT TURNER: TEN BLACK WRITERS RESPOND, 1968
MALCOLM X: THE MAN AND HIS TIME, 1969

Acknowledgment
The material in this book is reprinted with permission from *Freedomways,* a Quarterly Review of the Negro Freedom Movement, published at 799 Broadway, New York, N. Y. 10003.

THIRD PAPERBOUND EDITION, 1970
Copyright © 1964, 1969 by Freedomways Associates, Inc.
All rights reserved
Manufactured in the United States of America
Published by Citadel Press, Inc.
222 Park Avenue South, New York, N. Y. 10003

ISBN 0-8065-0132-4

INTRODUCTION

In the years before the Montgomery Bus Boycott and the rise of the Southern Freedom Movements that initiated the prevailing phase of history known as "The Negro Revolution," Harlem was the nerve center of advancing black America: Harlem is more than a community—it is a city within a city—the most famous ethnic city in the world. Among black communities in the United States, Harlem is unique. It is the only large community of this nature that is not on the "other side" of town. Harlem is located in the heart of Manhattan Island. It is probably the most written about and the least understood community in the world.

Roi Ottley, writing about Harlem in 1943, says: "It is the fountainhead of mass movements. From it flows the progressive vitality of Negro life. Harlem is, as well, a cross section of life in Black America —a little from here, there and everywhere. It is at once the capital of clowns, cults and cabarets, and the cultural and intellectual hub of the Negro world. By turns Harlem is provincial, wordly, cosmopolitan and naive—sometimes cynical. From here, though, the Negro looks upon the world with audacious eyes. . . . To grasp the inner meanings of life in Black America, one must put his finger on the pulse of Harlem."

Claude MacKay, writing about Harlem in 1940, called it a "Negro Metropolis" and added: "Harlem is the most interesting sample of black humanity marching along with white humanity."

James Weldon Johnson, in the 1930's, found it different from any other black settlement in the northern United States cities. He found it an extremely healthy and attractive community and worried whether Negroes would be able to "always hold it as a residential section." Johnson's optimistic view continued: "Harlem is indeed the great mecca for the sightseer, the pleasure-seeker, the curious, the adventurous, the enterprising, the ambitious and the talented of the whole Negro world; for the lure of it has reached down to every island of the Carib Sea and has penetrated into Africa."

Harlem has been called, and may well be, the cultural and intellectual capital of the black race in the Western world. It has also been called other names less complimentary—names like: "a cancer in the heart of a city" . . . and "a large-scale laboratory experiment in the race problem." Some of the most colorful and dynamic personalities in the Negro world have used Harlem as a vantage point, a platform and proving ground for their ideas and ambitions. The "Back to Africa" movement and the more vocal aspects of Black Nationalism found a greater acceptance in Harlem than in any other place. This cannot be understood without some knowledge of how and why Harlem came into being in the first place.

Some time in 1626, when what is now New York City was a Dutch outpost called New Amsterdam, eleven Africans were imported and assigned quarters on the fringe of what is now The Bowery. These black laborers eventually built a wagon road to a place in the upper part of the settlement that the Dutch called "Haarlem." About 274 years passed before Harlem (now spelled with one "a") was changed into a black metropolis.

Eighteen years after their arrival, the eleven Africans petitioned the Dutch authorities, with the support of the rank and file colonists, and were finally granted their freedom. The liberated men, who now had wives, settled in a swamp, known today as Greenwich Village. They built this swamp into a prosperous community and attracted other settlers.

The peaceful relations between the Africans and the white settlers came to an end when the British gained control of New Amsterdam in 1664, and introduced chattel slavery.

In 1741, an African named Caesar led the first slave uprising in New York. In 1799, more than a half century before Lincoln's proclamation, a bill was passed in New York beginning the gradual emancipation of slaves.

Black slaves fought in the American Revolution in large numbers; some of them fought as replacements for their white masters who did not choose to fight.

The first independent act of these slaves after the end of slavery in the North was to break away from the Methodist Episcopal Church and start the African Methodist Episcopal Zion Church. After the

Civil War, Negroes moved further uptown, but they were still a long way from Harlem.

The mass exodus and settlement of Negroes in Harlem started in 1900, after New York's disastrous race riot. One of the spiritual leaders of the movement to Harlem was the Reverend Adam Clayton Powell, Sr., father of the Congressman. The Harlem they came to around 1900 was a cheerful neighborhood of broad streets, brownstone dwellings and large apartment houses. Thoroughbred horses were seen on Lenox Avenue and polo was actually being played at the Polo Grounds.

Bert Williams, the famous actor and comedian and Harry T. Burleigh, the composer, had moved to Harlem ahead of the mass movement. By 1910, the white residents of Harlem were in full flight.

The early Twenties was a time of great change and accomplishment in the Harlem Community. It was the period when Harlem was literally "put on the map." Two events made this possible—a literary movement known as the Harlem Renaissance, and the arrival in Harlem of the magnetic and compelling personality, Marcus Aurelius Garvey.

Among the numerous black Manassehs who presented themselves and their grandiose programs to the people of Harlem, Marcus Garvey was the most tempestuous and flamboyant. Garvey came to the United States from Jamaica, British West Indies, where he was born. He had grown up under a three-way color system—white, mulatto and black. Garvey's reaction to color prejudice and his search for a way to rise above it and lead his people back to Africa, spiritually if not physically, was the all-consuming passion of his existence.

Marcus Garvey's glorious, romantic and riotous movement exhorted the black race and fixed their eyes on the bright star of a future in which they would reclaim and rebuild their African homeland and heritage. Garvey came to the United States as a disciple of Booker T. Washington, founder of Tuskegee Institute. Unfortunately, Booker T. Washington died before Marcus Garvey reached this country. Garvey had planned to raise funds and return to Jamaica to establish an institution similar to Tuskegee. In 1914 he had organized the Universal Negro Improvement Association in Jamaica. After the failure of this organization, he looked to the United States, where he found a loyal group of followers willing to listen to his message.

Garvey succeeded in building a mass movement among American blacks while other leaders were attempting it and doubting that it could be done. He advocated the return of Africa to the Africans and people of African descent. He organized, very rashly and incompetently, the Black Star Line, a steamship company for transporting people of African descent from the United States to Africa. Garvey and his movement had a short and spectacular life span in the United States. His movement took really effective form in about 1921, and by 1926 he was in a Federal prison, charged with misusing the mails. From prison he was deported home to Jamaica. This is, briefly, the essence of the Garvey saga.

The self-proclaimed Provisional President of Africa never set foot on African soil. He spoke no African language. But Garvey managed to convey to members of the black race everywhere (and to the rest of the world) his passionate belief that Africa was the home of a civilization which had once been great and would be great again. When one takes into consideration the slenderness of Garvey's resources and the vast material forces, social conceptions and imperial interests which automatically sought to destroy him, his achievement remains one of the great propaganda miracles of this century.

Garvey's voice reverberated inside Africa itself. The King of Swaziland later told Mrs. Marcus Garvey that he knew the names of only two black men in the Western world: Jack Johnson, the boxer who defeated the white man Jim Jeffries, and Marcus Garvey. From his narrow vantage point in Harlem, Marcus Garvey became a world figure.

While the drama of Marcus Garvey's rise and fall was unfolding in Harlem, another event, less colorful, but equally important, was contributing toward making Harlem the center of racial awakening and literary activity. The period called the Negro Renaissance was reaching its zenith in Harlem. This was the richest and most productive period of Afro-American writing in the United States. The community of Harlem was the center, spiritual godfather and midwife of this renaissance, and the cultural emancipation of the Afro-Americans that began before the first World War was now in full force. The black writers discovered a new voice within themselves and liked the sound of it. The white writers who had been interpreting black American life with an air of authority and a preponderance of error looked at last to the black writer with a degree of respect.

Writers like Jean Toomer, Langston Hughes, Zora Neal Hurston, Rudolph Fisher and Countee Cullen produced a pyramid of imaginative and arresting literature. Strong voices from the West Indian community were heard. The Jamaican writer Claude MacKay finished a group of novels and short stories about his homeland before writing *Home to Harlem,* still the most famous novel ever written about this community.

Early in the Harlem literary renaissance period, the black ghetto became an attraction for a varied assortment of white celebrities and just plain thrill-seeking white people lost from their moorings. Some were insipid rebels, defying the mores of their upbringing by associating with blacks on a socially equal level. Some were too rich to work, not educated enough to teach and not holy enough to preach. Others were searching for the mythological "noble Savage"—the "exotic Negro." Some sophisticated and non-talented would-be black writers took advantage of the white visitors' gullibility and became professional "exotic Negroes."

These professional exotics were generally college-educated blacks who had become estranged from their families and the environment of their upbringing. They talked at length about the great books within them waiting to be written. Their white sponsors continued to subsidize them while they "developed their latent talent." Of course, the "great books" of these camp followers never got written and eventually their white sponsors realized that they were never going to write—not even a good letter.

Concurrently with the unfolding of this mildly funny comedy, the greatest productive period in Afro-American literature continued. The most serious and talented black writers were actually writing their books and getting them published.

The stock market collapse of 1929 marked the beginning of the Depression and the end of the period known as the Negro Renaissance. The "exotic Negro," professional and otherwise, became less exotic now that a hungry look was on his face. The numerous white sponsors and well-wishers who had begun to flock to Harlem ten years before no longer had the time or the money to marvel over black ghetto life. Many Harlemites lived and died in the community during this period without once hearing of the famous literary movement that had flourished and declined within their midst. It was not a mass movement. It was a fad, partly produced in Harlem and partly imposed on Harlem. Most of the writers associated with it would have written just as well at any other time.

In the years following the Harlem Literary Renaissance period, the Harlem community became a land of opportunity for new cultists and their leaders. George Wilson Becton, first of the famous cult leaders to excite the imagination and stir the enthusiasm of the entire Harlem community, died and left the field open to Father Divine, who expanded the domain of his Kingdom of Peace and found a way to feed Harlem's hungry people at a price they could pay.

The insecurity of the Depression years had produced widespread discouragement and apathy in Harlem. The mood of the people called for new leaders, and new leaders appeared—some were false and some were true. In the midst of this era, a young man born of poverty-stricken parents in the cotton fields of Alabama entered the prize-fighting ring of this nation and, figuratively, wrote poetry with his gloved fists. He was soon to be hailed as the greatest prize fighter of this century. His name was Joe Louis. In Harlem and in other black communities, he was the great symbol and the new hope. He lifted the spirit of an entire people and gave them a sense of self-importance.

Many aspects of Afro-American life totally removed from the boxing profession were influenced by the rise of Joe Louis. Dr. Alain Locke, a professor at Howard University, had recorded what he called "the dramatic flowering of a new race-spirit" in the book *The New Negro* (1925). Black scholars rewrote those chapters of history which ignored or minimized the part played by their people. "The American Negro must remake his past in order to make his future," said Arthur A. Schomburg, founder of the famous collection of literature that bears his name.

The economic dislocation of the Harlem community during the depression years motivated in Harlem, and in other black communities, the growth and development of a "Don't Buy Where You Can't Work" movement. The boycott and the picket line became the main weapons in a war against job discrimination. Some groups picketed City Hall and demanded that city agencies change their hiring policies.

In Harlem, and in other northern ghettos, most of the stores servicing the community were owned by whites who did not readily employ people from the community. The campaigns for jobs in these stores brought forth a number of remarkable and often colorful, new leaders. Sufi Abdule Hamid, who had been known in Chicago as Bishop Conshankin, started a new movement for jobs in Harlem. Also in Harlem the Citizens Committee for Fair Play and the Greater New York Coordinating Committee projected new ideas and methods into the fight for jobs. The political career of Adam Clayton Powell had its early development in these campaigns.

J. A. Rogers, lecturer and traveler and once a member of Marcus Garvey's staff of advisors, became the most widely read pamphleteer in Black America. During the Italian-Ethiopian War, J. A. Rogers and another Harlem resident, Dr. Willis N. Huggins, author of a remarkable book, *Introduction to African Civilizations,* were assigned to report and explain this war to the people of African descent in the United States. Dr. Huggins went to Geneva and reported on the League of Nations meetings concerning the Italian-Ethiopian War. J. A. Rogers went to the battlefront in Ethiopia. Both Rogers and Huggins saw behind and beyond the headlines and foretold the future repercussions of Ethiopia's betrayal. Their reports were a highwater mark in Afro-American journalism.

In Harlem and in other communities throughout the nation, the search for the lost African heritage continued.

The political arena in the world's largest black community represents a kind of underdeveloped area dominated, mainly, by messenger boys for the larger and richer political machine bosses in downtown New York City. There are two outstanding exceptions: Benjamin J. Davis, Jr., and Rev. Adam Clayton Powell, Jr.

The political career of Ben Davis started a long way from Harlem, where Adam Clayton Powell grew up. In 1943, under proportional representation, a progressive and democratic form of election, Benjamin J. Davis, Jr. was elected to the New York City Council to fill the seat vacated by Adam Clayton Powell, Jr., who had been elected to Congress. In the City Council, Ben Davis was a thorn in the side of machine politicians who were determined to silence him in order to get him out of the City Council and out of Harlem. Finally, these forces succeeded in bringing down their prey: first, proportional representation was abolished. Before his last term had expired, Davis was barred from the City Council because he had been convicted under the Smith Act.

Then in 1951, the Supreme Court upheld the Smith Act, and Ben Davis and his comrades were sent to prison. In prison, Ben Davis continued his lifelong fight against Jim Crow and second-class citizenship. The long prison term diminished his effectiveness but not his popularity in the Harlem community.

Adam Clayton Powell, Jr. was born into controversy and comfort. For more than thirty years, this self-proclaimed "Disciple of Protest" has been the most colorful and sometimes the most effective politician in black America. He has always been a man who provokes extreme reactions in most people. In Washington, reporters and legislators compete in denouncing him. In Harlem and in other black communities he is the deliverer of the word—spokesman of the black oppressed. As the Congressman from the 18th District in Harlem, he has been the creator of a political mystique and a dramatic enigma. This mystique and this enigma stand in the way of every attempt at making an objective appraisal of the adventurous career of Rev. Adam Clayton Powell.

In the years after the Second World War, Harlem became a community in decline. Many old residents, now successful enough to afford a better neighborhood, moved to Westchester, Long Island or Connecticut. The community leaders who had helped to make Harlem the cultural center of Black America had either died or moved away. Only one black writer of note, Langston Hughes, and two musicians of distinction, Duke Ellington and Lionel Hampton, still lived in Harlem.

Harlem is not a self-contained community. It is owned and controlled by outsiders. It is a black community with a white economic heartbeat. Of the major retail outlets, national chains and local merchants, only a handful are black-owned. In the raging battle for integration and equal job opportunities for blacks, little is heard about the blacks' long fight to gain control of their community. A system of pure economic colonialism exists in the Harlem community. This colonialism extends into politics, religion and every money-making endeavor that touches the life of a Harlem resident.

This kind of exploitation in Harlem, and in other black communities, has helped to produce a phenomenon called Black Nationalism. This phenomenon brings into focus the conflicts, frustrations and crises encountered by Harlem's inhabitants, both outside their immediate environment and among themselves.

For over a half century of Harlem's existence various local groups within the community have been planning and fighting to free the people of this—the world's most famous ghetto—from outside control. The creation of HARYOU-ACT in 1964 made some people of the community believe that this was possible.

The announced objective of the HARYOU-ACT programs was to place persistent emphasis and insistence upon social action rather than dependence upon mere social service. The ultimate goal was to develop in Central Harlem a community of excellence through the concern and initiative of the people of the community.

Three major components of HARYOU-ACT were developed as the vehicles for dynamic social change: The Community Action Institute, The Neighborhood Boards, and Harlem Youth Unlimited. The main functions of these components are to suggest, select and refine the types of services which particular families and individuals might require; and at the same time to provide the training, orientaton, and specific skills necessary for sustained and successful community action.

In the area of political action the intent of HARYOU-ACT was to show the people of Harlem how they can force governmental agencies to respond to their needs. The intent was also to show that this involves knowledge both of the formal political institutions, and of the groups and individuals who, for one reason or another, actually—or might potentially—determine and influence what occurs within the political structure. For Harlem this was meant to be a way of discovering its political self and how to make the most of it.

Unfortunately, the bright dreams of HARYOU-ACT faded before community support could be marshalled behind them. For a number of times the agency was harassed by lengthy investigations that proved nothing of consequence. By the end of 1968 HARYOU-ACT was only a shell of its former self. The community of Harlem was involved in a fight to control its school and to restore some of its lost political prestige.

Harlem, the six-square-mile area in Manhattan's geographical center, containing over half of New York's million-plus black people continues to grow and grapple with its problems. It continues to be a community in transition, searching for its proper place in the Black Revolution.

JOHN HENRIK CLARKE

December 1968

CONTENTS

TALKING ABOUT HARLEM

SYLVESTER LEAKS

I'M TALKING NOW about Harlem: A six square mile festering black scar on the alabaster underbelly of the white man's indifference.

HARLEM: A bastard child, born out of wedlock, baptized in the gut bucket of life, midwifed by oppression and fathered by racial hate, circumscribed by fear and guilt-ridden detractors.

HARLEM: A hot hearted, generously kind, and jovial black woman, whose blood-sucked veins are a playground, whose skinned and scarred, bruised and battered, used and tattered, seduced and raped body is a privileged sanctuary for that unholy trinity of rent gouging land-lords, graft grabbing cops, and usurious loan sharks; for silver tongued pimps and phony prophets, thieving politicians and vendors of sex and religion, fake healers and fortune tellers and atrocious peddlers of narcotics and death.

HARLEM: Whose expansive bosom is nestling place, hiding place, haven and hell, for her three hundred thirty-six thousand, three hundred sixty-four black and brown, tan and yellow children—thirty-one per cent of whom are either separated, widowed or divorced. And no matter how full her house gets she never refuses them a helping hand, never scorns, never complains, is always understanding.

HARLEM: Here slum life is the total sum of life for so many thousands of her children, with only fifty per cent of the children under eighteen years old living with both parents; here forty-nine per cent of the dwelling units is dilapidated, twenty-five per cent is over-crowded; here the average *family* income approximates $3,723, whereas statistics show the average family needs $6,000 just to make ends meet.

HARLEM: Here nine thousand eight hundred and eighty jobless souls exist, with no State Unemployment Office in the community to serve them; here twelve thousand, four hundred and fifty-four receive public assistance; here women constitute forty-eight per cent of the

13

labor force, twenty-five per cent of them married; four and a half per cent have children under six years of age.

HARLEM: A dingy-dirty cluster of roach crawling, rat infested brownstones and tenement flats, interspersed here and there with housing projects, creating a bizarre effect; here the birth rate is twenty-six per thousand, the death rate thirteen per thousand; here juvenile delinquency has escalated to one hundred thirty-five per thousand; from here came fifteen per cent of admissions to mental hospitals in 1957.

HARLEM: Here one hundred twenty-five thousand church members raise their voices in prayers and songs in two hundred fifty-six churches, imploring unknown gods for surcease to their man-made plights; while some of their ministers drive flashy cars and live in fancy homes, misery stalks the street and the blues is the only antidote to atavistic pain.

HARLEM: A lucrative colony for white retail merchants, whose three thousand eight hundred ninety-eight retail stores produce an annual gross sale of $345,871,000—exclusive of doctors, lawyers, undertakers, insurance, rent, utilities, dry cleaners, etc. While little, if any, of this wealth is left in the community for improvement. Most, if not all, of these merchants live in neighborhoods where black folks can't live, even if they could afford it.

HARLEM: Here the lust for life is infectious; one feels its accelerating rhythm and demoniacal beat of life the moment he enters the enfolding confines of her streets; here $34,368,000 worth of liquor is purchased annually in one hundred sixty-eight liquor stores, exclusive of the untold millions spent in bars. And the unpretentious purchasers thumb up their noses at their maligners and shout to the top of their voices, "It ain't nobody's business if I do!"

HARLEM: The home of Sugar Hill—but minus the dollar bills now; of City College and Lewisohn Stadium and its yearly concerts which every man can afford; The Grange (Alexander Hamilton's home); Schomburg Library, with its more than thirty-seven thousand volumes of material by and about black folks—the largest in the world; of Jumel Mansion (George Washington's Revolutionary War headquarters); of Delano Village, Lenox Terrace, Morningside Garden Cooperative, Bowery Savings Bank apartments, with their high rents which most of Harlem can't afford. Here one sees black knots of humanity on the street corners every day around 5:00 in the evening, waiting breathlessly and hopefully for the last number. And when the news is learned one hears subdued and oftentimes explosive imprecations from the unfortunate, as they dejectedly walk away.

Although I'm talking about you, dear Harlem, I love you just the same—with your woes and all, ills and all, laughter and all, your troubles and all. For I see in you a profound beauty, manifested by your ceaseless struggles to mold and fashion something good and meaningful out of it all, in spite of it all; in your Senior Choirs competing with the Usher Boards to see which will raise the most money for "the building fund"; in your picket lines, protesting this and demanding that; in your fifty-four social agencies, serving fifty-five thousand souls; in your pouring over books in libraries, unlocking the portals of knowledge; in NAACP meetings, planning legal assaults on the ramparts of jim crow; in the black Muslim Temple, demanding some of this good earth for ourselves; in the African Nationalist street meetings on Seventh Avenue and 125th Street, with the speaker exhorting his listeners to "buy black" and reminding them that "when you mess with the dollar, the white man will holler"; in the Negro American Labor Council, struggling to get us some jobs.

And, yes, I love the way you relax and enjoy life; twisting at Smalls on Wednesday nights, dancing at Rockland Palace and the Audubon Ballroom, the Renaissance and Connie's on Fridays, Saturdays, and Sunday nights; giving cocktail sips, teas, readings, fashion shows, beaux arts balls; forming a line a block long to see Jackie Wilson "work out" at the Apollo and to hear Moms Mabley say, "I got somp'n to tell ya" and explode in uninhibited laughter. You are a black wonder, Harlem. You survived.

The statistics on economics are from: *The Uptown Chamber of Commerce;* Statistics on social factors are from: *Harlem—Upper Manhattan,* a survey made by The Protestant Council of the City of New York.

HARLEM:
THE MAKING OF A GHETTO

GILBERT OSOFSKY

"It is evident to the most superficial observer that the centre of fashion, wealth, culture, and intelligence, must, in the near future, be found in the ancient and honorable village of Harlem. . . ."—*The Harlem Monthly Magazine,* 1893.

"The colored people are in Harlem to stay, and they are coming each year by the thousands."—John M. Royall, Negro realtor, 1914.

IN THE LAST THREE DECADES of the nineteenth century Harlem was a community of great expectations.* During the previous half-century it had been an isolated, poor, rural village inhabited largely by squatters who lived in cottages pieced together with any material that could be found—bits of wood, twigs, barrel staves, old pipes, tin cans hammered flat. The community was now, however, being transformed into an upper- and upper-middle-class suburb—New York's first suburb.

The phenomenal growth of Harlem in the late nineteenth century was a by-product of the general development of New York City. From the 1870's on, the foundations of the modern metropolis were laid. This urban revolution was characterized by improvements in methods of transportation, sanitation, water supply, communication, lighting and building. As the city expanded, so did its population. In 1880, for the first time in its history (and in the history of any American city), the population of Manhattan alone passed the one million mark (1,164,673). This increase in population coincided with an expansion of business and industrial activity; both made serious inun-

* This article is a brief sketch of some of the important factors that helped make Harlem a Negro community. For a full-length study of this subject, including the documentation for all the points mentioned here, see Gilbert Osofsky, *Harlem, The Making of a Ghetto: A History of Negro New York, 1900-1920* (Ph.D. dissertation, Columbia University, 1963); and "Race Riot, 1900: A Study of Ethnic Violence," *The Journal of Negro Education,* Vol. XXIII, No. 1 (Winter 1963), pp. 16-24. The word "Negro" has been capitalized where contemporary sources failed to do so.

dations on living quarters in formerly staid residential areas of the island. Many New Yorkers, attempting to avoid the bustle of the new metropolis and escape contact with its newest settlers, looked to Harlem as the community of the future: "In our family, we were careful to explain that we lived in Harlem, not in New York City," recalled a man whose family moved uptown in these years. "It was our way of avoiding contact with such uncouth citizens as might be found downtown. . . ." Harlem was to become "the choicest residential section in the city," remembered a man who settled there in the 1880's.

One great barrier to Harlem's development in the early nineteenth century had been its distance from lower Manhattan. Between 1878 and 1881, however, three lines of the elevated railroad reached 129th Street; by 1886 they had come even further north. From this point on Harlem's growth was amazing. Rows of brownstones and exclusive apartment houses appeared overnight: "Business grows, blocks and flats go up with apparently so little effort, that the average Harlemite is in a continuous swim of development and prosperity," editorialized the white *Harlem Local Reporter* in 1890. Practically all the houses that stand in Harlem today were built in a spurt of energy that lasted from the 1870's through the first decade of the twentieth century. The old shanties were doomed by "the wilderness of brownstone, brick and mortar. . . ." A man who had lived in Harlem since the 1840's saw a "one horse town . . . turned into a teeming metropolis."

Older and wealthier Manhattanites ("people of taste and wealth") were attracted to this new "residential heaven." In a society whose working-class families paid an average of $10-$18 a month rent, the rents for one group of apartments in Harlem in the 1890's *started* at just under $80 a month, and ranged between $900 and $1700 a year.

The homes of municipal and federal judges, mayors, local politicos, and prominent businessmen were scattered throughout Harlem. Their children could attend Grammar School 68, "referred to as the 'Silk Stocking School' of the City [because] the pupils were practically all from American families, and . . . more or less prosperous people." Young girls could go to "Mme. De Valencia's Protestant French and English Institute for Young Ladies." Local citizens, after attending a performance at the Harlem Opera House (built in 1889), might dine at the luxurious Pabst Harlem: "where gentlemen and ladies can enjoy good music and a perfect cuisine amid surroundings which have been rendered as attractive to the eye and senses [as] good taste, combined with lavish expenditure, could make them." Late nineteenth century Harlem was able to support a monthly literary magazine, a weekly magazine of local affairs and a bi-weekly newspaper. It certainly promised to be a vital, ever-growing, genteel community. Its future seemed boundless.

To the generation who remembered only this Harlem, who had never known the Harlem of squatters and shanties, its memory remained warm and bright. Few would have disagreed with the editor of *The Harlem Monthly Review* who saw Harlem developing as a "district . . . distinctly devoted to the mansions of the wealthy, the homes of the well-to-do, and the places of business of the tradespeople who minister their wants. . . ." "We have no adequate idea of . . . the greatness that lies in store for Harlem," thought another resident in 1890.

land speculation in Harlem

A few factors combined to alter Harlem life radically in the first decade of the twentieth century. Underlying them all was a wave of speculation in Harlem land and property that was set off by the construction of new subway routes into the neighborhood in the late 1890's. Land that had been left unimproved or undeveloped at that time— marshes, garbage dumps, empty lots—were bought up by speculators who intended to make astronomic profits when the subway was completed. Between 1898 and 1904, the year that the Lenox Avenue line was opened at 145th Street, "practically all the vacant land in Harlem [was] built over. . . ." "The growth of . . . Harlem . . . has been truly astonishing during the last half dozen years," commented a leading real estate journal in 1904.

It was taken as business gospel that investments would be doubled and trebled when the "tunnel road" was completed: "Even a 5-story single flat in Harlem would net . . . at the end of . . . three to five years . . . at the utmost . . . a very handsome unearned increment." A supposed expert in New York real estate concluded that no "other class of public improvements had such a great, immediate and permanent effect upon land values as rapid transit lines. . . ."

"The existing speculation in flats and tenements," wrote another observer, "surpasses . . . anything of the kind which has previously taken place in the real estate history of the city."

In West Harlem, along Seventh Avenue and Lenox Avenue in the 130's and 140's ("the best of Harlem," it was called), luxurious apartment houses were built. It was believed, in keeping with the traditions of the neighborhood, that West Harlem would be inhabited by richer people who wanted "high-class flats," "costly dwellings," and who earned enough money to afford them. Many of these buildings were equipped with elevators (then first being installed in better houses), maid's rooms and butler's pantries. In 1899 William Waldorf Astor erected an apartment house on Seventh Avenue which cost $500,000. Sunday real estate sections of New York City newspapers at the turn of the century bristled with full-page advertisements and pictures of the elegant homes in this part of Harlem. The building activity of these years created the physical foundations for what became, initially, the loveliest Negro ghetto in the world.

Speculation in West Harlem property at the turn of the century led to phenomenal increases in the price of land and the cost of houses there—increases inflated out of all proportion to their real value. John M. Royall, Negro realtor, recalled that from "1902 to 1905 real estate speculative fever seized all New York City. The great subway proposition . . . permeated the air. Real estate operators and speculators [imagined] becoming millionaires, and bought freely in the West Harlem district in and about the proposed subway stations. Men bought property on thirty and sixty day contracts, and sold their contracts . . . and made substantial profits. I have known buyers to pay $38,000 and $75,000 for tenements which showed a gross income of only $2,600 and $5,000 a year. On they went buying, buying. . . . [Houses] had been continually changing hands." Each time a building was sold it brought a higher price. In the urge to get rich quick on Harlem property few persons realized how artificial market values had become.

The inevitable "bust" came in 1904-1905. Speculators sadly realized afterward that too many houses had been constructed at one time. Harlem had been glutted with apartments and "excessive building . . . led to many vacancies." No one knew just how long it would take to construct the subway and many apartment houses had been built four and five years before it was completed. Some of these homes remained largely unoccupied. The first of them to be inhabited by Negroes, for example, had never been rented previously. Rents were too high for the general population ($35-$45 per month) and precluded any great rush to Harlem even after the subway was completed. There was, remembered one man, a widespread "overestimation of rental values" at first. When the market broke, landlords competed with each other for tenants by cutting rents or by offering a few months rent-free occupancy to them. Some local business groups attempted to get landlords to stabilize rental values, but this movement had little success. The formerly inflated prices asked for land and property in

Harlem "solemnly settled beneath a sea of depreciated values."

coming of the Negro population

The individuals and companies that were caught in Harlem's rapidly deflated real estate market were threatened with financial ruin. Rather than face destruction, some landlords and corporations were willing to rent their houses to Negroes and collect the traditionally high rents that colored people paid. Others, instead of accepting their losses, used the threat of bringing in Negro tenants to frighten their neighbors into buying them out at a higher than market price. Shrewder operators (present day realtors call them "blockbusters") hoped to take advantage of the unusual situation by "placing colored people in property so that they might buy other parcels adjoining or in the same block [reduced in price by] fear on the part of the whites to one-half of the values then obtaining." By using these techniques "a great number" of property owners were able "to dispose of their property or . . . get a . . . more lucrative return from rents paid by colored tenants." Negroes, offered decent living accommodations for the first time in the city's history, "flocked to Harlem and filled houses as fast as they were opened to them."

But not all property owners in the neighborhood were ready to open their houses to Negroes. It seemed unbelievable to some that theirs, one of the most exclusive sections in the entire city, should become the center of New York's most depressed and traditionally worst-housed people. Some owners banded together in associations to repulse what they referred to as the Negro "invasion" or the Negro "influx." The language they used to describe the movement of Negroes into Harlem (the word "invasion," for example, appeared in almost all denunciations of Negroes) was the language of war.

In the 1880's and 1890's Harlemites annually celebrated the historic Revolutionary Battle of Harlem Heights. These patriotic fetes were symbols of community pride, and pamphlets were widely distributed informing the neighborhood of all the organizations and dignitaries that participated in them. In the early twentieth century, however, Harlem's residents gathered, not to preserve the memory of a Revolutionary conflict, but to fight their own battle—to keep their neighborhood white.

The formal opposition to Negro settlement in Harlem centered in a number of local associations of landlords. Some were committees representing individual blocks, others were community-wide in structure. Between 1907 and 1915, the last year in which there was signifi-

cant organized opposition to Negro settlement, a number of protective associations were founded. Property owners on West 140th, 137th,
136th, 135th, 131st, 130th, 129th Streets (in descending order as the
Negro community spread southward) , and along the avenues, signed
agreements according to which each swore not to rent his apartments
to Negroes for ten or fifteen years—till when, it was thought, "this
situation . . . referred to . . . will have run its course": "The premises,
land, and building of which we . . . are the owners . . . shall not be
used as a . . . Negro tenement, leased to colored . . . tenants, sold to
colored . . . tenants . . . or all [other] persons of African descent."
"Each of the parties," reads another agreement, "does hereby covenant
and agree [not] to . . . hereafter . . . cause to be suffered, either directly or indirectly, the said premises to be used or occupied in whole
or in part by any Negro, quadroon, or octoroon of either sex whatso-
ever. . . ." Some covenants even put a limitation on the number of Negro janitors, bellboys, laundresses and servants that could be employed
in a home.

Following a pseudo-legal procedure which was supposed to make
these agreements binding, each signer paid all the others a fee of one
dollar. The finished products were notarized and filed at the County
Clerk's Office in the New York City Hall of Records (where they can
be read today) . The streets covered by such restrictive codes were
known in the Negro community as Covenant Blocks, and Negroes
took pride in being the first colored landlords or tenants to live in
them ("to knock [the covenants] into a cocked hat," said one) .

Other community groups led by white realtors tried to hold back
the Negro's "steady effort to invade Harlem." (One realty company
dealing in upper-Manhattan property was called the Anglo-Saxon
Realty Corporation.) These people formed such organizations as the
Harlem Property Owners' Protective Association, the Committee of
Thirty, the Harlem Property Owners' Improvement Corporation and
the West Side Improvement Association. Each group planned to
arouse the interest of all white Harlemites in "the greatest problem
that Harlem has had to face." Meetings were held and programs introduced which proposed the eviction of all Negroes already in Harlem or, failing this, at least to prevent the further sale and rental of
property to Negroes. A propaganda war was waged as "White Only"
signs were hung in the windows of Harlem apartment houses. Adver-
tisements were printed in the white *Harlem Magazine* asking all property owners to join the movement: "WILL YOU HELP YOURSELF?"; "HELP
PROTECT YOUR PROPERTY."

21

Negro realtors were contacted and told they would be wasting their time trying to find houses on certain streets: "We herewith resolve that every colored real estate broker be notified as to the following: That the owners of this section have unanimously agreed not to rent their houses for colored tenancy. . . ." Like an enemy negotiating a line of truce, the Committee of Thirty called a meeting of Negro real estate men to try to draw a voluntary boundary line that would permanently separate the white and Negro communities. Four members of Harlem's Church of the Puritans (white) attended meetings of the New York Presbytery to protest the proposed movement of St. James Presbyterian Church (Negro) into the neighborhood. Others called on city fathers to try to prevent the licensing of a Negro-owned movie house on Lenox Avenue. The Lafayette Theater, on Seventh Avenue, permitted Negroes to sit only in its balcony. People who signed restrictive covenants and subsequently broke them were brought into court.

All these movements failed. That it was necessary to found so many different organizations in a relatively short period of time was a reflection of the general failure of each. Racially restrictive housing covenants were unconstitutional and, although at least one person was sued, no one was ever convicted of violating them. Negro realtors, like John M. Royall, ridiculed the proposal for a voluntary line of segregation as an agreement to "capitalize on prejudice" and "a joke." In spite of the protests of Harlemites ("Can nothing be done to put a restriction on the invasion of the Negro into Harlem?"), St. James Church was permitted to move into the area and was even granted a large loan to build a new church. In 1913 the Lafayette Theater was sold to promoters who realized that it was foolish to run a segregated theater in "what is destined to become a colored neighborhood." The new owners opened their doors to Negroes (*"our doors are open to all"*), and even contributed regularly to Negro charities. The large basement of the building in which the theater was housed, Lafayette Hall, was later leased as a temporary armory to Harlem's Negro national guard unit. In 1919, the entire building, including the theater, was sold to a group of Negro businessmen. In the twenties, the Lafayette was noted for its fine troupe of Negro actors.

The basic cause for the collapse of all organized efforts to exclude the Negro from Harlem was the inability of any group to gain total and unified support of all white property owners in the neighborhood —and without such support it was impossible to organize a successful neighborhood-wide anti-Negro movement. Landlords forming associations by blocks had a difficult enough time trying to keep people on individual streets united. Nor was it possible—and this is the major point—to create a well-organized, well-financed movement of Negro restriction (one plan called for the contribution of one-half of one per cent of the assessed valuation of all property to a community fund) in the disrupted and emotional atmosphere that pervaded Harlem in the first two decades of the twentieth century. The very setting in which whites were confronted with Negro neighbors for the first time led to less than level-headed reasoning.

The first impulse of many whites was to sell out at whatever price their property would bring and move elsewhere. Realtors called this "panic selling" and, in spite of efforts to prevent it, it went on. Between 1907 and 1914 two-thirds of the houses in or near the Negro section were sold—practically all at substantial losses to the original owners. Since the already weak real estate market was flooded with property in a short time, and only a relatively few Negroes were wealthy enough to buy ("there was no market for real estate among the newcomers"), prices continued to depreciate rapidly: "realty values have tumbled by leaps and bounds." In the 1870's and 1880's fortunes were made from soaring Harlem land prices; by 1917 white realtors tried to encourage interest in the neighborhood by advertising how cheap property had become: "Changes in the character of Harlem population," wrote a member of the white Harlem Board of Commerce, have led "to remarkable bargains, both for rental and purchase. ... Such properties in good condition can now be purchased at less than the assessed value of the land alone."

The minority of Harlem landlords who tried to adhere to their original restrictive covenants suffered serious economic consequences. Many were unable to find white people willing to rent their apartments. To encourage white tenants already in them to remain, some were forced to reduce rents drastically: "The introduction of Negro tenants ... has caused ... many white tenants to move and [has] required a substantial reduction of rents to those who remained," complained a group of Harlem landlords in 1907. Those who had mortgage payments to meet were threatened with foreclosure by banks and other lending institutions, and many found it "impossible ... to hold out." The opponents of Negro settlement were faced with the dilemma of maintaining a "White Only" policy and probably losing everything, or renting to Negroes (at higher prices) and surviving. Most chose what seemed to them the lesser of two evils, and published or posted such revealing notices as this one which appeared in 1916:

"We have endeavored for some time to avoid turning over this house to colored tenants, but as a result of . . . rapid changes in conditions . . . this issue has been forced upon us."

Harlem: a unique community

The creation of Negro Harlem was only one example of the general development of large, segregated Negro communities in many American cities in the years preceding and following World War I. That Harlem became the specific center of Negro population was the result of circumstance; that some section of the city was destined to become a Negro neighborhood was the inevitable consequence of the migration of southern Negroes to New York City. Harlem was New York's equivalent of the Negro ghettos of the nation. "Niggertowns," "Buzzard's Alleys," "Nigger Rows," "Black Bottoms," "Smoketowns," "Bronzevilles," and "Chinch-Rows," had emerged elsewhere by 1913. "There is growing up in the cities of America a distinct Negro world," wrote Urban League director George Edmund Haynes in that year. These were neighborhoods "isolated from many of the impulses of the common life and little understood by the white world. . . ."

Of all the Negro ghettos, however, Harlem was unique. Its name was a symbol of elegance and distinction, not derogation; its streets and avenues were broad, well-paved, clean and tree-lined, not narrow and dirty; its homes were spacious, replete with the best of modern facilities, "finished in high-style." Harlem was not a slum, but an ideal place in which to live. For the first time in the history of New York City, Negroes were able to live in decent homes in a respectable neighborhood ("the best houses that they have ever had to live in") : "It is no longer necessary for our people to live in small, dingy, stuffy tenements," editorialized a Negro newspaper in 1906. Harlem was "a community in which Negroes as a whole are . . . better housed than in any other part of the country," concluded an Urban League report in 1914. "Those of the race who desire to live in grand style, with elevator, telephone and hall boy service, can now realize their cherished ambition."

Practically every major Negro institution moved out of its downtown quarters and came to Harlem by 1920: churches, insurance companies, small businesses, real estate firms, fraternal orders, settlement houses, social service agencies, the YMCA and YWCA, branches of the Urban League and NAACP. The "Fighting Fifteenth," Harlem's Negro national guard unit, was outfitted in 1916. Harlem's first Negro assemblyman was elected in 1917. Harlem Hospital hired its first

Negro nurses and a Negro doctor in 1919. P.S. 89, on Lenox Avenue (three-quarters Negro by 1915), opened a night school, reading rooms and a community center to keep Negro children off the streets. P.S. 68, the former "Silk Stocking School," became noted for its regular skirmishes between white and Negro pupils.

The community that had been advertised as a place of exclusive residence in the 1890's was now claimed to be the perfect area in which to locate factories. Land was cheap, it was argued, transportation was good, and the neighborhood was full of unskilled, lower-income families willing to accept any kind of employment. The heterogeneity of Harlem's population was then seen to be one of its principal assets: "Only 17 per cent of its people are native white of native parents," concluded a survey of the Harlem Board of Commerce in 1917. "Racial colonization shows distinctly." Parades were held on local streets to stimulate public interest in Harlem's business and industrial opportunities. The merchants adjusted as best they could to new conditions while those who remembered the expectations of previous generations sadly moved away: "Harlem has been devastated as a result of the steady influx of Negroes," bemoaned an old resident in 1913. The "best of Harlem was gone," thought another in the same year, and it "will be all colored in ten years."

In 1914 Negroes lived in at least 1100 different houses within a twenty-three block area of Harlem. The Negro population of Harlem was then conservatively estimated at just under 50,000—the entire Negro population of Manhattan in 1910 had been 60,534. By 1920 the section of Harlem bordered by 130th Street on the south, 145th Street on the north and west of Madison and Fifth Avenues to Eighth Avenue was predominately Negro—and inhabited by some 80,000 people. As the immigrants (Italians and Jews) who lived in surrounding areas moved to better quarters in other boroughs in the 1920's, their homes were filled by Negroes. The Negro section remained and expanded as the other ethnic ghettos disintegrated. By 1930 Negro Harlem had reached its southern limit, 110th Street—the northern boundary of Central Park. Its population was then approximately 200,000. Harlem became the "largest colony of colored people, in similar limits, in the world." And so it remains to this day.

THE LITERATURE OF HARLEM

ERNEST KAISER

O NE WAY of getting at the diverse and myriad writings about the tremendous community of Harlem in New York City is the chronological approach. In this way, the literary and sociological materials can be correlated, to some extent, with the social and economic changes over the decades of this Negro city within a city.

Harlem as a Negro community began around 1900. As early as 1912, the Negro sociologist, scholar and a founder of the Urban League, George Edmund Haynes, did a doctoral dissertation, *The Negro at Work in New York City; a Study in Economic Progress,* published by Columbia University, which included Harlem. James Weldon Johnson's early novel *The Autobiography of an Ex-Coloured Man,* also published in 1912, embraced New York City but did not touch the Negro community. A rather early publication of the National Urban League, founded in 1911, was a pamphlet report *Housing Conditions Among Negroes in Harlem, New York City* in January 1915. Another early piece specifically on the new and growing Harlem community was Rev. Charles Martin's article *The Harlem Negro* in *The A.M.E. Zion Quarterly Review* (Fourth Quarter, 1916).

But Harlem really got its first sizeable population influx and growth from the first great migrations of southern Negroes north during and after World War I. Between 1915 and 1925, over a million Negroes moved north. Rural Negroes flocked to Harlem in the twenties, says Margaret Just Butcher in her book *The Negro in American Culture* (1956) based on materials left by the late Dr. Alain Locke. Several things important to Negro culture generally and to Harlem culture in particular occurred around this period. The pioneering and prolific Negro cultural and social chronicler, Benjamin Brawley, brought out his *The Negro in Literature and Art in the United States* in 1910 with another edition following in 1918. The NAACP magazine *Crisis,* founded in 1910 in New York City and edited by Dr. W. E. B.

Du Bois (who earlier, in 1903, had brought out his literary classic, *The Souls of Black Folk*), was publishing poetry, fiction and essays by Negro writers. Charles S. Johnson of the National Urban League began editing in 1923 that organization's new magazine *Opportunity: Journal of Negro Life* which was also a literary as well as a sociological organ for Negroes. *Crisis* and *Opportunity* prizes for creative expression were announced in 1924 and continued for several years. In these two New York magazines a literary movement had gathered momentum.

literature of early nineteen hundreds

James Weldon Johnson's book of poems *Fifty Years and Other Poems* containing *O Black and Unknown Bards* appeared in 1917 and his pioneering anthology *The Book of American Negro Poetry* appeared in 1922. The first edition of the Negro historian Carter G. Woodson's *The Negro in Our History* was published in 1922. He had already founded the *Journal of Negro History* in 1916. Claude McKay, a young poet who had come from Jamaica in the West Indies to America to study at Tuskegee Institute in 1912 and whose great poem *If We Must Die* appeared in the magazine *The Liberator* in 1919 about the time of the murderous Chicago and Washington (D.C.) race riots, published his powerful book of poetry about social and economic injustice *Harlem Shadows* also in 1922. Jean Toomer, that wonderfully talented, poetic Negro writer, startled literary America with his book *Cane*, a collection of sketches, short stories and poems in 1923. Jessie Fauset, a Negro woman novelist concerned with the Negro middle class, published her first book *There Is Confusion* in 1924. W. E. B. Du Bois, whose book *Darkwater*, published in 1919, contained his passionate poem *A Litany of Atlanta* about the terrible Atlanta (Ga.) riot of 1906, brought out *The Gift of Black Folk*, a book of historical and cultural essays, in 1924. (John Henrik Clarke's essay *Transition in the American Negro Short Story* [*Phylon*, 4th quarter, 1960] should be mentioned here as quite good in giving the literary backdrop as well as a vivid description of the Harlem Renaissance.)

This was the background for the assorted anthology of Negro creative and historical writing, *The New Negro,* edited by Alain Locke and published in 1925. With the publication of this book, as all of the voluminous writings on the Harlem Renaissance period of the 1920's have pointed out, Harlem as a cultural and pulsating community really came into its own. *The New Negro* used the special number of *Survey Graphic* titled *Harlem: Mecca of the New Negro* (also edited by Alain Locke in 1925) as its nucleus and enlarged the Negro Renaissance to its national and international scope. A large portion of the poetry, fiction and essays of *The New Negro* was either about Harlem or written by Harlem authors. Harlem was the cultural capital where the New Negro, whom this volume documented socially and culturally, lived. This interpretation of the Harlem Renaissance became a landmark of the movement. The largest Negro community in the world became a subject and theme for poets, novelists, essayists, painters, sculptors and musicians, Negro and white. Harlem began to have an impact upon the national American culture.

Many other books either about Harlem or by Harlem writers were published in 1925 and after as the New Negro movement burgeoned to full flower. Countee Cullen, the lyrical and technically dazzling Harlem poet published *Color* which won great critical acclaim in 1925. Other Cullen books of poetry were *The Ballad of the Brown Girl* and *Copper Sun* in 1927 and *The Black Christ* in 1929. His novel about Harlem, *One Way to Heaven,* appeared in 1932. Cullen served as assistant editor of the magazine *Opportunity* and in 1927 edited *Caroling Dusk,* an anthology of verse by Negroes. Charles S. Johnson, the editor of *Opportunity,* brought out *Ebony and Topaz* (1927), an anthology of writings by about twenty young unknown Negro writers: poets, social scientists and journalists (also Negro artists) such as Langston Hughes, Sterling Brown, Arna Bontemps, Abram Harris, Zora Neale Hurston, Frank Horne, E. Franklin Frazier, Ira De A. Reid and George Schuyler. In this same year 1927, the New York Urban League issued a short study and interpretation of the living conditions of small Harlem wage earners titled *Twenty-Four Hundred Negro Families in Harlem,* and Ira De A. Reid published his article *Mirrors of Harlem—Investigations and Problems of America's Largest Colored Community* (*Social Forces,* June 1927) dealing with the growth of Harlem, its employment, health and housing problems.

The Long Island University English professor Eugene Arden's article *The Early Harlem Novel* (*Phylon,* 1st quarter, 1959) points to Paul Laurence Dunbar's naturalistic novel *The Sport of the Gods* (1902), about Negro migrants in urban New York, as the first novel to treat Negro life in New York seriously and at length. But, as Arden says, Dunbar's novel borrowed from the despicable white plantation-school writers in whose novels the north destroyed the Negro migrants who yearned for the south. The Negroes Dunbar wrote about were not in Harlem then, but down near the Pennsylvania Station, on San Juan Hill (West 64th Street) or in West 53rd Street. The Negroes in these Manhattan areas were written about in Mary White Ovington's article *The Negro Home in New York*. This piece, by a social worker and a founder of the NAACP, appeared in a special number (Oct 7, 1905) of the early magazine *Charities* (later to become *Survey Midmonthly*, the twin publication of *Survey Graphic*) titled *The Negro in the Cities of the North*.

The white writer Carl Van Vechten, Prof. Arden says further, expressed the indebtedness of his novel *Nigger Heaven* (1926, paperbacked in 1951) to Dunbar's *The Sport of the Gods* in the Introduction Van Vechten wrote to the 1927 edition of James Weldon Johnson's novel *The Autobiography of an Ex-Coloured Man* (paperbacked in 1948). Van Vechten, says Arden, as well as Claude McKay, Rudolph Fisher, Wallace Thurman and Countee Cullen were all following Dunbar. *Nigger Heaven* attempted to describe the Harlem urban Negro in human, realistic terms rather than as a stereotype. But its unfortunate title, its emphasis on the flamboyant and exotic, and the dissolute Negro life and characters it depicted led to severe Negro criticism of the book. Nevertheless, several Negro writers did imitate Van Vechten's novel in one way or another.

Claude McKay's naturalistic, primitive novel *Home to Harlem*, published in 1928 (paperbacked in 1951), and six of his twelve sexy, exotic short stories in the book *Gingertown* (1932) that were about Harlem, show Van Vechten's influence. The Negro writer Rudolph Fisher's novels *The Walls of Jericho* (1928) and *The Conjure-Man Dies* (1932) and his short stories give the lighter side of Harlem also in the realistic, satiric tradition. Another satiric Negro author who wrote about Harlem was Wallace Thurman whose article *Negro Life in New York's Harlem* appeared originally in the *Haldeman-Julius Quarterly* (Oct.-Nov.-Dec. 1924) and was published in 1928 as a 64-page Little Blue Book (No. 494) edited by E. Haldeman-Julius. In this booklet, the author describes the 200,000 Negro population of Harlem at that time, the social life, the Negro church, the Negro journalism and the New Negro in Harlem. Thurman wrote the novels *The Blacker the Berry* (1929) and *Infants of the Spring* (1932) and a highly sensational play *Harlem* (written in collaboration with W. J. Rapp) which had a successful run on Broadway also in 1929. He also helped found the short-lived Harlem magazines of this period *Fire* and *Harlem*.

The winner of the first prize in the *Opportunity* poetry contest of 1925 was Langston Hughes. His poetry books of this period, *The Weary Blues* (1926), *Fine Clothes to the Jew* (1927) and other books, dealt in part with Harlem, celebrated Negro beauty, and expressed race pride, a romantic interest in Africa and Negro history—all important ideas in the New Negro movement. The Negro woman novelist Nella Larsen's two books *Quicksand* (1928) and *Passing* (1930) describe upper-class Negro life in Harlem especially passing for white. The novels of Jessie Fauset, *Plum Bun* (1928), *The Chinaberry Tree* (1931) and *Comedy, American Style* (1933), and those of Walter White, *Fire in the Flint* (1925) and *Flight* (1928), though not specifically about Harlem, were authored by Negro writers who spent some time in New York City and therefore belong to the New Negro movement. T. B. Campbell's novel *Black Sadie* (1928) was a terribly stereotyped white southerner's attempt to debunk the Harlem of the twenties. Maxwell Bodenheim's naturalistic novel *Naked on Roller Skates* (1931), on the other hand, shows the harsher aspects of Harlem night life.

James Weldon Johnson's book *Black Manhattan,* published in 1930, was a long-awaited, popular history of Negroes in New York City as well as a history of Negroes on the stage in New York. It was also around 1930 that the great Spanish poet Garcia Lorca's book *Poet in New York* came out with these perceptive lines about Harlem:

> Ay Harlem, Harlem, Harlem!
> There is no sorrow like your oppressed eyes,
> like your blood shuddering in the dark eclipse,
> Your garnet violence, deaf in shadow and dumb,
> like your great king, prisoner in a janitor's uniform.

The white American poet William Rose Benét brought out a small book *Harlem and Other Poems* in 1935.

Clyde V. Kiser's doctoral dissertation, *Sea Island to City*, was published by Columbia University in 1932. It was a study of St. Helena islanders of South Carolina in Harlem and other urban centers.

literature of the depression years

The unemployment, dispossession, suffering and rioting of Harlem Negroes during the Great Depression led to pamphlets like James W. Ford's *Hunger and Terror in Harlem* (1935) about the causes and remedies of the March 19, 1935, Harlem riot, and prepared for the Mayor's Commission to Investigate Conditions in Harlem. E. Franklin Frazier's article *Negro Harlem: An Ecological Study (American Journal of Sociology,* July 1937) traced Harlem's physical expansion and demographic growth from its beginning around 1900 and particularly from 1910 through 1934. This article was based on the materials Frazier collected when making a survey of Harlem also for the Mayor's Commission to Investigate Conditions in Harlem (1936) following the March 1935 riot.

About this time, two master's theses were done about Harlem by Negro graduate students at Columbia University and C.C.N.Y. respectively: Barrington Dunbar's *Factors in Cultural Backgrounds of the British West Indian Negro and the American Southern Negro that Condition their Adjustment in Harlem* (1936) and Myrtle E. Pollard's big, two-volume *Harlem As Is* (1936-37), a sociological study with emphasis on Negro business and the economic community.

Alain Locke's article *Harlem: Dark Weather Vane* (*Survey Graphic*, Aug. 1936), eleven years after the 1925 special issue of this magazine on Harlem and over a year after the Harlem riot of 1935, stated that the New Negro hopes of the twenties then seemed like illusions and mirages in the depth of the depression and social unrest. For no cultural advance is safe, said Locke, without some sound economic underpinning, that is, without the foundation of a decent standard of living.

The *Harlem Digest* was a magazine published from 1937 to 1939 by A. Merral Willis's Colonel Young Memorial Foundation. The outstanding Negro playwright Theodore Ward's play *Big White Fog* (1938) about the problems of poverty, unemployment, prejudice, Garveyism and Communism, was equally applicable to Negroes in Chicago or New York. It was produced in both places. In 1940 Claude McKay's third book about Harlem appeared, titled *Harlem: Negro Metropolis*. This book was exotic, bizarre and rather superficial; it dealt with Father Divine, the cultists, the occultists, number-playing, Marcus Garvey and the other early Harlem nationalist Sufi Abdul Hamid. The American Negro Theatre created a hit in Harlem with the Negro writer Abram Hill's play *On Strivers Row: A Comedy of Sophisticated Harlem* in the early 1940's. This play was a satirical, social comedy of Negro middle class life in Harlem

literature of the nineteen forties

Harlem As Seen by Hirschfeld, a book of caricatured drawings with text by the American novelist and playwright William Saroyan, was published in 1941.

Langston Hughes, rapidly becoming the poet laureate of Harlem, brought out *Shakespeare in Harlem* in 1942 which contained this poem *Evenin' Air Blues* about the frustrations of the southern Negro when he migrates north:

Folks, I come up North
Cause they told me de North was fine.
I come up North
Cause they told me de North was fine.
Been up here six months—
I'm about to lose my mind.

This mornin' for breakfast
I chawed de mornin' air.
This mornin' for breakfast
    Chawed de mornin' air.
But this evenin' for supper,
I got evenin' air to spare.

The Negro novelist and short story writer Carl Offord's book *The White Face,* about a Georgia Negro family's woes in Harlem during World War II, came out in 1943. Bucklin Moon, a sensitive, progressive white writer and book editor, brought out his first book *The Darker Brother,* a novel about a Florida Negro migrant fighting for life in Harlem, in 1943 (paperbacked in 1949). Moon later published another novel about Negroes *Without Magnolias* (1949), which also touched on Harlem, and edited a very didactic and perceptive book of writings on the Negro titled *Primer For White Folks* (1945). Also published in 1943 was the white American novelist Ira Wolfert's *Tucker's People* about the underworld rackets in Harlem. This novel was issued in paperback in 1950 with the title *The Underworld.* The Right Rev. John H. Johnson, a long time Harlem minister, brought out his book *Harlem, The War and Other Addresses* in 1942.

The Negro Quarterly, a review of Negro life and culture, was published during 1942-43 with offices at 125th Street and Lenox Avenue in Harlem. This magazine was edited by two Harlemites, Angelo Herndon and Ralph Ellison who later became famous as a novelist and short story writer. It was national and international in scope and published only a few things about Harlem such as the poems *Lenox Avenue* and *Pawnbrokers* and the article *Anti-Semitism Among Negroes.* But many of the Negro writers who contributed to *The Negro Quarterly*, such as Langston Hughes, Harcourt Tynes, Carl G. Hill and L. D. Reddick, either resided in Harlem or were known Harlem figures.

The late Negro journalist and author Roi Ottley, who lived and worked in Harlem for many years, published his first book *New World*

A-Coming; Inside Black America in 1943. This book, as its bibliography clearly showed, was a sort of jazzed up, condensed version of the massive boxes of unpublished material written and collected by the scores of Negro writers who worked on the Federal Writers' Project's book *Negroes in New York* which was never published because Congress killed all appropriations for the federal cultural projects. This material on the history, development, institutions, organizations, culture and personalities of Harlem is now catalogued and available at the Schomburg Collection of Negro Literature and History of the New York Public Library in Harlem. Ottley merely skimmed over this material (probably under his publisher's pressure) and he gave no credit to the many Negro writers who had compiled and written the unpublished papers. However, his eternally sanguine, optimistic book, coming during World War II and pointing to a new world for Negroes after the War, enjoyed a tremendous success especially among white Americans whose uneasy, guilty consciences about Negroes and the defense of American democracy were somewhat assuaged by this sort of book by a Negro.

literature of the war years

But the war and civilian issues were not so easily resolved by Negroes. The anti-Negro riots by whites in Bessemer, Alabama, Philadelphia, Pennsylvania, Detroit, Michigan, and other cities against the upgrading of Negroes on their jobs, plus the widespread discrimination against Negroes in war plants everywhere and the Negro press' constant reports of Negro soldiers being beaten, denied service and even killed on southern buses and in southern camps and restaurants led to the devastating Harlem riot of August 1 and 2, 1943. Two of the reports written about this Sunday night-Monday morning riot are Harold Orlansky's pamphlet *The Harlem Riot: A Study in Mass Frustration* (1943), a social anthropological analysis, and the then publishing progressive New York City newspaper *PM's* big 19-page picture and text coverage titled *The Whole Story of the Harlem Riot* (Aug. 3, 1943). Also around this time during World War II the NAACP published a pamphlet *Food Costs More in Harlem,* a comparative survey of retail food prices after the O.P.A. had frozen prices at very high levels. In the fall of 1943, spurred no doubt by the August 1943 Harlem riot, the City-Wide Citizens' Committee on Harlem got busy with its proposed projects for Harlem. The Committee had already issued in 1942 three good, critical reports of its subcommittees on employment, education and recreation and housing in Harlem. It followed these up with another report on health and hospitals in Harlem in 1945.

The late Dan Burley, a well-known Harlem figure, published in 1944 his *Original Handbook of Harlem Jive* illustrated by the *New York Amsterdam News* cartoonist Melvin Tapley with a learned foreword by Earl Conrad. The talented Negro woman novelist Ann Petry brought out her first book *The Street* in 1946. While, like most novels about Harlem, *The Street* may be too naturalistic and slice-of-life in spots, it is nevertheless an honest attempt to sum up what the author saw and heard during the six years she lived in Harlem and worked as a reporter for a Harlem newspaper: the ancient, evil housing; the tragic, broken families; and the high death rate. This book, which won a Houghton Mifflin Literary Fellowship award, has been through several hard and paperback editions and is still on the paperback stands.

The *Harlem Quarterly* was published in 1949-50 edited by the Negro writer and now militant Negro leader of Brooklyn CORE, Benjamin A. Brown. The magazine carried symposia, short stories, poetry, articles, features and book reviews. Among the editors and contributors were many Harlem writers such as John H. Clarke, Ricardo Weeks, Willard Moore, John Hudson Jones, Gene Holmes, Waring Cuney, Langston Hughes, William Attaway and Ernest Kaiser. A *Who's Who in Harlem* for 1949-50, the biographical register of a group of distinguished persons of New York's Harlem, was edited and published by B. S. B. Trottman. It contained many of the Harlem personalities alive at that time. Trottman also brought out *New York's Harlem Business Register* in 1951, a listing of virtually all Harlem businesses of that time. Also following up on the *New Harlem Blue Book* (1940), a directory of organizations, businesses and professionals, which was long out of print, Constance Curtis, Adele Glasgow and Carl Lawrence brought out *Harlem's Top Thousand,* a similar directory, in 1949 and *Harlem's Top People,* a larger, more classified directory, in 1953. Olivia P. Frost, who had done an analysis of the characteristics of the population in Central Harlem for the New York Urban League published in 1946, completed her master's thesis, *Some Sociological Aspects of the Realty Investment Market in New York's Harlem,* in 1951.

Every book written about New York City as a whole has a section or sections on Harlem. This holds for books like the Federal Writers' Project's *New York City Guide* (1939), Eleanor Early's *New York Holiday* (1950), Kate Simon's *New York, Places and Pleasures* (1959) and Gay Talese's *New York: A Serendipiter's Journey* (1962). Some of these sections on Harlem are pretty good and some are exotic in their approach to Harlem.

white writers on Harlem

Many white writers like Hal Ellson, Wenzell Brown, Evan Hunter, Jack Lait and John Henry Hewlett have maligned Harlem, its youth and adults with their derogatory novels and inside and confidential books. Robert Lowry's novel *The Violent Wedding* (1953), a very crude take-off on Harlem's Ray Robinson, John H. Hewlett's novel *Harlem Story* (1948), Jack Lait's *New York: Confidential* (1948), Wenzell Brown's terrible paperback *The Big Rumble* (1955) subtitled *Teen-age Gangs in the [East] Harlem Jungle,* are some examples of this. Also William Arnold's *Harlem Woman* (1952) and Floyd Miller's *The Dream Peddlers* (1956) are paperback novels about Puerto Ricans, prostitution and dope in East Harlem; Earl Conrad's *Rock Bottom* (1952), a novel about a Negro woman's experiences from Mississippi to Harlem; William Krasner's *North of Welfare* (1954), playing up Harlem gangs and violence and Evan Hunter's sensational novel *The Blackboard Jungle* (1954) (later made into a motion picture) through which the author tried to get attention by exploiting the deprivations of Harlem's school children. This book was supposed to show a public school classroom of juvenile delinquents in a terrible Harlem neighborhood.

Hal Ellson's paperback novels *Duke* (1949), *Rock* (1955), *I'll Fix You* (1956) and *This Is It* (1956) have been particularly vicious in their treatment of Harlem youth as only juvenile delinquents. We must also include in this category of deleterious books about Harlem the works of several Negro writers. George W. Henderson's novel *Jule: Alabama Boy in Harlem* (1946), Philip B. Kaye's novel *Taffy* (1950) (both also paperbacked), Robert Lucas's paperback *Harlem Model* (1953), and Chester Himes's recent paperback novels written in France about Harlem—*The Real Cool Killers* (1959), *The Crazy Kill* (1959), *All Shot Up* (1960) and *The Big Gold Dream* (1960) — are all novels by Negro writers that denigrate and demean Harlem youth and adults.

the Harlem of Langston Hughes

Arthur P. Davis, one of the editors of that huge anthology of American Negro writing, *The Negro Caravan* (1941), wrote an article for the magazine *Phylon* (4th quarter, 1952) titled *The Harlem of Langston*

Hughes' Poetry. Hughes has mirrored Harlem rather faithfully in his poetry through the years. One of these poems titled *Harlem* in his book of poems mostly about Harlem—*Montage of a Dream Deferred* (1951) —goes like this:

> What happens to a dream deferred?
> Does it dry up
> Like a raisin in the sun?
> Or fester like a sore—
> And then run?
> Does it stink like rotten meat?
> Or crust and sugar over—
> Like a syrupy sweet?
>
> Maybe it just sags
> Like a heavy load.
>
> *Or does it explode?*

Hughes's book about the now famous Harlem character Jesse Semple began as a series in *The Chicago Defender,* a Negro newspaper. These articles were collected and published as the book *Simple Speaks His Mind* in 1950 followed by two other collections *Simple Takes a Wife* in 1953 and *Simple Stakes a Claim* in 1957. Hughes has selected his favorite Simple stories from these three volumes in *The Best of Simple* (1961). The book *Simple Takes a Wife* became the basis for the Langston Hughes and David Martin musical comedy *Simply Heavenly* of 1957. The text of this musical was published in 1959. Alice Childress, the outstanding Negro woman playwright and Harlemite, adapted the text of the Harlem-produced, Committee For the Negro in the Arts musical *Just A Little Simple* (1950) from Hughes's *Simple Speaks His Mind.* Her book *Like One of the Family* (1956), conversations from a Harlem domestic's life, is really the female Harlem counterpart of Hughes's "Simple" sketches. Hughes did the text for a book of Harlem photographs, *The Sweet Flypaper of Life* (1955), by that gifted Harlem photographer and Guggenheim Fellowship winner Roy De Carava. Hughes also brought out a novel *Tambourines to Glory* (1958) about pentecostal religion in Harlem. Often called the O. Henry of Harlem, he has written several of his short stories in *The Ways of White Folks* (1934), *Laughing to Keep from Crying* (1952) and in magazines, about Harlem. He has chosen 37 of these stories and vignettes with various locales for *Something in Common and Other Stories* (1963).

other writers about Harlem

Around the World with the Harlem Globetrotters, a book about those zany clowns of basketball, appeared in 1953 and *I Always Wanted to Be Somebody,* Althea Gibson's autobiography of her tremendous rise from the slums of Harlem to the women's tennis championship of the world, was published in 1958. Samuel B. Charters and Leonard Kunstadt's recent book *Jazz: A History of the New York Scene* (1962) has material, historical and current, on Harlem jazz music and musicians. Bruce Kenrick's book *Come Out the Wilderness* (1962) is the dramatic story of the interracial East Harlem Protestant Parish.

There are some novels by Negro and white writers about Harlem which, while not of the worst type, are so naturalistic, slice-of-life or distorted that Harlem could have done very well without them. In fact, the paperback reprints of these books show that they lend themselves to the usual damaging stereotypes of life in Harlem In this category fall National Book Award winner Ralph Ellison's *Invisible Man* (1953) (about distorted Negro nationalism and nightmarish riot in Harlem) ; Julian Mayfield's two books *The Hit* (1957) and *The Long Night* (1958) ; Warren Miller's *The Cool World* (1959) (about youth gangs) that later had a very short run as a Broadway play; William Fisher's *The Waiters* (1953) (about the numbers racket) ; Arthur Joseph's *Volcano in our Midst* (1952) ; Sheila S. Klass's *Come Back on Monday* (1960) (a novel written by a white teacher in Harlem about public schools there with an anti-Harlem Negro press slant) ; and Eugene Brown's *Trepass* (1952) (about interracial love).

The magazine and newspaper articles and series on Harlem have been many in number. We shall run through some of them along with some longer studies of Harlem. The now defunct magazine *Collier's* carried a terrible article *Harlem—Dense and Dangerous* in its September 23, 1944, number. Ann Petry's piece *Harlem* with beautiful pictures in rich color (*Holiday,* April 1949) was a kind of Cook's tour of Harlem with some interpretation. The famous liberal novelist Lillian Smith's article *Strange Fruit in Harlem* (*Ebony,* June 1950) gives impressions of her visit as a white southerner to the New York Negro community: of the children, the mothers and also the blighted areas of Harlem. The *New York Sunday News* ran a series of brief picture stories on Harlem from February to October 1953 which emphasized the way the community's Negroes study, train and work. The Negro free-lance journalist Alex Haley, who today, the Negro press says, is aiming for the top, published an article in 1954 titled *The*

Harlem Nobody Knows (*Christian Science Monitor*, May 6, 1954). This article tells a dream-like, grossly exaggerated, everything-is-rosy story of what it calls the community's great progress over a fifty year period from about 1900 to about 1954. The piece was, naturally, immediately reprinted (if not planted originally in the *Monitor*) by *The Reader's Digest* (June 1954) and also by the *New York Amsterdam News*. In 1955, the research department of the Welfare and Health Council of New York City brought out studies of population characteristics and social and educational services in Central Harlem and East Harlem and in other Negroes areas of the borough of Manhattan.

The veteran Negro reporter Ted Poston's long *New York Post* series *Prejudice and Progress: The Negro in New York* (April 1956 deals in part with Harlem. One article of the series is titled *How Harlem Got that Way*. The *New York Post* carried another long series of articles this time on Harlem by the white reporter and writer Stan Opotowsky, in March 1958 These articles maligned and denigrated Harlem and its people past and present. Mrs. Anna A. Hedgeman wrote a long reply to this series in which she tried to describe the positive, dignified, hard-working, "struggle" side of the Harlem Negroes' story left out by the *Post* reporter. She discussed the Harlem community with Opotowsky on a television program. But Opotowsky insisted to the end that he would write the series a second time exactly as he had already written it, and Mrs. Hedgeman's reply to his Harlem slander was never published in the *Post*. However, the *Post's* next series, *Inside Bedford-Stuyvesant* (May 1958) on Negroes in Brooklyn, was much better than its Harlem series by Opotowsky; and the newspaper later apparently tried to make amends for the earlier series with the short series on *Harlem and Beyond*, about the new Negro middle class, in April 1962.

Peter Abrahams, the South African colored journalist and writer now living in Jamaica in the West Indies, contributed an article *The Meaning of Harlem* to *Holiday* (June 1960) after having his original piece on Harlem written for *Holiday's* New York number (October 1959) rejected as too sociological. The Abrahams piece, as revised to meet *Holiday's* demands, still had more depth and interpretation than most *Holiday* pieces. About the same time the famous Negro novelist and essayist, James Baldwin, contributed an article *Fifth Avenue Uptown* to *Esquire's* special New York number (July 1960). This was an angry piece which told of the Harlem people's silent contempt for and hatred of their oppression. Baldwin, a native son of Harlem, has written extensively on Harlem from his early essay *The Harlem Ghetto* reprinted from *Commentary* (February 1948) in his book *Notes of a Native Son* (1955), through his largely auto-biographical novel *Go Tell It on the Mountain* (1953) which delves deeply and with much insight into the religion and life of the people of Harlem's store front churches, to his popular novel *Another Country* (1962) about Harlem and Greenwich Village, although here he has been charged with creating stereotyped Negro characters such as white and Negro writers create when pandering to the public's distorted conception of Negro life.

Harlem of the sixties

The liberal southern journalist and writer Harry S. Ashmore's book *The Other Side of Jordan* (1960), which stemmed from a series of articles in the *New York Herald Tribune,* describes Negro life in the northern communities with a section on Harlem. The Harvard historian and sociologist Oscar Handlin's book *The Newcomers: Negroes and Puerto Ricans in a Changing Metropolis* (1959, paper-backed in 1962) also deals in great part with the housing, employment, education and welfare problems of Harlem. The Urban League of Greater New York brought out in 1960 a survey of *Gaps in Services to Children and Parents in Harlem: Your Agency's Role* when so many social agencies had either moved out of Harlem or closed down. The Teamsters Joint Council 16 released in June 1962 a report on New York City family income whose statistics on non-white income in the borough of Manhattan relate largely to Harlem. The Protestant Council of the City of New York published in September 1962 a two-part report, *Harlem—Upper Manhattan,* the most exhaustive study that has been made of Harlem in many years.

Finally, we have the *Ebony* (April 1963) article *Harlem's Antique Collector* about Mrs. W. D. Finkley, who collects antique furniture, china, silver and glassware; the Negro novelist Chester Himes' long essay *Harlem or the Cancer of America* written after his visit to New York City from France (during the latter part of 1962) and translated into French for the magazine *Presence Africaine* (1st quarter 1963); Conrad Kent Rivers' book of poems in preparation *The Still Voice of Harlem* whose title poem has already been published in Paul Bremen's second volume *Sixes and Sevens* (1963) of his projected four-volume Heritage (London) series of poetry by American Negroes; and Gay Talese's article *Harlem for Fun* (*Esquire,* September 1962).

In April 1955, almost a year after Dr. Alain Locke's death in June

1954, the Howard University Graduate School published *The New Negro: Thirty Years Afterward.* This book, coming exactly thirty years after Locke's book *The New Negro* (1925), consisted of papers read at the 16th annual spring conference of the University's Social Sciences Division. These papers were eulogies of Dr. Locke with a pretty good bibliography of his diverse writings and discussions of the historical setting, the political ideologies, the middle class, the modern art, the literature and the New Deal period of the New Negro by Rayford W. Logan, E. Franklin Frazier, Charles S. Johnson, Emmett E. Dorsey, James A. Porter, Sterling A. Brown, Eugene C. Holmes and John Hope Franklin sweeping back in some instances to 1877 and forward three decades after 1925.

present parallels with earlier writers

Arna Bontemps, the versatile Negro novelist, poet, historian and anthologist, in an article *The New Black Renaissance (Negro Digest,* November 1961) which is similar to some of the papers in *The New Negro Thirty Years Afterward,* says that the current Negro writers (Baldwin, Hansberry, Ellison, etc.) resemble the Harlem Renaissance writers more than they do the Negro writers of the late thirties and forties, their immediate forerunners (Willard Motley, the late Richard Wright, Margaret Walker, Gwendolyn Brooks, etc.). With the possible exception of Lorraine Hansberry *(Raisin in the Sun)* (and I would add John O. Killens, author of the novels *Youngblood* and *And Then We Heard the Thunder)* as descendants of Richard Wright, Bontemps sees some parallels between Ralph Ellison and Jean Toomer, James Baldwin and Wallace Thurman, Louis E. Lomax *(The Reluctant African, The Negro Revolt)* and the late Walter White *(Rope and Faggot* [1929]), Alston Anderson, author of *Lover Man* (1959), a book of short stories, and Eric D. Waldron whose book of short stories, *Tropic Death,* pleased the critics in the Harlem Renaissance period. Both Alston and Waldron have the West Indies and Panama in their backgrounds. Bontemps also brackets the Harlem flavor of Julian Mayfield's novels with that of Rudolph Fisher's short stories and novels; and novelist Paule Marshall, author of *Brown Girl, Brownstones* (1959) and *Soul Clap Hands and Sing* (1961) with the late Zora Neale Hurston who worte *Mules and Men* (1935), *Their Eyes Were Watching God* (1937) and other works. (And I would bracket the novelist John A. Williams [*Night Song, Sissie*] and novelist Arna Bontemps [*God Sends Sunday, Black Thunder*].)

And if the Harlem Renaissance group had no Lorraine Hansberry

(I would also add no John O. Killens) and no journalist like Carl T. Rowan (author of *South of Freedom, Go South to Sorrow* and other works), says Bontemps, neither have the present group of Negro writers any poets comparable to Claude McKay, Countee Cullen and Langston Hughes. The Harlem Renaissance group, he says, also included Helen Johnson, Dorothy West, Frank Horne, Sterling Brown, Nella Larsen, Jessie Fauset and Arthur Huff Fauset. Our current crop of Negro writers, Bontemps says further, also includes the late Frank London Brown, LeRoi Jones, Gloria Oden, Herbert Simmons and William Melvin Kelley. (I would add the poet Conrad Kent Rivers, author of *Perchance to Dream, Othello* [1959] and *These Black Bodies and This Sunburnt Face* [1962]). But, says Bontemps probably correctly, it will take the best of all of these to fill the firmament as did the literary stars that brightened the Harlem sky in the twenties.

But if, as Locke has pointed out, no Negro cultural advance is safe without a sound foundation of a decent standard of living for Negroes generally, it is also true that a powerful Negro culture of novels, poetry, plays and the like can develop out of and also give direction to the current great struggles and protests of Negroes everywhere in our country against the injustices and denials of their rights. This is the tradition of Richard Wright in which John O. Killens with his novels, Lorraine Hansberry with her plays, and other Negro writers are working.

Alain Leroy Locke

THE LEGACY OF
ALAIN LOCKE

EUGENE C. HOLMES

THE RISE OF A GENUINE New Negro Movement was fostered and encouraged by one person, Alain Leroy Locke, who became its creative editor and its chronicler. It may be true that the term Renaissance, as Sterling Brown has so perceptively pointed out, is a misnomer because of the shortness of the life span of the Harlem movement. Also, the New Negro writers were not centered only in Harlem, and much of the best writing of the decade was not always about Harlem, for most of the writers were not Harlemites. Yet Harlem was the "show window," the cashier's till, though it is no more "Negro America" than New York is America. The New Negro had temporal roots in the past and spatial roots elsewhere in America and the term has validity only when considered to be a continuing tradition.

It may be argued that the so-called Negro Renaissance held the seeds of defeat for a number of reasons, among them being the general anti-intellectualism of the new Negro middle class. But it was, by every admission a representation of a re-evaluation of the Negro's past and of the Negro himself by Negro intellectuals and artists. For the rise of the New Negro Movement coincided with an ever increasing interest in Negro life and character in the twenties. American literature was being re-evaluated and overhauled as a revolt against the genteel tradition and the acquisitive society of the last decades of the nineteenth century.

Charles Johnson characterized Alain Locke as "the Dean of this group of fledgling writers of the new and lively generation of the 1920's." Johnson wrote, "A brilliant analyst trained in philosophy, and an esthete with a flair for art as well as letters, he gave encouragement and guidance to these young writers as an older practitioner too sure of his craft to be discouraged by failure of full acceptance in the publishing media of the period."[1] Johnson referred to Alain

1. *The New Negro: Thirty Years Afterward,* The Howard University Press, 1955, p. 84.

Locke as "an important maker of history" of a "dramatic period in our national history." Locke had this to say about these young writers being launched on their careers: "They sense within their group—a spiritual wealth which if they can properly expound, will be ample for a new judgment and re-appraisal of the race." This, then, is only a part of the backdrop of what has been called the Negro Renaissance. What Charles Johnson referred to as "that sudden and altogether phenomenal outburst of emotional expression unmatched by any comparable period in American or Negro American history."

No one, not even the older Du Bois, could have been better equipped to have been the architect of the New Negro Movement and maker of history. Philadelphia, Locke's birthplace, was the one city where one could speak of a culture. Negro artists were encouraged and Negro literary, musical and painting groups were encouraged. Young Locke was aware of this personally and always kept these artists in mind as reminders of the awakening of Negro art in America. The literary movement had many of its origins in Philadelphia, but, because of social, economic and political reasons, it flowered in New York. For a racial dilemma in Negro art, a racial solution was necessary. This came in the mid-twenties from the inspiration of the New Negro Movement with its crusade of folk expression in all of the arts, the drama, painting, sculpture, music and the rediscovery of the folk origins of the Negro's African heritage.

The racial dilemma was a distinct carryover from the same dilemma encountered by the Negro writers of the late nineteenth century. In most of these writers, there was to be found the same tendentious, pedestrian and imitative style as observed in many of the painters. There was the dialect poetry of Dunbar and his later English poems in which he was the exponent of the romantic tendencies which were to be decried by the next generation of Negro poets. There were the propaganda novels of Frances Harper, Martin Delaney, Frank Webb and William Wells Brown. The novels of Charles Chestnutt were outstanding for their genre, style and impact. The political essays, the pamphleteering, the autobiographical slave accounts, the polemical essays were all to be merged with and channelized into that renascence which came to be known as the New Negro Movement.

Locke's early years

As a burgeoning critic and student of Negro life in Philadelphia, in Boston and New York, at Howard University where he had gone to teach in 1912, Locke had been working in his way, in concert with many friends, to help lay to rest the mawkish and moribund dialect school of poetry. William Stanley Braithwaite, Locke's friend and mentor while he was at Harvard; William Monroe Trotter, the editor; W. E. B. Du Bois, all helped in hastening the demise of Negro dialect poetry. Friendly critics such as Louis Untermeyer also helped by labeling the traditional dialect as "an affectation to please a white audience." And, along with James Weldon Johnson, who had genuine poetic talent, this critics' coterie saw that dialect poetry had neither the wit nor the beauty of folk speech, but was only a continuation of the stock stereotypes about gentility, humility and buffoonery, and an evasion of all of the realities of Negro life.

One counteraction, however, to this dialect poetry was a conscious reverting to Romanticism and neo-Romanticism which reflected a middle-class recognition of Europeanized esthetic values. In some ways, this was a result of the rejection of the minstrel-buffoon stereotype. In addition, as the middle class Negro became better educated, there was an increase in his desire to share in the legacy of general culture, to participate in it, even though in a lesser fashion. As Sterling Brown put it, in too many instances "these poets were more concerned with making copies of the 'beauty' that was the stock-in-trade of a languishing tradition." These imitators were, for the most part, only too anxious to avoid any mention of a Negro tradition or to look into their own experiences as Negroes. The result, in their poetry, was escapist, without vitality or understanding.

Along with this counteraction there developed in the same period, the movement which assisted in the Negro writer's spiritual emancipation. As Locke himself put it in his last published account (1952) of the movement: "For from 1912 on, there was brewing the movement that in 1925, explicitly became the so-called Renaissance of the New Negro. The movement was not so much in itself a triumph of realism, although it had its share of realists, but a deliberate cessation by Negro authors of their attempts primarily to influence majority opinion. By then, Negro artists had outgrown the handicaps of allowing didactic emphasis and propagandist motives to choke their sense of artistry. Partly in disillusionment, partly in newly acquired group pride and self-respect, they turned inward to the Negro audience in frankly avowed self-expression."

Langston Hughes, one of their number, thus phrased this literary declaration of independence:

"We younger Negro artists who create now intend to express our individual dark-skinned selves without fear or shame. If white people are pleased, we are glad. If they are not, it doesn't matter. We know we are beautiful. And ugly too. If colored are pleased, we are glad. If they are not, their displeasure doesn't matter either. We build our temples for tomorrow, strong as we know how, and we stand on the top of the mountain, free within ourselves."

Once again, there was a common denominator between the advance-guard elements of the majority and the minority. The anti-slavery collaboration had forged a moral alliance; this was an esthetic one, which spelled out a final release from propaganda and its shackling commitments both for Negro materials in American art and literature and for the Negro artist and writer. And from 1925 to the present, realism and Southern regionalism on the one side, and the promotion of racial self-expression on the other, have informally but effectively combined to form a new progressive atmosphere in American letters.

One of the then new poets, James Weldon Johnson, sensitive, socially aware, and a founder of the N.A.A.C.P., had a considerable influence on the younger generation of Negro poets. His poems of race consciousness, his fine commemorative elegy of the fiftieth anniversary of Negro freedom, praised the Negro's contribution to the American heritage and they were more militant than anything heretofore written. After Du Bois' *Litany of Atlanta,* Johnson depicted the horrible brutalization of lynching in his poetry, "grimly prideful and resistant to the lynch-mad South."

Although the younger Locke had not always seen eye to eye with the older Du Bois on every issue concerning the Negro's struggle for artistic emancipation, he had always admired *The Souls of Black Folk* and *Darkwater.* He had only sympathy for the *Litany* from whose loins "sprang twin Murder and Black Hate." He knew of Du Bois' biography of John Brown, he sympathized with the Du Bois attack on the philosophy of Booker T. Washington. He supported the Niagara movement and voiced his support for the intellectual and literary leadership which signalled Du Bois' founding of *Crisis,* the journal of the N.A.A.C.P. In the early years, Locke supplied the journal with an annual review of Negro literature, art and music. And Locke joined with those Negro intellectuals who supported Du Bois as the leader of the "talented tenth" movement and of Negro liberalism.

Under the directorship of Du Bois, *Crisis* became the instrument which led to the vocal and verbal expression of Negro political and artistic leadership. Du Bois was one of the first American scholars to turn to the new scientific approach in the social sciences and this meant new approaches in history and sociology by way of philosophy and scientific method. All of this appealed to the philosophically trained Locke who knew of Du Bois' history of *The Suppression of African Slave Trade to America,* where he was anxious to employ the techniques of scientific research and its results for the settlement of the Negro problem in America. Locke knew of Du Bois' investigations of the treatment of Negro soldiers by the American army in 1918. Locke supported Du Bois' calls for the Pan-African Congress of 1919, 1921 and 1923. And Locke withdrew from his active role in the N.A.A.C.P. when its Board refused to support Du Bois' Pan-Africanism. He maintained this support until Du Bois' return to Atlanta and supported the "old man's" founding and editorship in 1940 of *Phylon, The Atlanta Review of Race and Culture.* To this journal Locke contributed another annual critical review of literature by and about Negroes.

Opportunity, An American Journal of Negro Life, the organ of the National Urban League, was first edited by Charles S. Johnson. This organ was another impetus to the literary movement with the establishment in 1924 of cash prizes for original literary work. The *Crisis* prizes were established through the sponsorship of Mrs. Amy E. Spingarn and the *Opportunity* prizes through that of Caspar Holstein. Additional prizes were offered later by Carl Van Vechten through *Opportunity* and by Carl Brandt through *Crisis.* Also through *Crisis,* the Charles W. Chestnutt Honorarium was given. These prizes were given for many years and had quite an effect upon the younger writers. The title poem to Langston Hughes' first volume won an *Opportunity* prize. "The *New Negro* was the distillation of the ferment of the preceding decade."

The post-war decade which ushered in the Harlem Renaissance was the age of triumph for big business and the consolidation of industry and monopoly capitalism on a world wide scale. This was conducted by white capital with Negro and immigrant labor, a mass of cheap and potentially efficient labor, unlimited natural power and a use of unequalled technique, reaching all of the markets of the world and leading to the emergence of America as a force in twentieth century world imperialism.

The profits promised by the exploitations of this quasi-colonialism were endangered by labor difficulties; wholesale scabbing by Negroes threatened to flare into race war. Relations between Southern poor whites and Negroes became increasingly exacerbated. The northward emigrations to the cities depleted the rural south and made new ghettoes in the north. The shadows of race riots and lynchings remained. And they seared. The Vardamans and Tillmans still ruled the Congress. The Thomas Nelson Pages and Dixons were in the ascendancy in literature. There was bound to be an inevitable conflict between the new graduates of the Negro colleges and the northerners who had supported the new schools, all of which was symbolized in the struggle and conflicts between Booker T. Washington and Dr. W. E. B. Du Bois. The organization of the Rockefeller-supported General Education Board and the Rosenwald Foundation launched the new racial educational philosophy of the south. By the second decade a legal caste system based on race and color had been openly grafted on the democratic conscience of the United States. And the representatives of the New Negro Movement allied themselves to a man with Du Bois, Locke, Charles Johnson and James Weldon Johnson.

Locke's leadership at Howard

Locke had the auspicious fortune to begin his educational experience at Howard University, where, as an instructor in education and philosophy, he came into contact with many scholars who greeted the Harvard, Oxford, Berlin trained youth of twenty-five. Meeting and working with Ernest E. Just, the English teacher turned zoologist, was an event and the two became inseparable friends until Just's untimely death in 1941. The young Locke was accepted and acclaimed by the first Negro to teach sociology, the former classicist and mathematician, Kelly Miller. There were many others such as his classmate, Montgomery Gregory, with whom he organized the Howard Players. Together these Negro scholars organized into a group known as the Sanhedrin under the joint leadership of Locke and Miller. Locke organized the first literary movement at Howard and remained the faculty adviser of the university literary journal, the *Stylus*, from its beginning until its demise. He helped in the organization of the art gallery and the music department for he saw that general and cultural education was a desideratum for Negro students. His own educational philosophy predisposed him to manifest the broad approach and an interdisciplinary point of view. In so doing, he devoted much of his own teaching to the new science of anthropology, social conflict and social theory. He wrote *Race and Culture Conflict* in 1916.

No one could have been better equipped for the leadership and sponsorship of the New Negro Movement than Locke, who described himself "more of a philosophical midwife to a generation of younger Negro poets, writers and artists than a professional philosopher." For years he had been encouraging artists and musicians to study the African sources at first hand. He was an avid collector of Africana. He wrote expertly about the lost ancestral arts of Africa and traced the influence of African art on European artists in the early twentieth century. He knew a great deal about African influences in Haiti and other Caribbean islands and he consistently pointed out African influences on the Negro American, both before and after the abolition of slavery.

Alain Locke did not make many original researches into American Negro history or into the golden lore of African history, but he grew in stature as he learned more and more of this history. It taught him that the Negro scholar's ability to withstand the infirmities of the American scene is a dialectic phase of the democratic process. And this dialectic must necessarily aid in bringing into fruition the dream of a community of Negro scholars. This was his sensitivity about American history and it led him to an identity with the great leader, the self-taught Frederick Douglass, about whom he wrote a biography. Locke was deeply appreciative of Du Bois' scientific approach to history and Carter G. Woodson's pioneer scientific work in the history of slavery and the Negro past. His contributions to the New Negro Movement always turned out to be re-evaluations of Negro history as it affected the Negro writer, the Negro scholar, and the lives of all sensitively aware Negroes.

As an author, Locke knew that the story of the Negro writer had to be told, because of the social history involved. He came to see that the position of the Negro in American culture had come to mean a great deal more than merely the artistic activity of the Negro minority. It came to mean for him a pointing toward a goal of a "natively characteristic national literature as being one of the crucial issues of cultural democracy." And this had to be evaluated against the slavery and anti-slavery background from which this literature emerged.

The harsh effects of slavery had to be viewed as contributing to the recognition of the Negro's role as participant and contributor to American culture. "Just as slavery may now (1952) in perspective be viewed as having first threatened our democratic institutions and then forced them to more consistent maturity, the artistic and cultural impact of the Negro must be credited with producing unforeseen constructive pressures and generating unexpected creative ferment in the literary and artistic culture of America. In cutting the Negro loose from his ancestral culture, slavery set up a unique and unprecedented situation between the Anglo-Saxon majority and the Negro minority group. The peculiar conditions of American slavery so scrambled Africans from the diverse regions and culture of our entire continent that with the original background culture, tribal to begin with, neither a minority language nor an ancestral tradition remains. The American Negro was left no alternative but to share the language and tradition of the majority culture."[2]

The Negro had never set up separate cultural values, even though he had been forced on many occasions to take on defensive attitudes of racialism, "an enforced, protective, counter-attitude, stemming the worst of proscription and discrimination." Locke believed that, despite historical interludes, the Negro's values, ideals and objectives, have always been integrally and unreservedly American. He wrote, "The crucial factors in group relationships are social attitudes and literature—recording and reflecting these in preference even in social fact—becomes the most revealing medium."[3]

the works of Locke

Locke wrote more than a dozen books and articles since 1921 on Negro art, music and literature, tracing these developments from the earliest times, from 1760 up to 1920. He began with the first Negro poets, essayists and novelists, showing that the earliest indictments of slavery from the articulate free Negro displayed signs of a strong race consciousness. He showed that if slavery had molded the emotional and folk life of the Negro, that also it was the anti-slavery movement which developed the intellect of the Negro and pushed him forward to articulate, disciplined expression. The edifice of chattel slavery was shaken to its foundation by the combined efforts of the literary and oratorical efforts of Negro leaders and self-taught fugitive slaves. The emergence of the "slave narrative" supplied the incandescent spark, to be added to the abolitionist tinder.

In making America aware of the Negro artist and his work, an important part was played by the *Harlem Number* (1925) of the *Survey Graphic* which was edited by Locke. This issue of the *Survey* contained a hundred pages. There were twenty contributors, fifteen Negro and five white and twelve belonged to the Harlem group. Among the

2. Locke, *The Negro in American Literature, New World Writing*, New American Library, p. 19.
3. *Ibid.*

articles were, *Enter the New Negro, The Making of Harlem, Black Workers and the City, Jazz at Home, Negro Art and America, The Negro Digs Up His Past, The Rhythm of Harlem,* and many others appertaining to Harlem. This issue of the *Survey* had the largest circulation of any in its history. Several editions had to be run off before the demand was satisfied. In *Black Manhattan,* James Weldon Johnson in 1926, wrote, "It was a revelation to New York and the country. Later the symposium, somewhat enlarged, was brought out as a book, entitled *The New Negro,* under the editorship of Alain Locke. It remains one of the most important books on the Negro ever published."

The movement, for a while *did* thrive in Harlem. Then the "influence of Locke's essays and of the movement in general, spread outward over the country, touching writers in Missouri, Mississippi, in Boston, Philadelphia and Nashville and Chicago."[4]

Unknowingly, there was being cultivated a middle class nationalism within the protective folds of the capitalist ethos. The majority did not rebel, but rather hearkened to the voice of bourgeois authority. American capitalism had prospered in the redivision of the profits and spoils of the war. In too many instances, the "New Negro" had served in too large a measure as a means of amusement, to be fawned upon and idolized. Many of the New Negroes were unwilling victims of an inverted racialistic nationalism, looking upon themselves as having arrived, and priding themselves that they could sing, paint and write as well as their white-skinned patrons.

rediscovery of African past

But, the movement was a true "renaissance" in another sense—the antiquity which Negroes wanted to revive from a "lost" African past. However they might share in the leavings of their new found prosperity, if they were to rediscover their racial souls, they had to go back, at least mentally, to the African past. There were the successes and the failures of Du Bois' leadership in the 1921, 1923 and 1925 Pan-African Congresses. The efforts of Locke to instill in the younger poets, artists and musicians, some sense of this African heritage bore fruit in the work of Toomer, Cullen, McKay and Hughes.

The most developed poet and literary figure of the New Negro movement, Langston Hughes, wrote on all manners of subjects and always movingly of Africa. In 1926, *Weary Blues* and in 1927, *Fine*

4. *Negro Caravan,* edited by Sterling Brown, Arthur P. Davis and Ulysses Lee, p. 16.

Clothes to the Jew, Hughes displayed his artistry of particular power and beauty pursuing his own course more than any other of the New Negroes. Hughes' antecedents were bound up in a family tradition where the struggle for freedom was always a strong memory and inspiration. A grandfather died fighting beside John Brown. An uncle was a Reconstruction Congressman and the first Dean of the Howard Law School. Even Hughes' blues, melodious and rhythmic are full of African feeling as in *Homesick Blues*:

> De railroad bridge's
> A sad song in de air
> Every time de trains pass
> I wants to go somewhere.

The black world of America and Africa came to have a new meaningful nationalistic pride for so many of these poets. It was not always very deep or couched in any scientific anthropological understanding, but no matter, there was precious little understanding at the time for anyone. What mattered was that this flowering was a true renaissance of feeling, a prideful evocation of the dark image of Africa, germinated from a fructified seedbed but one which took on a new form and content.

literary renaissance and the "new Negro"

The Harlem Renaissance, substantively, transformed the Negro as subject and as artist from the old stereotype into the New Negro, militant, no longer obsequious, more of a paragon because he had shown that he was nearly on equal terms with his white counterpart. He won coveted prizes, fellowships, he was being published and he won his spurs the hard way in creative writing. These artists were not organized but theirs was a strong spirit of cohesion, a bond of group consciousness, toward some goal of achievement which would make the Negro artist proud of his work. It was a self-confidence which grew and proliferated into an outburst of emotional expression, never matched by any comparable period in American history. The new generation of writers began to carve out a niche in the hitherto impermeable walls of American literary culture. Hence the self-confidence, the self-assurance and the pride of craftsmanship.

The New Poetry Movement embraced every facet of Negro experience from lyricism, African heritage, social protest, folk song and blues, Negro heroes and episodes, lynchings, race riots, treatment of the Negro masses (frequently of the folk, less often of the workers), and franker and deeper self-revelation, social injustice and intolerance. Claude McKay's famous *If We Must Die* became the touchstone for the dynamics of the social forces and conflicts of the twenties. His was an answer to the growing crescendo of race riots and lynchings which characterized the times. Toomer's eloquent outcries in *Cane* were race conscious and challenging. In Cullen's *Shroud of Color,* his sense of race is one of loyalty, pride and group consciousness, "almost the tone of a chosen people."

> Lord, I would live persuaded by mine own
> I cannot play the recreant to these:
> My spirit has come home, that sailed the doubtful seas.

Hughes' *Brass Spittoons* tells of the distasteful tasks of menial labor:

> Hey, Boy!
> A bright bowl of brass is beautiful to the Lord
> Bright polished brass like the cymbals
> Of King David's dancers
> Like the wine cups of Solomon.

These poets, in their different ways, were all influential in the twenties and thirties, influencing an entire generation of younger poets. Cullen and Toomer in New York and all over America, Hughes in New York and all over the world, McKay in New York and the socialist world, Sterling Brown at Howard and all over the south, all expressing ideas that were representative of the Negro movement. In *Strong Men,* Brown pens:

> They dragged you from your homeland,
> They chained you in coffles
> They broke you in like oxen
> They scourged you
> They branded you
>   You sang:
>   Keep a-inchin' along
>   Lak a po' inch worm . . .
>   You sang:
>   Walk togedder, chillen,
>   Dontcha get weary
> The strong men keep a comin' on
> The strong men get stronger.

After Frederick Douglass' fictionalized *Madison Washington* and the short stories of William Wells Brown and Chestnutt, the Negro as short story writer could only emerge from a vacuum even though the short story as literary genre had taken creditable form in America. Negro writers were unable to gain any entree into the magazines. Charles Chestnutt's experiences in 1887 with the *Atlantic Monthly* when the editors did not wish to publicize his racial identity was an infamous blot on American literature. Chestnutt's story *The Goophered Grapevine* was accepted by Walter Hines Page and later Page accepted *The Wife of His Youth,* and only belatedly admitted that the author was a Negro, claiming to the editor of the magazine *Critic* that he did not want to do damage to the author's reputation. Dunbar's stories were popular because of the plantation tradition of his dialect style and they did not offend.

In the late twenties, Langston Hughes faced the problem when *Esquire* published *A Good Job Gone.* Hughes wrote about this in *Fighting Words:*

"Here are our problems: In the first place, Negro books are considered by editors and publishers as exotic. Negro material is placed, like Chinese material or Bali material into a certain classification. Magazine editors will tell you, 'We can use but so many Negro stories a year.' (That 'so many' meaning very few.) Publishers will say, 'We already have one Negro novel on our list this fall.'

"When we cease to be exotic, we do not sell well."

These have been the circumscriptions placed on the Negro short story writer on all sides in the publishing world.

When the Negro writer published in either *Crisis* or *Opportunity*, the pay was paltry and the stories were typed. The stories were concerned with lynchings, race riots, race praise or passing. Rudolph Fisher's *High Yaller* won the first prize in the 1925 *Crisis* contest. Later in the same year, *Atlantic Monthly* published his story, *The City of Refuge.* Many other new writers of the Movement wrote well constructed stories which won *Crisis* and *Opportunity* prizes—Arthur Huff Fauset, John Matheus, Eugene Gordon, Marita Bonner, Edwin Sheen and Jean Toomer. Unlike Fisher, most of these writers did not continue their careers of writing. Eric Walrond's *Tropic Death,* Langston Hughes' *Ways of White Folks* came close to penetrating into the innermost workings of Negro life which were overlooked by the racial idealists who wrote cloyingly of the new Negro middle class escapists.

Perhaps the novel as an art form was grist to the mill of the Negro writer at any time or place, whenever he began to write about his own experiences or those of others.' The earliest Negro novelists, William Wells Brown and Martin Delaney, wrote as pleaders for a cause and as Sterling Brown wrote, "their successors have almost followed their example." The inferior propaganda novels such as Frances Harper's *Iola Leroy* or *Shadows Uplifted* and Dunbar's four conventional novels were not comparable to Chestnutt's novels of social realism.

James Weldon Johnson's *Autobiography of an Ex-Coloured Man* was a purpose work, the first "passing novel," Du Bois' *Quest of the Silver Fleece* had virtues but it was not artistic. Nella Larsen's *Quicksand*, Jessie Fauset's *Plum Bun* and Walter White's *Flight*, all written in the twenties, were "passing" novels. White's *Fire in the Flint* had the virtue of being the first anti-lynch novel written by a Negro in the twenties. Du Bois' *Dark Princess* (1928) part fantasy and part fiction, called for a union of the darker nations and also criticized the weaknesses of the Negroes' struggles for freedom and America's handling of the race problem.

The New Negro Movement produced the first really competent novelists—Fisher, Walrond, Cullen, McKay, Thurman and Hughes. The forefield of this New Negro literature was an artistic awakening. Publishers may have had only one Negro on their lists, but as the late E .Franklin Frazier pointed out, the audience was not Negro, but white. These writers were very important in the development of the Negro novelist as a craftsman. With these new writers there was great fire and enthusiasm, a creative dynamism of self-conscious racialistic expression which at the time was a healthy manifestation of the problems which beset the Negro people. Thurman, in *Infants of the Spring* satirized the exaggerations and Bohemian aspects of the movement. Fisher, a physician, the first Negro to write a detective story and a writer of social comedy, in *Walls of Jericho*, wrote of Harlem jive, a socially intelligent satire of the foibles of the new Negro middle class.

The Negro had come to stay as a novelist and the novelists of the New Negro Movement prepared the way for all of those who were to come later. The genius of Wright burgeoned out of the thirties. Many, like Ellison, relied heavily on the New Negro novelists' experiences. The writers of the Federal Writers Project of the thirties looked back only a decade to their New Negro precursors. As Sterling Brown wrote in his essay, *The New Negro in Literature* (*1925-1955*),[5] "Negro au-

5. *The New Negro Thirty Years Afterward,* The Howard University Press, 1955, p. 62.

thors of the thirties, like their compatriots, faced reality more squarely. For the older light-heartedness, they substituted sober self-searching; for the bravado of false Africanism and Bohemianism, they substituted attempts to understand Negro life in its workaday aspects in the here and now. . . . Alert to the changing times, a few critics—Alain Locke among them—charted new directions."

In 1930, James Weldon Johnson in *Black Manhattan* wrote: "Harlem is still in the process of making. It is still new and mixed; so mixed that one may get many different views—which is all right so long as one view is not taken to be the whole picture. This many-sided aspect, however, makes it one of the most interesting communities in America. But Harlem is more than a community, it is a large-scale laboratory experiment in the race problem and from it a good many facts have been found."

And Alain Locke, more prophetic and Cassandra-like than he could have ever known, in the last article written before his death said, "It is to this mirror that I turn for the salient changes of majority attitudes toward the Negro, and equally important, for a view of the Negro's changed attitude toward himself. For the Negro seems at last on the verge of proper cultural recognition and a fraternal acceptance as a welcome participant and collaborator in the American arts. Should this become the realized goal, the history of the Negro's strange and tortuous career in American literature may become also the story of America's hard-won but easily endured attainment of cultural democracy."

THE HARLEM RENAISSANCE
—A PERSONAL MEMOIR

GLENN CARRINGTON

THE HARLEM of the 1920's, the decade of the New Negro, recovered very slowly from the disorganization of World War I. When northern capital had needed Negro labor to fill gaps caused by military conscription and the falling off of migration from Europe, no plans were made for housing the additional thousands who were to pour into the already overcrowded area from 125th to 145th Streets, and from Fifth to Eighth Avenues, and, of course, fair housing and fair employment practices had not been written into the law.

Lynching, peonage, disfranchisement and other evils in the south caused large numbers of Negroes to come northward, as there was promise if not fulfillment in places like New York. Just as New York City has attracted migrants from all over the world, Harlem has long had a lure for Negroes. Claude McKay called it "the queen of black belts, drawing Afroamericans together into a vast humming hive." Alain Locke, in the Harlem issue of the *Survey Graphic* for March 1925 described it thus:

"Here in Manhattan is not merely the largest Negro community in the world, but the first concentration in history of so many diverse elements of Negro life. It has attracted the African, the West Indian, the Negro American; has brought together the Negro of the North and the Negro of the South; the man from the city and the man from the town and village; the peasant, the student, the business man, the professional man, artist, poet, musician, adventurer and worker, preacher and criminal, exploiter and social outcast. Each group has come with its own separate motives and for its own special ends, but their greatest experience has been the finding of one another."

Harlem has never had any outstanding educational institutions of its own, and yet living within its borders are numerous representatives of "the talented tenth." Few of its business establishments are owned by Negroes, but a sizeable number of its residents have amassed a measure of wealth, and a few have even been rumored to be "millionaires." The value of church property owned by the major denominations runs into many millions of dollars, but the moral tone of the community still needs considerable revamping.

During the twenties Harlem was looked upon by many downtowners as an exotic, bizarre area. It was considered as one of New York's playgrounds, and attracted many whites who wanted to go slumming or merely wished to see how the "other half" of the old town lived. On the other hand, there were serious-minded, non-patronizing whites who, while appreciating the spirit of abandon found uptown, accepted Negroes as friends and equals, and did not hesitate to associate with them in their own homes downtown.

white involvement in Harlem

In this connection, one immediately thinks of Carl Van Vechten and his wife, Fania Marinoff. Van Vechten's interest in Negro life began around 1902 when he was a student at the University of Chicago. Possessed of a keen critical faculty, he presented several promising Negro writers and artists to the public through his articles in *Vanity Fair* and introductions written for their books, attended hundreds of plays, concerts, dance recitals and other events in which Negroes performed, founded the renowned James Weldon Johnson Memorial Collection of Negro Arts and Letters at Yale University, and smaller collections at Fisk and Howard Universities. His portrayal of life in Harlem in his 1926 novel *Nigger Heaven* is well known. He has made thousands of photographs of Negroes in various walks of life, but particularly in the arts.

Another able white interpreter of Harlem is Nancy Cunard, English by birth but cosmopolitan by nature, whose gigantic anthology, *Negro,* contains a wealth of material dealing with Negro life of the twenties, much of which she collected during extended stays in Harlem.

Mention should also be made of the Mexican artist, Miguel Covarrubias, whose book, *Negro Drawings,* published in 1927, contains some exceptional Harlem portraiture. While some of the drawings are slightly satirical, they are not in any sense caricatures. Covarrubias was a frequent visitor to Harlem, and his work is much more than surface-deep. The same can be said of the excellent illustrations he made for Taylor Gordon's autobiography, *Born to Be,* and the Limited Editions publication of René Maran's *Batouala.*

One cannot catalogue here all the white New Yorkers who had wholesome racial attitudes in the early days of the struggle for equality. The name of the Community Church as a center that has practiced equality cannot, however, be forgotten. Its pastor for several decades was the Rev. Dr. John Haynes Holmes, a founder and moving spirit in the N.A.A.C.P., who, soon after the publication of Alain Locke's *The New Negro,* made the book's title the subject of one of his sermons.

Continuing our recollection of some of the oases in the desert of the 1920's, there was the Civic Club on Tenth Street in lower Manhattan, which included many Negro figures of the Renaissance in its membership. It was located not far from the 14th Street headquarters of the N.A.A.C.P., and staff members from that organization, Dr. W. E. B. Du Bois, Augustus Granville Dill, Jessie Fauset, and James Weldon Johnson, often ate lunch there. White liberals, among them Lewis Mumford, Stuart Chase, Heywood Broun, Martha Gruening, Clarence Darrow and Arthur Garfield Hays were to be seen mingling and chatting with Alain Locke, Langston Hughes, Countee Cullen and Harold Jackman (the late Harlem school teacher and devoted patron of the arts).

cultural centers in other cities

Although Harlem continued to be considered the "cultural capital" of the New Negro Movement, there were a few other cities which can be called outposts of this literary headquarters. Mrs. Georgia Douglas Johnson, distinguished poet and playwright, has lived in her Halfway House in Washington for about half a century. And if Dr. Alain Locke was godfather to the younger writers and artists, Mrs. Johnson was certainly their godmother.

At Halfway House groups would gather on Saturday evenings to listen to the reading of their works or just to chat with Mrs. Johnson and each other. There one met the brilliant Rudolph "Bud" Fisher, who (circa 1924) was a Howard medical student, and who, before his untimely death in New York a decade later, was to achieve recognition as a short story writer and novelist; Langston Hughes and Countee Cullen when they were in town; Lewis Alexander, the poet; Jean Toomer, *avant garde* writer of poems, short stories and plays; Angelina

Grimké, poet and playwright; Clarissa Scott Delany, poet, and many more. Each of these writers, except Toomer, Alexander and Mrs. Johnson herself, resided later in Harlem.

Boston had its Saturday Evening Quill Club, founded by Eugene Gordon, journalist and short story writer. Among the contributors to this group's several issues of the *Saturday Evening Quill*, published in the late twenties, were Waring Cuney, poet, Dorothy West, short story writer and novelist, and Gertrude Parthenia McBrown, writer of poems for children and elocutionist.

Another center of literary activity was Philadelphia, which in 1927 published *Black Opals,* including contibutions by Arthur Huff Fauset, folklorist, biographer and essayist; Mae Cowdery, poet, Allan R. Freelon, artist, as well as a greeting from Alain Locke to his native Philadelphia!

In the field of the performing arts, the Negro's abilities and the folk material he had to offer have long been given grudging, if not open, recognition. Even in the slave era, Negroes were called upon to amuse or entertain their masters. While the age of minstrelsy both prior to and following the Civil War abounded with Negro jokes, Negro dances, Negro songs and Negro mimicry, much of that presented on the stage was done by whites in black face. The early nineteen hundreds saw the more frequent emergence of the Negro performer, the Negro composer and the Negro musician. The story of Williams and Walker, Cole and Johnson, S. H. Dudley and Ernest Hogan belongs to the pre-Renaissance period, and not to the period of the twenties. The great Bert Williams lasted until the beginning of our era, however, as witness his last performance in *Broadway Brevities* in 1920, and *The Pink Slip* (later renamed *Under the Bamboo Tree*) in 1921. But Williams was already a sick man, and died in 1922.

A great event in the New York theatre was the discovery of Paul Robeson. In 1924 he was presented in *All God's Chillun' Got Wings,* an O'Neill play. Though some members of its audiences were shocked because Robeson had to kiss Mary Blair, the white actress playing opposite him, his performance established his stature in the theatre, and led to his being cast later in *The Emperor Jones, Showboat, Porgy, Othello, Black Boy,* and *Stevedore.* He has also starred in numerous films. His wife, Eslanda Goode Robeson, is a talented writer, and except when the Robesons were traveling abroad during the twenties with their son, Paul Jr., they were popular figures in Harlem.

It will be recalled that the nineteen twenties were years of prohibition. That "noble experiment" was a complete failure in Harlem, where speakeasies flourished by the hundreds. Not all of their patrons, it must be admitted, were from the "lower classes." Some of them furnished entertainment by artists later acclaimed in musical comedy and on the legitimate stage, and they were patronized by many of our "better" citizens. They had colorful names, like the "Glory Hole," the "Blue Room," the "Air Raid Shelter" (which, appropriately enough, was a celler "dive"), "Basement Brownie's Coal Bed," etc.

Then there were the legitimate night spots. One of the popular ones of the period was Leroy's, on 135th Street near Fifth Avenue, which Langston Hughes has immortalized in his poem *To Midnight Nan at Leroy's*. This place was owned by Leroy Wilkins, and the music was furnished, as was the custom, by a six-piece jazz combination. There were many, many more, like Smalls', Happy Rhone's, Connie's Inn, the Nest, and Lulu Belle's.

Entertainment was also furnished at the endless house rent parties, an institution peculiarly Harlemesque, persisting even to the present day, though far less popular now than formerly. Among the "delicacies" offered at these gatherings were chitterlings, pig snouts, black eyes (short for black eyed peas, often cooked with rice and bacon to form the popular "hopping John"), and collard greens. An article in the *New York Sunday Times* for July 15, 1928, speaking of food in Harlem, related that "collards are said to have a peculiar affinity for the negro (sic) palate. . . . What broccoli is to Park Avenue the select collards are to the colony of upper Manhattan." We need not comment on this opinion. Suffice it to say that many who gave these parties took pride in their cooking, and many well-known figures attended or sponsored these events. Upright pianos were in fashion then, and pianists of the James P. Johnson and Fats Waller school of piano playing furnished music for the dancing or as background for the eating and drinking.

These are only one person's recollections of an era that brings back inevitable reactions of nostalgia. Harlem was good. Harlem was bad. Harlem was everything. It was colorful in more than one sense!

MY EARLY DAYS IN HARLEM

LANGSTON HUGHES

O N A BRIGHT September morning in 1921, I came up out of the subway at 135th and Lenox into the beginnings of the Negro Renaissance. I headed for the Harlem Y.M.C.A. down the block, where so
many new, young, dark, male arrivals in Harlem have spent early
days. The next place I headed to that afternoon was the Harlem
Branch Library just up the street. There, a warm and wonderful librarian, Miss Ernestine Rose, white, made newcomers feel welcome,
as did her assistant in charge of the Schomburg Collection, Catherine
Latimer, a luscious café au lait.   That night I went to the Lincoln
Theatre across Lenox Avenue where maybe one of the Smiths—Bessie,
Clara, Trixie, or Mamie—was singing the blues. And as soon as I could,
I made a beeline for *Shuffle Along,* the all-colored hit musical playing
on 63rd Street in which Florence Mills came to fame.

I had come to New York to enter Columbia College as a freshman,
but *really* why I had come to New York was to see Harlem. I found
it hard a week or so later to tear myself away from Harlem when it
came time to move up the hill to the dormitory at Columbia. That
winter I spent as little time as possible on the campus. Instead, I spent
as much time as I could in Harlem, and this I have done ever since.
I was in love with Harlem long before I got there, and I still am in
love with it. Everybody seemed to make me welcome. The sheer dark
size of Harlem intrigued me. And the fact that at that time poets and
writers like James Weldon Johnson and Jessie Fauset lived there, and
Bert Williams, Duke Ellington, Ethel Waters, and Walter White, too,
fascinated me.   Had I been a rich young man, I would have bought
a house in Harlem and built musical steps up to the front door, and
installed chimes that at the press of a button played Ellington tunes.

After a winter at Columbia, I moved back down to Harlem. Every-

PICTURES
FROM HARLEM
The work
   The children
The play
   The issues
The joy and sadness
   and watchful waiting

PHOTOGRAPHS BY JOHN TAYLOR

where I roomed, I had the good fortune to have lovely landladies. If I did not like a landlady's looks, I would not move in with her, maybe that is why. But at finding work in New York, my fortune was less than good. Finally, I went to sea—Africa, Europe—then a year in Paris working in a night club where the band was from Harlem. I was a dishwasher, later bus boy, listening every night to the music of Harlem transplanted to Montmartre. And I was on hand to welcome Bricktop when she came to sing for the first time in Europe, bringing with her news of Harlem.

When I came back to New York in 1925 the Negro Renaissance was in full swing. Countee Cullen was publishing his early poems, Aaron Douglas was painting, Zora Neale Hurston, Rudolph Fisher, Jean Toomer and Wallace Thurman were writing, Louis Armstrong was playing, Cora La Redd was dancing, and the Savoy Ballroom was open with a specially built floor that rocked as the dancers swayed. Alain Locke was putting together *The New Negro*. Art took heart from Harlem creativity. Jazz filled the night air—but not everywhere —and people came from all around after dark to look upon our city within a city, Black Harlem. Had I not had to earn a living, I might have thought it even more wonderful than it was. But I could not eat the poems I wrote. Unlike the whites who came to spend their money in Harlem, only a few Harlemites seemed to live in even a modest degree of luxury. Most rode the subway downtown every morning to work or to look for work.

Downtown! I soon learned that it was seemingly impossible for black Harlem to live without white downtown. My youthful illusion that Harlem was a world unto itself did not last very long. It was not even an area that ran itself. The famous night clubs were owned by whites, as were the theatres. Almost all the stores were owned by whites, and many at that time did not even (in the very middle of Harlem) employ Negro clerks. The books of Harlem writers all had to be published downtown, if they were to be published at all. Downtown: *white*. Uptown: *black*. White downtown pulling all the strings in Harlem. Moe Gale, Moe Gale, Moe Gale, Lew Leslie, Lew Leslie, Lew Leslie, Harper's, Knopf, *The Survey Graphic*, the Harmon Foundation, the racketeers who kidnapped Casper Holstein and began to take over the numbers for whites. Negroes could not even play their own numbers with their *own* people. And almost all the policemen in Harlem were white. Negroes couldn't even get graft from *themselves* for themselves by themselves. Black Harlem really was in white face, economically speaking. So I wrote this poem:

Because my mouth
Is wide with laughter
And my throat
Is deep with song,
You do not think
I suffer after
I have held my pain
So long?

Because my mouth
Is wide with laughter,
You do not hear
My inner cry?
Because my feet
Are gay with dancing,
You do not know
I die?

Harlem, like a Picasso painting in his cubistic period. Harlem—Southern Harlem—the Carolinas, Georgia, Florida—looking for the Promised Land—dressed in rhythmic words, painted in bright pictures, dancing to jazz—and ending up in the subway at morning rush time—*headed downtown*. West Indian Harlem—warm rambuctious sassy remembering Marcus Garvey. Haitian Harlem, Cuban Harlem, little pockets of tropical dreams in alien tongues. Magnet Harlem, pulling an Arthur Schomburg from Puerto Rico, pulling an Arna Bontemps all the way from California, a Nora Holt from way out West, an E. Simms Campbell from St. Louis, likewise a Josephine Baker, a Charles S. Johnson from Virginia, an A. Philip Randolph from Florida, a Roy Wilkins from Minnesota, an Alta Douglas from Kansas. Melting pot Harlem—Harlem of honey and chocolate and caramel and rum and vinegar and lemon and lime and gall. Dusky dream Harlem rumbling into a nightmare tunnel where the subway from the Bronx keeps right on downtown, where the money from the nightclubs goes right on back downtown, where the jazz is drained to Broadway, whence Josephine goes to Paris, Robeson to London, Jean Toomer to a Quaker Meeting House, Garvey to the Atlanta Federal Penitentiary, and Wallace Thurman to his grave; but Duke Ellington to fame and fortune, Lena Horne to Broadway, and Buck Clayton to China.

Before it was over—our New Negro Renaissance—poems became placards: DON'T BUY WHERE YOU CAN'T WORK! Adam Powell with a picket sign; me, too. BUY BLACK! Sufi long before the Black Muslims. FIRST TO BE FIRED, LAST TO BE HIRED! The Stock Market crash. The bank failures. Empty pockets. *God Bless The Child That's Got His Own*. Depression. Federal Theatre in Harlem, the making of Orson Welles. WPA, CCC, the Blue Eagle, Father Divine. In the midst of the Depression I got a cable from Russia inviting me to work on a motion picture there. I went to Moscow. That was the end of the early days of Langston Hughes in Harlem.

THE MUSIC OF HARLEM

WILLIAM R. DIXON

THE MAIN difficulty one encounters when attempting to write about the music of Harlem is that unlike the other arts, the dance, theatre, literature and so on, the *music* of Harlem did not necessarily concern itself only with Harlem in Manhattan but was involved with all the other "Harlems" that were and are abundant in America. With the possible exception of Bud Powell (piano), Sonny Rollins (tenor saxophone), Jackie McLean (alto saxophone), Bennie Harris (trumpet)—and of course there are others—the musicians who made this music were not from Harlem at all, but they did come there, at first to live and then to explore and develop their music.

A strange paradox is that the music which did much to shape contemporary music and dance, which was largely created in Harlem, is not to be found on a large scale in Harlem today. Any student of jazz history has heard of the golden days of jazz in Harlem, when the Cotton Club was housing the early Ellington band—the days of Smalls, Connie's Inn, the Elk's Rendezvous and others. The legends of the house-rent parties are legion, where such pianists as Willie ("the Lion") Smith, James P. Johnson, Willie Gant, Fats Waller and others vied for the plaudits of the audiences.

> It was at Leroy's that I first saw piano battles. Players like Willie "the Lion," James P., Fats Waller, Willie Gant. They'd last for three or four hours. One man would play two or three choruses, and the next would slide in. Jimmy was on top most of the time. Fats was the youngest, but he was coming along. They played shouts and they also played pop tunes. You got credit for how many patterns you could create within the tunes you knew, and in how many different keys you could play.[1]

1. "Garvin Bushell and New York Jazz in the 1920's," by Nat Hentoff, *The Jazz Review,* February, 1959.

And of course the old Savoy Ballroom, that home of "happy feet," which today is no more, did much to bring people from other parts of the city, country and even the world, to hear this music and to see experts perform dances to it.

Much of the world's important music, music that has lasted and endured, has been concerned a great deal of the time with the dance, and if not with a specific dance, at least with that *kind* of movement. The early days of jazz were not to be an exception to that rule. In the beginning everybody danced to the rhythm of jazz, and by their dancing to it, by their participating in it, such new dance steps as the Lindy Hop, the Big Apple, the Charleston were created.

> From 1916 to 1930, James P. Johnson was the outstanding rag-time pianist and composer for piano in New York. During that time, he developed the New York style of "stride" piano from the rags of Scott Joplin and the southern Negro cotillion and set dances. . . .[2]

The first dance I ever went to was at the Renaissance Ballroom, known affectionately as the "Rennie," located at 137th Street and Seventh Avenue. At that time I had absorbed much more about the art of music through listening than I had by participating through dancing. The band was that of Jimmie Lunceford, whose music was later to become a heavy influence on the music of Stan Kenton and others. I can remember standing all night long at the bandstand, completely enthralled, listening to the music of that marvelous band. But then those bands were not dance bands in the way that a dance band is thought of today. Those bands were good jazz bands and the music they played was good music, suitable for both listening *and* dancing. A few weeks ago, a friend of mine played some tapes made by the Ellington band at a dance in Fargo, North Dakota, and in the light of what is played for dancing today, this was indeed a marvel. The band was simply playing Ellington's music, with such as Jimmie Blanton, Rex Stewart and others, in the way that they play. And the people danced.

> Yes, dancing is very important to people who play music with a beat. I think that people who don't dance, or who never did dance, don't really understand the beat. What they get in their

2. "Conversations with James P. Johnson," by Tom David, *The Jazz Review*, June, 1959.

minds is a mechanical thing not totally unacademic. I know musicians who don't and never did dance, and they have difficulty communicating.[3]

It has been offered as argument that the "new music," or bebop—later just plain bop—was created to discourage inferior players from participating, and also to keep "outsiders" off the crowded bandstand at Minton's. But I can't fully accept this. No art is deliberately created on so small a basis. It is possible that some of the rather unusual harmonies (for the time) employed were so devised for the purpose of making it difficult for non-"in" musicians to play, or even *want* to play, but the over-all idea of the music—a music that was to change the direction or, rather, further reinforce the direction of the older music—was much more profound in concept and, like all art, was simply created by doing.

There are certain advantages about the ghetto, although one who is compelled against his innate desires to live in it may not view them in this manner. Because the Negro musician was relegated to jazz, and jazz only, it is easy to understand why all the main innovators and important creators of this music have been Negro. The Negro jazzman has never (until very recently) really played anything but jazz. And when I say jazz, I mean that he has, for the most part, only played that music which he himself created. All of his creativity, concentration and sensitivity went into this music and this *kind* of playing. Unlike white musicians, he could not work both in the symphonic or non-jazz world *and* the jazz world. And this had nothing to do with his ability, or even his desires. As a result, his entire concept of music, braced and supported by a background of spiritual music, work songs, field hollers and, of course, the blues, was a concept steeped in a musical form that first of all demanded strong emotional giving and response. In jazz, unlike other forms of music, the composer, the man who wrote the music (in a literal sense) was not *that* important. To the jazz player a piece of music simply meant that he was to extract from it those elements which *he* felt, and responded to. In fact, in jazz the player *always,* if he was true to his art, played himself and his own feelings.

In the ghetto this kind of emotional playing flourished. There was no time or inclination to intellectualize the music. Either it "moved" you or it didn't, and if a player failed to "get to the people" he would

3. "It's Really A Twisting World," by Duke Ellington, in an interview with Stanley Dance, *Jazz*, October, 1962.

most certainly find it difficult to work. All jazz was not played in the clubs, at dances or in the other places commonly assumed to be *the* places where jazz was heard. Who is to say that it was *not* jazz that I heard as a child in those Baptist churches? It made *my* foot pat!

It is amazing to me how the full significance of the music of Parker and Gillespie has managed to escape the majority of people who lay strenuous claim to being art and music "lovers." It is a rare thing that in one's own time one is able to witness so much innovation, transition, so much change and so much creativity. After the initial impact of Parker and Gillespie (and of course I am not leaving out Powell, Monk, Clarke or Lester Young) had sort of infiltrated into the noncreative areas of music, the commercial big bands and the radio and television "jingle" field (which, incidentally, were to reap large financial rewards for *their* "work," while Bird was to die a premature death and Gillespie was unable to keep a large band together because of the financial strain), it became pretty safe to play *like* Parker and Gillespie. (Monk's music, for some reason or other, never permitted that kind of "borrowing" and familiarity.) Horn men, pianists, arrangers, composers, and so on, drew excessively from not only the grammar and musical language of these men, but also from some of their actual works. It reached the state, which jazz had had the fortunate pleasure to do every now and then, where the "borrowers" thought they'd solved it all, where much of the music produced in and out of jazz became highly predictable. At the apogee of this period another addition to and extension of this vital music was made on the appearance of composer-saxophonist Ornette Coleman.

Ornette, like most of the revolutionaries in jazz—Parker, from Kansas City; Gillespie, from Cheraw, South Carolina; Monk, from Rocky Mount, North Carolina; Christian, from Dallas, Texas—came to New York from Fort Worth, Texas, with his own ideas of what should be the ultimate in a person's application to jazz music. He indicated that the old way of playing, interpreting and composing would no longer suffice if further creativity and extension of the music was to be desired and obtained.

With his arrival all the old stock arguments concerning his ability to play, and so on, were again heard. Every innovator has had the same experience. Ornette was both hailed and reviled, idolized and sneered at, understood and misunderstood. His music, however, left no one who heard it passive. And now, if being aped musically is the sign of arrival, then he most certainly has arrived. But this is in the *musical* sense, certainly not in the financial sense. Those very musicians who at first contested even Ornette's ability to play his instrument have found it necessary to re-evaluate their own musical statements. Each day finds a new fragment of his music cropping up in someone else's work. (The writer copied part of the music for a concert of avant garde, non-jazz music recently held at Carnegie Hall and conducted by composer-conductor Gunther Schuller, and at least one of the compositions was based on the concept and approach of Ornette's playing and writing.) So it is apparent that not only has his presence been felt in the jazz world, but in the non-jazz music world as well.

Had it not been for the early Cotton Club, it is quite possible that Duke Ellington might never have formulated the style of music that he did. Of course this is highly speculative because Ellington would most certainly have created some *kind* of important music. But the question Gunther Schuller poses, "How did Ellington develop into one of America's foremost composers?" has the following highly informative answer:

> It was precisely due to the fortuitous circumstances of working five years at the Cotton Club. There, by writing and experimenting with all manner of descriptive production and dance numbers, his [Ellington's] inherent talent and imagination found a fruitful outlet.[4]

That the music which virtually supports the musical theatre, television, radio, commercial jingle field, and in some instances even supplies the lifeblood for "serious" music, exists as a nonfunctional art form for so many who profess love of folk music, seems to me a ridiculous situation. As Louis Armstrong has so aptly put it, "All music's gotta be 'folk' music. I ain't never heard no horse sing a song." And with the emergence of spring there is hardly a Sunday that Washington Square Park in Greenwich Village doesn't play host to thousands of folk singers and folk song lovers. Of course we know that jazz, especially that of today, is no longer folk music in the sense that defines folk music, but the noted British writer-critic Francis Newton has made this observation on the work of Duke Ellington:

> ... he [Ellington] solved the unbelieveably difficult problem of turning a living, shifting and improvised folk music into composition without losing its spontaneity.[5]

4. "The Ellington Style, Its Origins and Early Development," by Gunther Schuller, *Jazz*, edited by Nat Hentoff and Albert McCarthy.
5. Article by Francis Newton, *New Statesman*, October 11, 1958.

When I was coming up, every beginning Negro band, composed of youngsters, was always formed with a dancing audience in mind. Sol Moore always had a good musical band and George Smith always played at the functions we went to as kids. Strange—as I write this, I'm recalling that both these musicians are now dead and I think we were all of the same age.

Of course, much of the self-consciousness that is attached to a great deal of today's playing was absent in the beginning for several reasons. In the beginning, art for art's sake was not a dominant factor. Well, maybe it was, deep down inside, but the thing that came through was the fact that these "cats" had a story to tell, they wanted to play and they wanted more than anything to play *themselves,* without restrictions. And this was the most important thing.

But music was plentiful in Harlem in those days (as it was everywhere else) in the late twenties and thirties up to the early forties. And while it was necessary to go "downtown" to make a living, the real "living" for these people was when they returned home. What was it that Bessie Smith said about Saturday night? It was music, dancing, dancing and music. Not that that was *all* there was to life. But, to face reality, who could view *only* the bad and sometimes terrible things and injustices twenty-four hours a day, seven days a week, three hundred and sixty-five days a year? Who could think *all* the time that in all those banks in New York not one black person would ask for your deposit book?

I can remember when we came from Massachusetts to Harlem in 1934. I had never seen so many *people* before, let alone black people. And it never really occurred to me until I went "downtown" to high school that every person in authority that I'd seen in Harlem—the butcher, the grocer, the policeman, the man who came to read the gas meter, and even the vendor of fruit and vegetables in the block—were all white. It did seem, to a little boy, that these white people *really* owned everything. But that wasn't entirely true. They didn't own the music that I heard played. And although I did like Harry James (that was when I first decided I wanted to learn to play the trumpet) and the Glenn Miller band, it was Count Basie, Earl Hines, Les Hite and Duke Ellington that I "dug." I didn't really *understand* them but I most certainly liked them.

> In 1937, in three weeks, I heard a dozen big bands of quality (Duke Ellington, Jimmie Lunceford, Fletcher Henderson, Chick Webb, Earl Hines, Basie, Corsey, Goodman, Shaw, Millinder,

Willie Bryant and Luis Russell). In 1958, in six weeks, I heard only two, both of which were assembled solely for recording purposes.[6]

At one time all the bands (Negro and white) were large bands, and this served a twofold purpose. It enabled a musician to learn. He learned music and musicianship. He learned to play *with* other musicians. He learned to play in a section. He learned to be a "lead" man and a soloist. It was a kind of apprenticeship. Also, a bandleader was able to employ more men. The average band was composed of from twelve to around seventeen men. There was more employment and a younger, inexperienced musician could find work much more easily than today. At the end of World War II, most of the large bands were unable to continue. Musical tastes had changed; the concept of what a large band should play, as indicated by the younger players, was difficult for the older leaders to fathom and, more than anything, the economics of the situation could no longer provide for the big payrolls which a large band needs. Where formerly bands had broadcast "live" from clubs and dances, recordings began to be played as a substitute for the in-person performance. And if white bands suffered, Negro bands suffered even more. In the first place, they'd always been restricted in their playing to certain areas. That was *real* segregation. And of course there came the decline in vaudeville, the change-over of the downtown movie houses that used to have bands. Finally, with the ushering in of television, the death of the large jazz band became official.

But when the big band was in its heyday (in the thirties and early forties), the music that was played generally bore the stamp of one individual—the arranger. It was his job to create the style of the band. Such men as Don Redman, Fletcher Henderson, Eddie Barefield, Bud Johnson and Benny Carter were the deciding factors in how a band should play and, in most instances, what. It was the Henderson arrangements played by the Henderson band almost a decade before that enabled Benny Goodman to become "King of Swing." Sy Oliver, who had written for the Lunceford band, started to write for and shape the musical thinking in the Tommy Dorsey band. It was, in fact, really Don Redman who actually introduced the style of orchestration that was to become the modus operandi of all the orchestras utilizing jazz. Thus the large band served some of the more creative players as a kind of tyrannical parent. It provided him with food and

6. "All Too Soon," by Stanley Dance, *The Jazz Review*, December, 1958.

shelter (almost literally) but he was rarely able to play as much individual jazz as he wanted to play. Because of this situation the "jam session" (also called "after hours session" and later called simply "session") was born.

> The afternoon I walked into the Rhythm Club, the corner and street was crowded with musicians with their instruments and horns. I was introduced and shook hands with a lot of fellows on the outside. Then we entered the inside which was crowded. What I saw and heard, I will never forget. A wild cutting session (a term for a session where the big achievement was to better, or "cut," all the other players) was in progress and sitting around the piano were twenty or thirty musicians, all with their instruments out waiting for a signal to play choruses of Gershwin's "Liza."[7]

The "after hours" session was just what its name implied. It was a place where musicians gathered after their regular working hours (generally after three in the morning) to play specifically for their own pleasure.

> One factor in the development of many a jazz artist, a factor frequently ignored, is the now almost obsolete custom of sitting in [jamming], and the interchange of ideas between musicians in sessions has been beneficial to the development of many jazz styles.[8]

Those bystanders other than musicians who were in attendance at these sessions were usually as creative in listening as the musicians were in playing. There were also "after hours spots." These were places that opened after the regular places closed. Admittance to them was often viewed as a high status symbol in the days when Harlem was *the* place to go for the people who lived "downtown"—and "downtown" meant any place that was not Harlem. Monroe's Uptown House, then located on 134th Street off Seventh Avenue, was one of the more popular places, and the music was generally of the kind that was not to be found in the more ordinary establishments.

With all of this background and development, however, jazz to

7. "Jelly Roll Morton in New York," by Danny Barker, *The Jazz Review*, May, 1959.
8. "Little Jazz—The Early Days," by George Hoeffer, *Down Beat*, January 31, 1963.

many people is apparently not music at all. To them it is not the expression of a people, the collectivization of a group experience, coupled with a strong desire to live and enjoy living within the confines of a social system which has not completely allowed them their birthright, which has resulted in a form of musical expression indigenous in the first instance only to America. For without America there could never have been jazz, such as we know it, that is, and those of us who are indeed fortunate in knowing it, love it and try to understand it.

Many great composers have, at one time or another, drawn on folk tradition for their sources of inspiration. Bela Bartok has made use, extensive use, of this source. Vaughan Williams, Igor Stravinsky and Aaron Copland are but three others who have extended some of the folk tradition by infusing it with their own personalities and experiences. But jazz, another *kind* of folk music, has seemingly eluded the "serious" composer. And I mean such composers as Milhaud (although his "Création du Monde" is considered to be a jazz-"influenced" piece), Stravinsky (the same holds true for his "l'Histoire du Soldat"), Copland and the Negro composer William Grant Still.

Where these men have made their mistakes has been in their attitudes that jazz music is something that is a smidgin less valuable and important than *their* music. Their approach has always embodied the idea that they can be *influenced* by the music to write much *longer* "serious" pieces. As if longevity had *anything* to do with music! They almost always "love" the "quaintness" of jazz. It is always "novel" to them. There isn't a "serious" composer who isn't "fascinated" by the rhythms of jazz. It is, however, never really *music* to them. For some strange reason it never really lives and breathes life to them. They can never glean the hope, despair, love, hate and *all* that man does, and consequently is, that is imbued in the music. It is always "exotic."

The insatiable curiosity of a gourmet anxious to try everything had brought him closer, as early as 1913, to Pierrot Lunaire, with the result that polytonality itself was for him an untried and particularly subtle form of pleasure. In fact Schoenberg interested him as much as Gershwin: for this same hunger for NOVELTY [the writer's capitals] took him also to the music hall and to JAZZ; he certainly revelled in American Negro music, as can be seen from the fox trots and boston two-steps of

L'Enfant et Les Sortilèges . . . and the nostalgic blues which serves as andante to the Sonata for piano and violin.[9]

When Igor Stravinsky composed the "Ebony Concerto" for the Woody Herman band it was because he had been so enthralled and excited about the sound of the Herman group with its exuberance and vitality. That same Herman band, however, owed much of its raison d'être to the writing and creativity of John Birks ("Dizzy") Gillespie. The now famous unison trumpet passage in "Caldonia" was lifted directly from the work and playing of Gillespie. And I often wonder how the sound of Gillespie's own orchestra playing such works as George Russell's "Cubano Be, Cubano Bop" would have affected him.

I think that the jazz composers and improvisers have utilized the techniques and approaches of non-jazz music much more definitively than has been the reverse case. In fact, jazz and the jazz language have made themselves felt, if not entirely loved and understood, by the "serious" composer.

> Even in self-consciously academic compositions we are used to hearing quarter-tones, glissandos, Moorish wailing on the clarinet and oboe, "dirty" tones, overblowing of trumpets in screeching registers, and the other instrumental effects once exclusively associated with jazz. All are now assimilated into the common language of contemporary music.[10]

It is indeed a sad commentary when the people who created and fostered this music now feel that in order to "better" themselves today they have to deny jazz and its creators. It was painful to read recently that William Grant Still had put down hard the efforts of individualism in musical expression of many of today's younger jazzmen, both instrumental and compositional. How far can one go from what he is? Whether Still likes it or not his roots are also located in that field holler—*and* the blues.

It was composer George Russell who said: "Jazz is the Negro's most important gift to American culture.[11] I find it doubly sad that the community and the people who formerly housed this music have for some reason or other found it necessary to reject it. Jazz is *their* con-

---

9. *Ravel* by Vladimir Jankelevitch, New York, Grove Press.
10. "Comments on Classics," by Donald J. Henehan, *Down Beat*, January 17, 1963.
11. *The Jazz Review,* 1959.

tribution to the arts. Jazz *is* America. The music of Duke Ellington, Miles Davis, Charlie Parker, heard around the world, is rarely thought of as being *their* music, but the music of America. All Americans should be proud of this, but the proudest should be the Negro. For he has contributed when his contributions were thoroughly undesirable as gifts. He gave when both he as the giver and what he had to give were unwanted. But the gift was too big to lie in the shadow. It sought the sun and the sun sought it.

There was a time around the late forties and early fifties when sessions could be found all over Harlem. There was a rehearsal studio at 315 Lenox Avenue, between 125th and 126th Streets. Newby's studio was located on 116th Street. At that time Fritz Pollard had a studio next door to Loew's Victoria on 125th Street. And jazz could be heard at Club Harlem (sometimes referred to as the "Heat Wave") on 145th Street, at Connie's at 135th Street and Seventh Avenue, Minton's on 118th Street, the Paradise at 110th Street and Eighth Avenue, the "L" bar at 146th Street and Broadway. A private club called The Sportsmen at 145th Street and Seventh Avenue, next to the Roosevelt Theatre, had jazz on weekends. There was also a very colorful bar with the misleading name Lotus at Lenox Avenue and 131st Street. Showman's on 125th Street, next to the Apollo Theatre, also had jazz, and there were many others. For dancing, of course, there was the Savoy Ballroom at 140th Street and Lenox Avenue, the "Rennie" on Seventh Avenue at 137th Street, and the list goes on.

But what happened? What Ed Cambridge has said:

> It's a good thing Jesse Shipp didn't go up there [Harlem] this year looking to work in theatre. He'd be hungry as hell!!![12]

Yes, I hear much of the music emanating from the record shops on 125th Street and I don't feel elated when I hear in quantity all of the cheap, gaudy—yes, music *can* be gaudy—sentimental hit-parade and sub-hit-parade pap and garbage that Madison Avenue has decreed must be accepted as music. It does indeed sadden the heart to know that if one wants to hear jazz, he can't, as Thomas Wolfe put it, "go home again." But then, perhaps that too is good. Harlem, although it doesn't appear to have jazz today, at least *did* and in its way gave jazz to us.

12. *Freedomways,* Summer, 1963.

CHARLIE PARKER ("BIRD")

He sang—as a bird does—
Not intent on rhyme,
But content to climb,
Note by note,
High as any bird's wing
Could carry him.
Sometimes his song was
Sheer prettiness—
As if from some starling—
Then, suddenly,
As if he were some
Earth-ridden bird
Bewailing his plight,
His song was blue,
And bottomless . . .
And yet, he was no prisoner of earth—
Of time perhaps, but not of earth.
I know, because there were other times
When he would soar way above
The could-have-beens; the would-have-beens,
The times-when . . .
And just be!

RALPH GERVIN

AFRICA CONSCIOUS HARLEM

RICHARD B. MOORE

C ONSCIOUSNESS OF AFRICA, if not coeval, certainly existed very early in the development of the Afroamerican community in Harlem. This consciousness grew almost as rapidly as the community itself expanded. From the few occupants of two houses on 134th Street west of Fifth Avenue in 1900, this unique community had grown by 1920 into a city within the City of New York. Embracing many thousands, this Harlem enclave then reached from 127th Street on the south to 145th Street on the north and from Fifth to Eighth Avenues. Now some 300,000 people of African descent reach down below 110th Street and up into the Washington Heights area, spread almost from the East to the Hudson Rivers.

Harlem's main thoroughfare in 1920 was 135th Street between Lenox and Seventh Avenues, with an almost solid block of houses and stores on its north side owned by St. Philip's Protestant Episcopal Church. In one of these stores, number 135 to be exact, sharing space with the weekly *New York News*, George Young conducted the first Afroamerican book shop in Harlem. A pullman porter who had made good use of his travels through the country to assemble a fine collection of Africana and Afroamericana, Young also endeavored to supply such literature to his people.

In Young's Book Exchange, known then as *The Mecca of Literature Pertaining to Colored People*, there was to be seen what would seem to many, even today, an astonishing array of material treating of Africa and her dispersed descendants. In this small establishment during 1921, a visitor would have seen several copies of the compact book by Dr. W. E. B. DuBois, which bore the all too current title *The Negro*, though this was chiefly devoted to Africa. Alongside would be seen *From Superman to Man* by J. A. Rogers, which exposed racism and pointed to the ancient history and culture of the African peoples.

On the shelves at Young's there reposed histories written by Afroamericans such as George W. Williams, *History of the Negro Race in America.* These generally followed the pattern set by William Wells Brown in *The Black Man, His Antecedents, His Genius, and His Achievements* and *The Rising Son,* which began with an account of the African background. *A Social History of the American Negro* by Prof. Benjamin Brawley of Howard University, then just published, also included an entire chapter on Liberia.

Books by African authors included the older *Letters of Ignatius Sancho* and the *Life of Olaudah Equiano* or *Gustavus Vassa.* Beside these were more recent treatises: Duse Mohamed, *In the Land of the Pharaohs;* Sol T. Plaatje, *Native Life in South Africa;* Casely Hayford, *Ethiopia Unbound, Gold Coast Native Instituitons,* and *The Truth About the West African Land Question;* Dr. James Africanus B. Horton, *West African Countries and Peoples* and *A Vindication of the African Race;* John Mensah Sarbah, *Fanti Customary Laws;* Bishop Samuel Adjai Crowther, *Journal of an Expedition Up the Niger and Tshadda Rivers.*

Numerous books by European and Euroamerican authors included important references to Africans by Abolitionists such as Granville Sharp, Thomas Clarkson, Wilson Armistead, Abbe Gregoire, Anthony Benezet, Mrs. Lydia Maria Child, and Charles Sumner. Beside these were accounts of explorers, travelers, missionaries, and investigators—Mungo Park, Livingstone, Moffat, Bruce, Speke, Baker du Chaillu, Reclus, Barth, Schweinfurth, Caillie, Du Bois, Burton, Crawford, Talbot, Ellis, Cardinall, Duff Macdonald, Bleek and Lloyd, Pitt-Rivers.

Specially emphasized were Frobenius, *Voice of Africa;* Ratzel, *History of Mankind;* Mary Kingsley, *West African Studies;* Flora L. Shaw (Lady Lugard), *A Tropical Dependency;* Dennett, *At the Back of the Black Man's Mind;* Morel, *Red Rubber* and *The Black Man's Burden.* George Young's signed personal copy of this last, purchased from his widow, is still among the highly prized books in my collection. As a special indulgence to those who evinced great interest, Young would exhibit such rare, old, large tomes as Ludolph's *History of Ethiopia* and Ogilby's *Africa.*

Expressing the consciousness of Africa already existing among Afroamericans, there were revealing volumes like *The African Abroad* by Prof. William H. Ferris, and *Negro Culture in West Africa* by George W. Ellis which recorded the alphabet and script invented by a genius of the Vai-speaking peoples. There, too, was the masterful work of the Haitian scholar Anténor Firmin, *De l'égalité des races humaines,* which marshalled evidence of early African culture and its significant contribution to Europe and the world in a crushing refutation of the racist theories of inequality propounded by Gobineau.

Though written in 1886, the challenging book *Liberia: The Americo-African Republic* by T. McCants Stewart urged Afroamericans to "put their own ships upon the sea. . . . We must have our own vessels carrying our African workers, our civilization, and our wares back to the 'Fatherland,' and bringing back its riches." This exhortation concluded with the confident vision of a great "Americo-African Republic," extending 'into the Soudan, throughout the Niger and into the Congo; and under a mighty African ruler, there will arise a stable and powerful Government of Africans, for Africans, and by Africans, which shall be an inestimable blessing to all mankind."

Likewise far-visioned were the writings of Alexander Crummell: *The Future of Africa* and *Africa and America.* This last contained his classic essay on *The Relations and Duties of Free Colored Men in America to Africa,* originally published in 1861. This dedicated thinker affirmed "a natural call upon the children of Africa in foreign lands, to come and participate in the opening treasures of the land of their fathers."

Further indicative of this consciousness of African provenience and common heritage were typical writings by scholars native to the African motherland, the Caribbean areas, and the American mainland. Pointed to with particular pride by George Young would be such books as the *History of the Yorubas* by Rev. Samuel Johnson, *Glimpses of the Ages* by Theophilus E. Samuel Scholes, *The Lone Star of Liberia* by F. A. Durham, and especially *African Life and Customs* and *Christianity, Islam and the Negro Race* by Edward Wilmot Blyden.

That this consciousness of Africa was active and widespread was perhaps significantly shown in the reprinting and distribution by George Young in 1920 of *The Aims and Methods of a Liberal Education for Africans,* the Inaugural Address delivered by Edward Wilmot Blyden, LL.D., President of Liberia College, January 5, 1881. Nor was this interest in Africa a new thing. For despite ruthless repression under the chattel slave system, the transplanted Africans could never be reduced to total cultural blankness.

early ties to Africa

Consciousness of their ancestral homeland has thus been historically evident from the first arrivals when some of these Africans, brought as slaves into the Americas, killed themselves believing that they would thereby return to Africa. Awareness of their heritage of culture and dignity continued during the colonial period and the early days of this republic. The name *African* was then preferred and used instead of the slave-masters' degrading epithet "negro." Witness thus The Free African Society, founded in Philadelphia in 1817 by Richard Allen and Absalom Jones. This was the forerunner of the African Protestant Episcopal Church of St. Thomas and also of the African Methodist Episcopal Church. Note also the African Lodge of Prince Hall Masons in Boston; the African Methodist Episcopal Zion Church, African Society for Mutual Aid, African Grove Playhouse in New York; and many so named throughout the country.

As early as 1788 an organized body of Afroamericans in Newport, R. I., which included Paul Cuffee who was soon to make history in this respect, wrote to the Free African Society of Philadelphia proposing a plan for emigration to Africa. In 1811 Paul Cuffee sailed in his own ship to Sierra Leone to investigate the feasibility of founding a settlement there. In 1815 at his own expense amounting to some $4,000, Captain Paul Cuffee, consummating twenty years of thought and effort, sailed forth again to Sierra Leone, this time commanding the good ship *Traveler* with 38 Afroamerican emigrants aboard, which included several whom he had boldly rescued from slavery along the Atlantic seaboard.

Paul Cuffee's achievement gave impetus to the founding of the American Colonization Society in 1817. But this body was dominated by slaveholders with the object of getting rid of free Afroamericans whose very presence and example encouraged the slaves to seek freedom. Hence the American Colonization Society was powerfully opposed by free-spirited Afroamericans and their Abolitionist allies.

Nevertheless, several Afroamerican leaders took advantage of the operation of the American Colonization Society to foster self-government in Africa through the founding of Liberia. Outstanding among these were Daniel Coker, Elijah Johnson, Lott Cary, Colin Teague, John B. Russwurm, Hilary Teague, and Joseph Jenkins Roberts who was elected first president of Liberia in 1848. By this time the population of Liberia included some 3,000 persons of African descent who had emigrated from the United States of America and the Caribbean.

The distinguished Afroamerican scholar, Rev. Alexander Crummell, after graduating from Cambridge University in 1853, spent 20 years teaching and laboring in Africa. Commissioned by a convention of Afroamericans held in Chatham, Canada West, in 1858, Martin R.

Delany led an expedition into what is now Nigeria and published his *Official Report of the Niger Valley Exploring Party* in 1861. This mission had even signed a treaty with African rulers at Abeokuta which authorized a projected settlement, but this project lapsed after the outbreak of the Civil War in the U.S.A. The other commissioner of this expedition, Professor Robert Campbell, published his report in *A Pilgrimage to My Motherland.*

After the Civil War and Reconstruction, interest was revived in African settlement as a great exodus began from the south, due to the wholesale massacre of some 40,000 Afroamericans by such terrorist organizations as the Ku Klux Klan. This reign of terror reached monstrous proportions after the withdrawal of federal troops from the south. A new movement for migration to Africa was fostered jointly by Afroamerican Baptists and Methodists; Bishop H. M. Turner played a leading part in this endeavor. Organizations were established in several states, notably the Liberian Exodus and Joint Stock Company in North Carolina and the Freedmen's Emigration Aid Society in South Carolina. This last acquired the ship *Azor* for $7,000 and this ship actually carried 274 emigrants to Africa on one of its trips, despite the efforts of prejudiced European Americans to impose outrageous costs and to hinder its operation. The *Azor* was soon stolen and sold in Liverpool; the attempts to recover it failed when the U.S. Circuit Court refused even to entertain the suit brought to this end.

About 1881 a descendant of Paul Cuffee, Captain Harry Dean, sailed to Africa commanding his ship the *Pedro Gorino* with the object "to rehabilitate Africa and found an Ethiopian Empire as the world has never seen." Another expedition took 197 emigrants from Savannah, Georgia to Liberia. "Chief Sam" of Kansas launched a movement to sail ships and build a state in Africa but this movement failed to achieve its goals.

role of speakers and press

This tradition was known in Harlem and interest in Africa was constantly stimulated by the generally well-informed outdoor speakers of the twenties. Free lance advocates such as William Bridges, Strathcona R. Williams, Alexander Rahming, Edgar M. Grey, Arthur Reid, and the Basuto "Prince" Mokete M. Manoede held forth constantly on African history and stressed unity with the African people.

Militant socialists like Chandler Owen, A. Philip Randolph, Rev. George Frazier Miller, Grace P. Campbell, Anna Brown, Elizabeth

Hendrickson, Frank Poree, Otto Huiswoud, W. A. Domingo, Tom Potter, Frank D. Crosswaith, Rudolph Smith, Herman S. Whaley, John Patterson, Victor C. Gaspar, Ramsay, Ross D. Brown, and the writer of this account—all steadily emphasized the liberation of the oppressed African and other colonial peoples as a vital aim of their world view. Above all Hubert H. Harrison gave forth from his encyclopedic store, a wealth of knowledge of African history and culture which brought this consciousness to a very great height.

A vigorous press which circulated widely in Harlem also intensified this consciousness of Africa. Notable among these journals were *The Amsterdam News* while edited by Cyril V. Briggs, the *Crisis* magazine under Dr. Du Bois, the *Challenge* of William Bridges, the radical *Messenger* magazine projected by Chandler Owen and A. Philip Randolph, the *African Times and Orient Review,* published by Duse Mahomed in London, imported by John E. Bruce, and distributed by this writer, the *Crusader* magazine edited by Cyril V. Briggs as the organ of the African Blood Brotherhood, the powerful *Voice* of the Liberty League of Afro-Americans then being led by Hubert H. Harrison. Later the *Emancipator* conducted chiefly by W. A. Domingo and this writer, warned against the weaknesses of the Garvey movement, while striving for an end to colonialist subjugation and all forms of oppression.

Vibrant echoes too had reached Harlem of the Pan African Conference, organized in London during 1900 by Henry Sylvester-Williams, a barrister-at-law born in Trinidad of African ancestry. This Conference elected as general chairman Bishop Alexander Walters of the African Methodist Episcopal Zion Church and Dr. W. E. B. Du Bois chairman of the Committee on Address to the World. Stimulating news had come also of the Second Pan African Conference organized by Dr. Du Bois and held in Paris early in 1919, following the significant though unsuccessful attempts made independently by William Monroe Trotter and Dr. Du Bois to present the case of the oppressed peoples of African descent before the Versailles Peace Conference in 1918.

Several distinguished visitors to Harlem contributed greatly to this ever growing consciousness of Africa, among them F. E. M. Hercules, a native of Trinidad and founder of an organization seeking to unify all the descendants of Africa everywhere. Dr. J. Edmeston Barnes, born in Barbados, came directly from London with a similar program calling also for the rejection of the disrespectful and denigrating name "Negro," which he condemned as "a bastard political colloquialism." Likewise, Albert Thorne of Barbados and Guiana projected the ideas of his African Colonial Enterprise which was designed to embrace all peoples of African origin.

arrival of Marcus Garvey

Harlem had thus become considerably Africa conscious and this consciousness was soon to build the movement which was carried to great heights of mass emotion, widespread projection, and stupendous endeavor by the skillful propagandist and promoter, Marcus Garvey. When Garvey arrived from Jamaica in 1916, Harlem was emerging as the vanguard and focal point, "the cultural capital" of ten million Afroamericans and to some extent also of other peoples of African origin in the Western Hemisphere. The demand for labor, due to the first World War, rapidly augmented the growth of Harlem, as thousands poured in from the south, the Caribbean, and Central America.

Harlem then seethed with a great ferment, bitterly resenting oppression and discrimination, particularly the treatment meted out to its crack Fifteenth Regiment. Harlem reacted vigorously also against the brutal lynchings then growing throughout the country, and especially against the frightful wholesale massacre in East St. Louis in July 1917. Some 10,000 of Harlem's citizens marched down Fifth Avenue carrying placards in the Silent Protest Parade led by the National Association for the Advancement of Colored People. The hanging of 13 Afroamerican soldiers following the Houston affair, when they had retaliated against wanton attack by prejudiced southerners, stirred mounting anger, frustration, and despair.

Marcus Garvey saw the opportunity to harness this upsurge against oppression and to direct the existing consciousness of Africa into a specific organized movement under his leadership. Realizing the deepseated if unconscious desire of the disinherited people of African origin for equal or similar status to that of others in every phase of human thought and endeavor, Garvey projected various means and enterprises which appealed to and afforded expression of this basic human desire.

After a poor initial meeting at St. Mark's Hall and some outdoor attempts, Marcus Garvey secured his first favorable public response when introduced by Hubert H. Harrison, leader of the Liberty League of Afro-Americans, at a huge meeting at Bethel A. M. E. Church. Following several abortive attempts, Garvey finally launched the reorganized New York Division of the Universal Negro Improvement Association and African Communities League. With the publication of the *Negro World* in January 1918, carrying sections in French and Spanish as well as in English, the movement spread through the United States and abroad.

The founder of the *Negro World* was astute enough to secure the editorial services of Professor William H. Ferris, graduate of Yale University and well versed in African lore, of the able and erudite Hubert H. Harrison, and of such skillful writers as W. A. Domingo, Eric Walrond, and Hudson C. Pryce. Duse Mohamed, the Sudanese Egyptian nationalist who had formerly employed Garvey in London, and from whom Garvey derived the slogan "Africa for the Africans," also worked for a time on the *Negro World*. Contributors like John E. Bruce (Grit), William Pickens, T. Thomas Fortune, Anselmo Jackson, and Hodge Kirnon presented various aspects of the ancient history, noteworthy achievements, and the current aspirations of people of African origin.

The convention held in August 1920 in Liberty Hall, Boston, the dramatic, colorful, and impressive parade, costumes, and pageantry, and the mammoth meeting at Madison Square Garden, established the Garvey movement as a powerful international force. Stirring hymns with African themes, especially the U.N.I.A. anthem composed by Rabbi Arnold J. Ford of Barbados, were rendered by choral groups and massed bands. Thousands joined the U.N.I.A., the African Legion, the Black Cross Nurses, and later the African Orthodox Church. Enthusiastic supporters poured their savings into the enterprise started by Garvey, the restaurants, hotel, grocery, millinery, tailoring and dressmaking establishment, publishing concern, and finally the Black Star Line, and the Negro Factories Corporation.

estimate of Garvey

It is difficult and still perhaps somewhat hazardous to attempt an objective estimate of the Garvey movement, yet this is necessary if we are to learn from its lessons and to apply them wisely in our present endeavors. To the present writer it appears that the founder and leader of the U.N.I.A. demonstrated two powerful drives which were basically opposed to each other. One was clearly the progressive tendency which projected "the redemption of Africa" and the "Declaration of Rights of the Negro People of the World." The other was obviously reactionary in its Napoleonic urge for personal power and empire, with the inevitable accompaniment of racial exclusiveness and hostility. This latter tendency was evident when Garvey declared, on taking the title of Provisional President of Africa in 1920, "The signal honor of being Provisional President of Africa is mine. . . . It is like asking Napoleon to take the world."

Unfortunately, Marcus Garvey veered evermore toward the more extreme forms of empire building, unlimited individual control, and unrestrained racism. At length these destructive forces were allowed to overshadow and outweigh the constructive, pristine ideas of African nationalism, liberation, and independence. Stridently advocating "racial purity," Garvey came at length to agree openly with the worst enemies of the Afroamerican people—the white supremacist leaders of the Anglo-Saxon clubs and even of the murderous Ku Klux Klan—in declaring America to be "a white man's country."

Besides, the constant attacks which Marcus Garvey made upon people of both African and European ancestry, whom he derisively called "the hybrids of the Negro race," did not conduce to the unifying of all people of African descent, who, regardless of varying shades of color and other physical characteristics, were compelled to suffer similar oppression whether as colonial subjects or as oppressed minority groups. Likewise, Garvey's condemnation of the principal leaders and organizations who were striving for human rights and equal citizenship status for the Afroamerican minority group in this country, was bound to arouse opposition and internal strife.

Finally, the open condemnation of Liberian officials by Marcus Garvey, his severe reprisals against several of his chief associates, his poor choice of certain officers, and the inept conduct of the business enterprises which he controlled, left the movement wide open to the disastrous blows of those who began to fear its growing power. Following his conviction and imprisonment on February 8, 1925, upon a charge of using the mails to defraud in connection with the sale of Black Star Line stock, the Garvey movement split into wrangling factions, and despite efforts to revive it only a few splinter groups remained. Nevertheless, the Garvey movement did heighten and spread the consciousness of African origin and identity among the various peoples of African descent on a wider scale than ever before. This was its definite and positive contribution.

Harlem literary renaissance

Developing almost parallel with the Garvey movement was what has come to be known as the Harlem Literary Renaissance. A number of creative writers of poetry, fiction, essays, and criticism then emerged: Claude McKay, Langston Hughes, Countee Cullen, Jean Toomer, Eric Walrond, Rudolph Fisher, Wallace Thurman, Nella Larsen,

Zora Neale Hurston, James Weldon Johnson, Jessie Fauset, Georgia Douglas Johnson, Lucian B. Watkins, Walter White, and others.

This literary movement was no Minerva sprung full-fledged from the head of Jove, for while its immediate inspiration lay in the surrounding social conditions, its roots, too, went back through earlier Afroamerican writers to the bards of ancient Africa. Alain Locke in his preface to *The New Negro* which proclaimed this movement in 1925, noted "the approach to maturity" and the role of *Crisis*, under the leadership of Dr. Du Bois, and *Opportunity*, edited by Charles S. Johnson, in fostering this movement by publishing many of the works of these budding authors. Locke further observed two constructive channels: "One is the advance-guard of the African peoples in their contact with Twentieth Century civilization; the other, the sense of a vision of rehabilitating the race in world esteem. . . ."

How these Harlem avant-garde writers felt, expressed, and stimulated consciousness of Africa may be observed in a few typical outpourings. In the sonnet *Africa* published in *Harlem Shadows*, the Caribbean born poet Claude McKay extolled:

> The sun sought thy dim bed and brought forth light,
> The sciences were sucklings at thy breast;
> When all the world was young in pregnant night
> Thy slaves toiled at thy monumental best.
> Thou ancient treasure-land, thou modern prize,
> New peoples marvel at thy pyramids!

The rather pessimistic note on which this sonnet ended still persisted in *Outcast* when McKay lamented the ancestral motherland in a mood of wistful nostalgia:

> For the dim regions whence my fathers came
> My spirit, bondaged by the body, longs
> Words felt, but never heard, my lips would frame;
> Thy soul would sing forgotten jungle songs.

In *Enslaved* the poet broods over his people

> For weary centuries despised, oppressed,
> Enslaved and lynched, denied a human place
> In the great life line of the Christian West;
> And in the Black Land disinherited,
> Robbed in the ancient country of its birth; . . .

At length this searing consciousness gave rise to that famous cry of passionate revolt in *If We Must Die—*

What though before us lies the open grave?
Like men we'll face the murderous, cowardly pack,
Pressed to the wall, dying, but fighting back!

And in *Exhortation: Summer, 1919* Claude McKay turns toward the future confidently with this clarion call:

From the deep primeval forests where the crouching
    leopard's lurking,
Lift your heavy-lidded eyes, Ethiopia! awake!

For the big earth groans in travail for the strong,
    new world in making—
O my brothers, dreaming for long centuries,
Wake from sleeping; to the East turn, turn your eyes!

Similarly, in *The Negro Speaks of Rivers* in his first published volume *The Weary Blues*, Langston Hughes sang profoundly:

I've known rivers
I've known rivers ancient as the world and older
    than the flow of human blood in human veins.

My soul has grown deep like the rivers.

I bathed in the Euphrates when dawns were young.
I built my hut near the Congo and it lulled me to sleep.
I looked upon the Nile and raised pyramids above it. . . .

Langston Hughes further expressed his retrospective identification with Africa:

We should have a land of trees
Bowed down with chattering parrots
Brilliant as the day,
And not this land where birds are gray.

Again, in the poem *Georgia Dusk* included in *Cane,* Jean Toomer, while etching the toilers in southern canefield and saw mill, recalls the ancestors from the long-past life of dignity and freedom in Africa:

Meanwhile, the men, with vestiges of pomp,
    Race memories of king and caravan,
    High priests, an ostrich and a ju-ju man,
Go singing through the footpaths of the swamp.

Countee Cullen mused long and lyrically in the poem *Heritage* which is outstanding in the book *Color:*

What is Africa to me:
Copper sun or scarlet sea,
Jungle star or jungle track,
Strong bronzed men, or regal black
Women from whose loins I sprang
When the birds of Eden sang?
One three centuries removed
From the scenes his fathers loved,
Spicy grove, cinnamon tree,
What is Africa to me?

Plaintively pondering his "high-priced conversion" to Christianity and humility, the poet needs must transmute this experience in terms consonant with his deeper ancestral self:

Lord, I fashion dark gods, too,
Daring even to give You
Dark despairing features where,
Crowned with dark rebellious hair,
Patience wavers just so much as
Mortal grief compels, while touches
Quick and hot, of anger, rise
To smitten cheek and weary eyes.
Lord forgive me if my need
Sometimes shapes a human creed.

The sense of dignity and power derived from Africa led this poet to an anguished effort to restrain with reason from a premature revolt against intolerable oppression:

All day long and all night through,
One thing only must I do:
Quench my pride and cool my blood,
Lest I perish in the flood,
Lest a hidden ember set
Timber that I thought was wet
Burning like the dryest flax,
Melting like the merest wax,
Lest the grave restore its dead.
Not yet has my heart or head
In the least way realized
They and I are civilized.

Finally, Lucian B. Watkins looked with serene confidence to Africa exulting in his *Star of Ethiopia:*

> Out in the Night thou art the sun
> Toward which thy soul-charmed children run,
>   The faith-high height whereon they see
>   The glory of their Day To Be—
> The peace at last when all is done.

Following the failure of the Garvey movement, consciousness of Africa was bolstered in Harlem by the campaign of the American Negro Labor Congress for the liberation of the colonial peoples of Africa and Asia. Representing this body, the present writer went as a delegate to the Congress Against Imperialism held in Brussels in 1927. As the forerunner of the Asian-African Conference held at Bandung in April 1955, the Brussels Congress was recalled and noted by President Sukarno of Indonesia in his opening address, "At that Conference many distinguished delegates who are present here today met each other and found new strength in their fight for independence."

The Commission on the African Peoples of the World elected at the Brussels Congress Against Imperialism included the brilliant Senegalese leaders Lamine Senghor, who unfortunately died shortly afterward in a French jail, and Garan Kouyatte who was shot by the Nazis during their occupation of Paris in 1940. Other outstanding members of this Commission were Mr. Makonnen of Ethiopia, J. T. Gumede, vice president of the African National Congress of South Africa, and J. A. La Guma, secretary of the South African Non-European Trade Union Federation. The writer of this present summary served as secretary of the Commission.

The resolution prepared by the Commission and adopted by the Brussels Congress Against Imperialism, called for the complete liberation of the African peoples, the restoration of their lands, and several other measures including the establishment of a University at Addis Ababa for the training of candidates for leadership in the trade union, cultural, and liberation movements of the oppressed African peoples.

reaction to Mussolini's aggression in Ethiopia

A new wave of consciousness spread through Harlem as the people reacted strongly against Mussolini's fascist, military aggression against Ethiopia in October 1935. Organizations were set up to mobilize support; the executive director of the International Council of Friends of Ethiopia, Dr. Willis N. Higgins, was commissioned to deliver an appeal on behalf of Ethiopia to the League of Nations in Geneva, Switzerland. Arden Bryan, president of the Nationalist Negro Movement, sent petitions to the League and protests to the British Foreign Office and the U. S. State Department against their failure to aid Ethiopia.

When invading Italian airplanes monstrously rained down deadly yperite gas on the Ethiopian people, huge protest meetings were organized. The Ethiopian Pacific Movement, from a gigantic rally at Rockland Palace, forwarded protests and also sent telegrams to Asian, African, Australian, Central and South American nations, appealing for action in defense of Ethiopia. Several organizations joined in the United Aid to Ethiopia with Rev. Wm. Lloyd Imes, chairman, Cyril M. Philip, secretary, and Dr. P. M. H. Savory, treasurer.

The officers just named were sent as a delegation to seek to influence the First Congress of the International Peace Campaign, which met at Brussels early in September 1936, to take action in support of Ethiopia. The delegation interviewed Emperor Hailie Selassie in London and requested him to send a representative to cooperate in the work here. Dr. Malaku E. Bayen, cousin and personal physician to the Emperor, was appointed and was greeted with acclaim at a great meeting at Rockland Palace. Meanwhile funds were raised and medical supplies sent through the Medical Aid to Ethiopia, of which body, Dr. Arnold W. Donawa was chairman and Dr. J. J. Jones, secretary.

The Ethiopian World Federation, then organized in Harlem, spread through the country, the Caribbean, and elsewhere. *The Voice of Ethiopia* published news from the Ethiopian front and further stimulated the campaign of resistance. J. A. Carrington and Dr. R. C. Hunt published the pamphlet *Yperite and Ethiopia,* with the full text of *Emperor Haile Selassie's Memorable and Immortal Speech at Geneva,* along with pictures of victims of the horrible yperite gas, so called because this gas was first used at Ypres in France. Volunteers generally could not secure passports to go to join in the military defense of Ethiopia, however, the Afroamerican aviator, Colonel John C. Robinson, known as the "Brown Condor," executed many heroic missions in that ravaged land. The *Pittsburgh Courier,* then directed by Robert L. Vann, sent J. A. Rogers as a war correspondent who on his return published the booklet *The Real Facts of Ethiopia.*

After the Italian invaders were driven out of Ethiopia in 1941, this intense fraternal consciousness in Harlem subsided into a residual sense of unity with all African peoples. But when Egypt was invaded in October 1956 by Israel followed by Britain and France, and ruthless massacre and destruction descended upon the people of Port Said, Suez, Alexandria, and Cairo, Harlem reacted with a rally organized by the Asian-African Drums and demonstrated its solidarity with President Nasser and the stricken people of Egypt. Harlem rejoiced when the note sent by Premier Khrushchev of the Soviet Union, demanding that withdrawal of the invading forces begin within 24 hours, led to the timely evacuation of these aggressors.

Harlem rallies to African freedom

Consciousness of Africa mounted again as more and more African nations regained their independence. The inhuman atrocities of the French colonialists against the Algerian people, who were struggling valiantly for their independence, aroused widespread sympathy and fraternal support among the people of Harlem. Active consciousness reached its zenith when the Congo was betrayed and dismembered and its dedicated leaders, especially the Prime Minister Patrice Lumumba, were foully and brutally done to death. Harlem boiled with fierce resentment against the failure of the United Nations to support the government of the Congo Republic and to prevent the murder of its Prime Minister and other officials.

This white hot indignation among the people of Harlem gave rise to the outburst in the visitors' gallery of the United Nations on February 15, 1961. Reactionary forces loudly denounced this protest upsurge and pseudo-liberals like Max Lerner in his *New York Post* column presumed to lecture and to condemn the protesting Afroamerican people while excusing the Belgian and other colonialist seceders and murderers. An open letter, exposing Max Lerner's hypocritical and racist attack, was addressed by this writer to him and to the editor and owner of the *New York Post*. But this answer to Lerner's diatribe has never been published or even acknowledged by them.

Harlem remains today quite conscious of its African heritage and basic kinship. This consciousness is by no means limited to the various groups which call themselves "nationalists," and who are quite vocal but who actually contribute little or no substantial, direct support to the African liberation movements. *Yet such effective support is vitally needed at this very moment in the present critical and decisive struggle now being waged for the liberation of the peoples of Central and South Africa.*

The limits of this article preclude more detail here. It should be stated, however, that these "nationalist" groups are as yet unable to unite among themselves, due largely, it appears, to self-centered power drives and competition for leadership. The tendency persists among them, unfortunately, to oppose other organizations which have the largest following of the Afroamerican people and to condemn these leaders caustically and constantly. Obviously, this hinders rather than helps to achieve essential *united action* either in support of the African liberation movements or to further the struggle for civil liberties and human rights here in the U.S.A.

Returning to the main currents of Harlem life, it is fitting to recognize the chief intellectual forces which have heightened consciousness of Africa since the 1930's. Outstanding is the Schomburg Collection of literature on Africa and people of African descent, brought together during a lifetime by Arthur A. Schomburg and established as a special reference library by the New York Public Library. The development of this institution has been carried forward by Mrs. Catherine Latimer and by the present genial curator, Mrs. Jean Blackwell Hutson. The Countee Cullen Branch, under the supervision of Mrs. Dorothy R. Homer, displays and features books on Africa for general circulation. Stimulating study classes were led by Dr. Willis N. Huggins and of special note were the several profound and scholarly lecture series given by Prof. William Leo Hansberry.

Significant also has been the activity of the Association for the Study of Negro Life and History, founded by Dr. Carter G. Woodson. This dedicated scholar published many volumes treating of Africa, notably his own *The Negro in Our History*, with its opening chapter emphasizing our African heritage, and the *African Background Outlined*. Among other widely read books were those by Dr. W. E. B. Du Bois, *Black Folk Then and Now* and the *World and Africa*: the writings of J. A. Rogers, *World's Great Men of Color, Sex and Race*, and *Africa's Gift to America*; Dr. Willis N. Huggins and John G. Jackson, *Guide to African History* and *Introduction to African Civilizations*; George G. M. James, *Stolen Legacy*, J. G. de Graft-Johnson, *African Glory*; Jomo Kenyatta, *Facing Mount Kenya*, Elton Fax, *West African Vignettes*; the writings of George Padmore, concluding with *Pan-Africanism and Communism*; and those of Dr. Kwame Nkrumah, *Ghana* and *I Speak of Freedom*. Making their contribution have been the works of the English author Basil Davidson, *Old Africa Rediscovered* and *Black Mother*, as well as that of the German writer Janheinz Jahn, *Muntu: An Outline of Neo-African Culture*.

Quite encouraging is the fact that today, in the main stream of life and thought in Harlem, interest as well as identification with Africa grows apace. In homes, more books on African life and development are seen and read. This concurs with the increasing sale of African literature in Harlem bookshops; the trend in the Frederick Douglass Book Center has been markedly away from general fiction and toward the history and culture of peoples of African origin. Among fraternal societies and clubs, in church and school, library and lecture hall, more programs than ever before are being presented on various aspects of African life and liberation.

To mention a few indications: A program for African diplomats organized by Sudia Masoud, secretary of the African-Asian Drums, began at the Prince Hall Masons' Auditorium and concluded with a dinner at the Hotel Theresa. The Seventh Day Adventist Church presented several representatives of African states. The Afro-Arts Cultural Center, Simon Bly, Jr., Executive Director, in cooperation with Dr. Charles M. Schapp, Assistant Superintendent of District Schools, has conducted In-Service courses on Africa for teachers for several years. Along with its work to emphasize the names *African* and *Afroamerican* as fitting and honorable designations, the Committee to Present The Truth About The Name "Negro" has conducted and plans more lecture series on *The History and Culture of African Peoples*.

in unity lies strength

Still more significant was the American Negro Leadership Conference held last November at Arden House in Harriman, New York. For this involved the principal Afroamerican organizations active or represented in Harlem and the country—the N.A.A.C.P., C.O.R.E., Brotherhood of Sleeping Car Porters, National Council of Negro Women, National Urban League, the Southern Christian Leadership Conference, and the American Society For African Culture. It has been alleged that these leaders suddenly evinced a new interest in Africa, but even in that case this interest definitely reflects the rising consciousness of Africa among the vast majority of the members and supporters of these organizations.

In any case such expressed concern for the African peoples should be welcomed and encouraged by all who are sincerely devoted to African liberation. If any of these Afroamerican leaders exhibit wariness or weakness, then those who honestly and wholeheartedly seek to aid Africa should, in order to infuse greater clarity and strength, indicate what they consider these weaknesses to be. Thoughtful supporters of African unity and progress must, therefore, regret the ill-advised, intemperate, and harmful attack made in the article entitled *Negro Stooges Bid For Africans Challenged,* which stands out offensively in the January 1963 issue of *Voice of Africa.*

When the leaders in the American Negro Leadership Conference are challenged on the ground that "they had the audacity to make attempts to move ahead of the African nationalists in America," this statement admits motivation from selfish considerations on the part of those who make this challenge. It is also obviously feared that these Conference leaders might get ahead in securing diplomatic posts or other prized considerations. Branding these Conference leaders as "opportunists," after making such a charge, will be logically regarded as an unconscious confession of competition in opportunism. Again, to affirm that "these organizations represent American colonialism, imperialism, and exploitation," is patently to go beyond the bounds of truth.

Moreover, such a statement is destructive of unity and must offend and repel the hundreds of thousands of members of the organizations in this Conference who are rallying to the cause of African freedom and progress. Thinking people, too, must pause to question the strange self-praise projected in this article by self-styled "Ghana patriots," who are not known to have given up their United States citizenship or to have been accorded citizenship by the government of Ghana. Likewise deplorable is the unwarranted use of the good name of Osagyefo of Ghana in these derisive proceedings which tend only to separate the Afroamerican leaders and people from the African statesmen and their peoples.

But utterly reprehensible is the disruptive campaign being waged by George S. Schuyler and his accomplices in mind-twisting which has rendered aid and comfort to the Belgian and other neo-colonialist oppressors in the Congo Republic and to the Portuguese imperialist butchers of the peoples of Angola and Mozambique.

Completely disproving the false and venomous general accusations made by George S. Schuyler et al. in the *N. Y. Courier* against African statesmen, of indifference and hostility against Afroamerican people, was the reported reaction of African Foreign Ministers at the Conference of African States held in Addis Ababa, Ethiopia. *The New York Times* of May 19th published their special correspondent's report that the Foreign Minister of Nigeria rose "to denounce racial discrimination in South Africa and the United States." This report also states, "American observers have been dismayed to hear Alabama linked with South Africa in attacks on apartheid inside and outside the conference hall," and further that "American correspondents approaching members of delegations frequently hear the question, "What's the latest news from Birmingham?"

The Ethiopian *Herald,* which is the official publication of the Ministry of Information, is quoted as having commented:

"What happened in Birmingham last week shows the United States in its true light. To be black is still a crime ... The colored American must fight hard for freedom rather than waste time and much needed energy bellyaching about Communism. The United States version of 'civilized apartheid' must be fought."

Acting on behalf of the 30 African nations assembled in this Conference at Addis Ababa, Prime Minister Milton Obote of Uganda sent a letter to President Kennedy of the U.S.A. which condemned the "most inhuman treatment" perpetrated upon Afroamericans at Birmingham, Alabama, and which further stated:

"Nothing is more paradoxical than that these events should take place in the United States at a time when that country is anxious to project its image before the world as the archetype of democracy and champion of freedom."

At a news conference held on May 23rd, as reported in the *New York Times,* Prime Minister Obote recognized that those "who had been doused with blasts of water from fire hoses in Birmingham were 'our kith and kin,'" and declared further that, the eyes of the world were "concentrated on events in Alabama and it is the duty of the free world, and more so of countries that hold themselves up as leaders of the free world, to see that all their citizens, regardless of color, are free."

It may be predicted confidently, despite the malicious efforts of a few venal slanderers, that consciousness of Africa will continue to grow in Harlem and among Afroamericans generally. An even more vigorous and healthy development of this consciousness will come when it is more fully realized that rationally no conflict really or properly exists between vital interest in our African heritage and the liberation of the African peoples and deep and active devotion to the cause of human rights and equal citizenship status here in the U.S.A. For the same social forces which spawned colonialist subjugation in Africa and other areas are the identical forces responsible for brutal enslavement and racist oppression in the Americas and elsewhere.

Freedom and the full development of the human personality, therefore, require independence for the African peoples as well as full citizenship rights with equal status and opportunity for the minority people of African descent wherever they now exist. The same inherent self-respect and will to be free, which led Paul Cuffee to wage a successful struggle for the vote and equal citizenship rights in Massachusetts, immediately after the American Revolution of 1776, also led this great pioneer leader to promote self-determination through migration and the development of Sierra Leone in Africa. An enlightened awareness of African lore and liberty is, and will continue to be, the inevitable expression of the indomitable will to self-knowledge, self-determination, self-realization, and self-development on parity with all mankind.

ON FREEDOM ROAD

"Sonneteer," said the traveller,
"Since you're going my way.
"Would you kindly help me onward,
"For I am old and grey?

"The trek is much too tedious,
"My wind is going fast.
"I want to see Utopia
"Before I breathe my last."

Sonneteer said, "Surely,
"I'll help you on, good friend.
"In fact, that's what I'm here for—
"My watch will never end.

"So lay aside your staff, sir,
"And put your trust in me.
"I'll take you to Utopia,
"Where every race is free!"

RICARDO WEEKS

THE NATIONALIST MOVEMENTS
OF HARLEM

E. U. ESSIEN-UDOM

A count of contemporary Afro-American "nationalist" organizations in Harlem discloses more than two dozen and a combined membership of about 5,000—considerably smaller than 30,000 membership scored forty years ago by the New York City division of the Garvey movement. They vary in size from crackpot-type sects, with a handful of members, to more serious, well-organized, and highly disciplined Muhammad's Mosque, No. 7, led by Minister Malcolm X. Shabbazz, or the Yoruba Temple of "New Oyo"—Harlem, informally renamed by this group after the historic Kingdom of Oyo in West Africa—led by the Babalosha (chief priest), Nana Oserjeman Adefunmi. Although space does not permit discussion of these organizations individually,* a partial listing which follows suggests the many in Harlem: African-American Cultural Foundation; African-American National Emancipation Proclamation Centennial and Reparation Committee; African Nationalist Pioneer Movement; Ethiopia Coptic Orthodox Mission, Inc.; Ethiopia World Federation Council, Inc.; First African Corps; Garvey Club; The Hearts of Africa Committee; Jamiyat Ill Fallah; Moorish-Americans; Nation of Islam: Muhammad's Mosque, No. 7; The National Muslim Improvement Association of America; The National Memorial Bookstore, also called the Home of Commonsense and Propaganda Headquarters of Back-to-Africa Movement; The Provisional Committee For a Free Africa; The United African Nationalist Movement; The United People of African Descent; United Sons and Daughters of Africa; The Universal Association of Ethiopian Women, Inc.; World Federation of African People, Inc.; The Yoruba Temple

---

* For discussion of some of these groups, see, John H. Clarke, "The New Afro-American Nationalism," FREEDOMWAYS, Fall, 1961; Peter Kihss, The *New York Times*, March 1, 1961, pp. 1 and 25, and Robert L. Teague, March 2, 1961, pp. 1 and 17; also see E. U. Essien-Udom's *Black Nationalism: A Search for an Identity in America* (University of Chicago Press, 1962).

of New Oyo; African Nationalist (Alajo) Independence-Partition Party of North America; Radio Free Africa, Inc.

These groups reveal a wide range of organizational patterns (most are run as petty "fiefs" of their leaders), ideologies, and objectives, though all pretend to have the same basic objective: Afro-American liberation. At any rate, they subscribe to one or more variants of Negro nationalism. Nearly all are woefully weak, insignificant organizations, and, apart from the Nation of Islam, they have been completely ineffective in evolving a nation-wide nationalist movement in the United States. On the whole, the leadership of these groups is inadequately educated or informed; hence, they tend to misunderstand their "gadfly," cultural, and "morale-uplift" role in contemporary Negro freedom movement in the United States; they are equally misunderstood by their countrymen.

If we are to comprehend the social manifestations generally called "black nationalism," among Afro-Americans in Harlem and elsewhere in the United States, if we are to appreciate its place in the Negro freedom movement, we must dispel a few prejudices which are obstacles to our understanding. First, a widespread belief that there exists in the United States a consolidated body of black nationalists, explicitly and unswervingly committed to a political program for achieving political self-determination. Our partial listing of nationalist organizations denies the existence of a monolithic "angry" black mass.

The second, derived from the first belief, is what I call the "conspiracy theory" of black nationalism. This theory explains nationalistic tendencies among Negroes as a vast conspiracy against the government and people of the United States. Evidence of this view is to be found in statements of some legislators, in at least one official report, viz., the *Eleventh Annual Report* of the State of California's Senate Committee on Un-American Activities, in newspaper and quasi-scholarly accounts, and in "trigger happy" attitudes of some local law enforcement officers, especially toward the Muslim movement. The conspiracy theory fails to recognize black nationalism as a variant of Negro protest, obscures issues, and tends to divert public attention from the deplorable conditions of the masses of Negroes. Implicitly, this theory explains away the legitimate protest of the oppressed against an unjust social situation, and helps to mask the absence of long-term self-help and "uplifting" programs for the social and cultural elevation of the masses of Negroes. Furthermore, the conspiracy theory serves to perpetuate the erroneous belief that the Negro will endure suffering with Job-like patience and sphynx-like silence.

A third obstacle to our understanding of Negro nationalism is widespread public ignorance of the history of Negro protest in the United States. This is because no serious effort has been made at any level of white-dominated educational institutions to incorporate the historic struggles of the Negro people in the learning experience of generations of white Americans. Had this been done, the conspiracy theory of black nationalism, the hysteria generated in the press, would have little currency. For this history would reveal, among other things, the basic and continuing theme of nationalism in Negro protest. It would show the fundamental weakness of Negro nationalism and its rejection by successive generations of Negro leadership. This point needs to be emphasized both for the "benefit of those who hate the Negro more than they love their country," as Frederick Douglass once said, and for apostles of a "black Zion."

The history of Negro nationalism during two "classical" periods testifies to the correctness of what may be called the "Douglass Dictum":

"It is idle—worse than idle, ever to think of our expatriation, or removal . . . *We are here,* and here we are likely to be. To imagine that we shall ever be eradicated is absurd and ridiculous. We can be remodified, changed, and assimilated, but never extinguished. We repeat, therefore, that we are here; and that this is *our* country; and the question for the philosophers and statesmen of the land ought to be, 'what principles should dictate the policy of action towards us?' We shall neither die out, nor be driven out; but shall go with these people, either as a testimony against them, or as evidence in their favor throughout their generations. . . . The white man's happiness cannot be purchased by the black man's misery. . . . It is evident that white and black 'must fall or flourish together.' "

Douglass' dictum, published in the *North Star,* November 16, 1849 under the heading, "The Destiny of Colored Americans," served two purposes. First, it was an expression of the overwhelming opposition of the freed African population against various emigration schemes sponsored by whites, and second, as a reply to a growing sentiment for voluntary emigration represented by a faction of Afro-American intelligentsia whose nationalistic agitation later found expression in the Cleveland (Ohio) National Emigration Convention, August 24-26, 1854. The period 1840-1858, may be said to represent the first classical period of Negro nationalism. This nationalism derived its inspiration in part, from the social unrest among freed Africans during the 1840's and 1850's and in part, from the theoretical nationalistic propositions advanced by Martin R. Delany in his book, *The Condition, Elevation,*

Emigration and Destiny of The Colored People of the United States, Politically Considered (1852). His views, setting forth the advantages of emigration to Central and South America and the West Indies, were adopted by the 1854 Convention as a "Report on the Political Destiny of the Colored Race on the American Continent." The movement failed for several reasons; principally, because nationalism or emigration was a peripheral objective to the overwhelming issue of the day, emancipation of the slaves. Douglass' dictum was unshaken during the second classical period, approximately 1915-1925, when the Garvey movement held considerable attraction for the Negro worker. Negro nationalism of this period derived significantly from the social unrest which accompanied intensive urbanization of Negroes, their continued subordination, and in part, from Garvey's theoretical formulation of the "Negro Problem," embodied later in the *Philosophy and Opinions of Marcus Garvey* (2 Vols. 1925). There appears to be no evidence that contemporary manifestations of Negro nationalism, as a political phenomenon, has better chance of success than it did during the previous periods.

variants of Negro nationalism

Nearly all Negro nationalist organizations incorporate explicit or implicit political goals. At any rate, they subscribe to one or more variants of Negro nationalism. These manifestations may be classified according to the degree of emphasis placed on political or other goals or with respect to their functions and ideologies. Those movements which have sought specifically political goals have been few. Both the National Emigration Convention movement during the 19th century and Garvey's "Back-to-Africa" movement in this century, may be said to have been largely political in objective. We should not, however, ignore the cultural and economic emphasis in the ideology of the Garvey movement. Neither succeeded. At best, both served during their respective periods as "gadfly" in the Negro protest, now against the ruling whites, then, against the conservative wing of Negro leadership. Garvey, moreover, is generally credited with instilling pride and morale in the urban Negro proletariat.

Contemporary nationalist organizations in Harlem which advocate political goals specifically are few and insignificant. Among these are splinter groups of the Garvey movement, e.g. African Nationalist Pioneer Movement or the recently founded African Nationalist (Alajo) Independence-Partition Party of North America. Some secular political goals are implied by the Nation of Islam, but its ideology is too ambiguous and confused, its leadership too uncommitted to a political program to warrant inclusion among movements with explicit political goals. It belongs, in part, to the religiously-oriented variant of nationalism discussed later. It incorporates, however, economic and cultural nationalism.

political goals listed

Political goals advocated by Harlem nationalists vary with organization, and in time. The most persistent of these goals has been emigration from the United States; in the 19th century the region of emigration preferred was to be Central and South America and the West Indies. During the twenties, Africa south of the Sahara has been advocated; the Muslims appear to prefer an area in the Nile valley. However, a new variation on the theme of emigration has been added by the Muslim movement and the Alajo Party: the partition of the United States between blacks and whites. The Muslims have suggested that they would be satisfied with five or seven states, although they have not specified which of the states they would prefer. The "Provisional Government of the African-American Captive Nation" arm of the Alajo Party, is more specific. In its "Declaration of Self-Determination of the African-American Captive Nation," issued January, 1963, the Provisional Government states:

Therefore, be it resolved, that this powerful nation (The United States of America), that was built with the unrequitted slave labor of our African ancestors, be as magnanimous as it is great, and relieve our oppression with restitution;

Be it further resolved that all land south of the Mason Dixon line where our people constitute the majority, be partitioned to establish a territory for Self-Government for the African Nation in the United States; and

Be it further resolved that the United States Government take full responsibility for training our people for self-government in all its ramifications, and

Be it finally resolved that the Provisional Government of the African American Captive Nation be recognized by the Government of the United States as of now.

Critics of these proposals argue that the partition goal is impracticable. Furthermore, they point out that the example of American tutelage over the Republic of Liberia for more than a century should discourage any idea of a black republic adjacent to the United States. In fact, it is argued that the overwhelming obstacles created by neocolonialism and neo-imperialism for African states thousands of miles away ought to dampen the enthusiasm of the partitionists.

Closely related to emigration or partition themes has been the nationalists' demand that the United States should pay reparations to Afro-Americans as restitution for the free labor of their ancestors during slavery. The sums demanded vary from $5,000 per Negro to a bulk sum of five billion for the entire Negro population in the United States. Some argue that the Negro question can properly be viewed as one of "under-development" just as much as those of countries in Africa, Asia, South and Central America. They claim that the purpose of American foreign aid, quite apart from making friends, is aimed at helping these countries and their peoples develop rapidly. Hence, they insist (and I believe with justification) that part of American foreign aid grants or peace corps arrangements could be utilized more profitably to attack the economic and cultural basis of inequality of the Negro people. They do not, however, consider restitution in cash or in kind to be full restitution—although it would be a step in the right direction. Others have demanded that the United States government should settle her "historic wrong" against Africa by payment of five hundred billion to all Independent African States. These, I believe, exhaust concrete political demands made by contemporary Harlem nationalists—one group has recently drawn up a petition which is intended to be submitted to the United Nations Refugee Committee ("as soon as we can find a sponsor among the U.N. delegations"), requesting that the Committee takes up the "Negro question" as an international problem of refugees.

religio-nationalism

A variant of Negro nationalism manifested itself earliest in religious terms. While this religiously-oriented nationalism has, in effect, tended to dissipate the emergence of secular political nationalism, it is significant that the organization of the Negro church as well as early African societies, during the 18th and 19th centuries, provided a viable framework for Negro self-assertion. It is my contention that a study of early literature of Negro religious bodies would reveal a high political and nationalistic content. Hence, the frequent appeal by many Negro Christians and nationalists to the Biblical statement, "Ethiopia shall stretch forth her hands..." interpreted by them as a promise of their liberation and emancipation. This religious nationalism is most central in the teachings of Mr. Elijah Muhammad, spiritual leader of the Nation of Islam. Religiously-oriented nationalism is, perhaps, the most widespread form of Negro nationalism. In practical terms, however, the separate Negro Church, like the Muslim movement, in the formative years provided a framework for self-assertion by the Negro people. The following passage from Benjamin T. Tanner's *An Apology for African Methodism* (1867) highlights an expression of the Negro's need for self-assertion as a group:

"*The* giant crime committed by the Founders of the African Methodist Episcopal Church, against the prejudiced white American, and the timid black—*the crime which seems unpardonable, was that they dared to organize a Church of men, men to think for themselves, men to talk for themselves, men to act for themselves. A Church of men who support from their own substance, however scanty, the ministration of the Word which they receive; men who spurn to have their churches built for them, and their pastors supported from the coffers of some charitable organization; men who prefer to live by the sweat of their own brow and be free.* Not that the members of this communion are filled with evil pride, for they exhibit a spirit no more haughty nor overbearing than Paul, who never neglected to remind the world that he was a man and a Roman citizen." (Emphasis added.)

The position of the AME Church then, like that of contemporary Muslims, was constantly branded by opponents as "ignorant, fanatical, and proscriptive." The AME Church was even attacked by better-placed Negroes as "ignorant and degrading." To this accusation, Tanner replied:

"Methodism, the organization that builds more churches, supports more preachers and missionaries, gives more money to the poor, and has done more to prove the absolute ability of black men to do everything which men do, than all the colored organizations in the United States—that is the organization, which in the eyes of Rev. Mr. (Charles H.) Thompson, demoralizes the Negro. And he a Presbyterian! Who built the Church in which the Reverend gentleman now ministers? The white Brethren. Who built four-fifths of all the colored Presbyterian Churches, and one-half of the other fifth? The white Brethren. Who is it that assists in the support of four-fifths, if not every individual one of the colored Presbyterian pastors? The white Brethren. Who is it that makes their books, good or bad? The white Brethren. Who edits their papers, ably or only to mediocrity? The ever present, ever generous white Brethren.

"And yet the religious organization that does all this, *inter se,* degrades itself by so doing, in the eyes of our wise Bro. Thompson. Surely from his standpoint, independency and suppliancy, freedom and bondage, have become inverted terms."

The sentiments expressed by Tanner, I believe, has been the most important theme of Negro nationalism. To this religio-nationalism which stresses not only worship but also self-assertion and self-help of the Negro people, should be added variants expressed in economic and cultural terms. However, all represent positive and constructive contributions to the Negro freedom movement.

The nationalists constitute that wing of Negro protest which is most insistent on self-assertion and self-help by the Negro people as a group—though they tend to undermine important contributions of Negro effort, energy, resources, and talent to this three-century old struggle.

A variant of this theme of self-sufficiency, stresses the economic position of Negroes in the United States. This, we call, "economic nationalism." It is advocated by nearly all Harlem nationalists and stridently voiced by the Muslims. The weaknesses of Negro economic nationalism have often been stressed. It is said that a separate Negro economy in the United States is a myth; that whatever capital exists within the Negro community is insignificant in the total economy of the United States. In any case, it is said that Negroes lack both capital and experience for effective participation with the giant corporations of America in large scale industrial and financial undertakings. There is no doubt that the improbability of the emergence of economically significant Negro capitalist class far outweights its probability.

I am convinced that the liberation of Afro-Americans in Harlem and elsewhere in America ultimately lies in an understanding, appreciation, and assertion of his Afro-American and African cultural heritage. It is the exploitation and assertion of cultural and spiritual heritage that will help to usher him into freedomland during the second century of emancipation. In this, he will be engaging in tasks comparable to those of his African brother. Herein lies the foundation of our freedom and liberation; and such is the meaning of the "voices from within the veil" represented, though inadequately, by the nationalist movements of Harlem.

ECONOMIC STRUCTURE
OF THE HARLEM COMMUNITY

HOPE R. STEVENS

IT IS AXIOMATIC that one who keeps his thoughts to himself preserves his claim to possible wisdom and I should perhaps have been more firm in my resistance when the editors of FREEDOMWAYS asked me to present a layman's view of the current economy of the Harlem Community. However, the prospect of commenting on those aspects of living directly concerned with economics in this area of "de facto" racial segregation, where I have had my being for nearly thirty-five years, proved to be too great a temptation. The facts and figures generally associated with economic analysis will not appear since a layman should not play with charts, tables and statistics, the tools of the scientist. But the right to think, each in his own way, interpreting one's observations or impressions within the limit of one's lights, remains a most valuable tool, unaffected by other un-American or unequal social attitudes. Every layman has the obligation to exercise that right.

economy of people of Harlem

How then is the economy of the people of Harlem to be described? In a capitalist society such as ours, we may begin by referring to the evidences of capital accumulation that are observable in the segregated community. In all frankness, such evidence is less than impressive. We talk of the purchasing power of the colored people in New York City and arrive by simple multiplication at figures running into billions of dollars representing their market potential. This is true only if we assume that by and large, the total income of the average black wage earner is spent to meet his needs and satisfy his wants. But in this assumption there is no room for savings, and capital can only be accumulated through retained earnings.

A small percentage of blacks do practice thrift. This number is responsible for the thousands of savings accounts in banks scattered

105

throughout the metropolitan area. In the main they prefer to save their money with large banks. In the late forties, Walter A. Miller, young West Indian realtor in Harlem, with the encouragement of fellow islanders Dr. Joseph D. Gibson and Dr. Charles A. Petioni, organized a group and secured a charter for the Carver Federal Savings and Loan Association. Shopping for a manager with experience was futile—there were very few colored persons who had been exposed to working in banking institutions above the level of porter. It was decided to employ a young man who had been in the mortgage department of a bank in a subordinate position for some years and to allow him to grow with the newly formed institution. Today with continuing community support, Carver has attracted savings accounts almost exclusively from non-whites totalling in excess of $21 million. The young mortgage assistant is now president of the institution; a branch has been established in Brooklyn and another branch in downtown Manhattan is about to be opened.

Contrasted with this is the experience of the only other Savings and Loan Association organized by colored persons in the State of New York—The Allied Federal Savings and Loan Association in Jamaica, Long Island. It is located in a comparatively prosperous area of colored homeowners. After some five years of operation, Allied has assets of less than $2 million. Various explanations have been given for Allied's failure to develop more rapidly but the fact remeans that it has not exactly been taken to the bosom of the Jamaica community.

credit chief method of purchase

Harlem lives on credit—its future wages are to a great extent pledged for the consumer goods purchased in the present. Afro-Americans are great shoppers. Most Harlem homes are equipped with television, hi-fi radios and refrigerators. These, together with the furniture, are usually bought on the credit installment plan covered by chattel mortgages. Clothing is bought on credit. The automobiles that line the streets of Harlem—Cadillacs and Chryslers, Volkswagons and Fords—are purchased, in most instances, on the credit plan.

This mortgaging of future income to provide the wants and luxuries of the present, while not confined to the blacks, has operated to prevent any considerable capital from being formed. Investment in the stocks and bonds of the industrial enterprises of the nation is minimal. There is little or no risk capital available in the colored community. Those who have more than average money are usually reported to have accumulated it in various unorthodox ways. In many instances, they are afraid to have their investments identified. Real estate was and still is the favorable kind of asset into which to convert money. Most capital controlled by whites is frequently held by the second, third or fourth generation of the accumulating family. Colored persons in Harlem with some money have generally saved it up over a long period of time, putting it together in small amounts on the basis of careful, thrifty practice and self-denial. Or they have acquired it in games or systems of chance, or through having managed to be identified with the proper political party in the days when liquor licenses were being issued.

Whatever the background or history of the individual may be, investment money, which is risk capital, is not in sight among colored persons of substance. There have been a few instances in which the public has been aroused to invest money, and lost—such as in the case of Marcus Garvey's Black Star Line—and the period of recovery from such disappointing experiences is understandably long. Business failures however are more frequent in American private enterprise as a whole than business successes, and yet the American public as a whole continues to invest—now more than ever. And to the extent that risk capital from non-white sources is unavailable, integration into the power structure of the economy will necessarily be deferred. The blacks have not yet been permitted to peer over the edge of the plateau on which the financial resources of the nation are constantly rearranged. They do not know what goes on there. They do not participate positively in influencing the economic shape of things to come. Nor is there any evidence that there will be more than token representation in this area for a long time yet.

shameful mortgage system

Mortgage practices in home financing provide an interesting study bearing directly on the comparative helplessness of colored homeowners or would-be buyers. Housing is and will remain in short supply in New York for the foreseeable future, according to the experts. First mortgages, by and large, are expensive but may be obtained with comparative ease generally for up to sixty-six per cent of the value of the property. When the colored home buyer applies for a first mortgage from a lending institution outside of Harlem, it is immediately assumed that there are no sources available to him in the local community. He is frequently required to pay a "commitment fee" in advance with his application which amounts to about three and one-half per cent. He is later required to pay a closing fee of about three and one half per cent. If he has been guided by a broker, he is faced with a brokerage fee which can run anywhere from two to five per cent. All of these percentages are computed on and deducted from the face amount of the mortgage and fall into the category of expenses. They do not affect the rate of interest which is usually six per cent annually on the total amount of the loan as this is reduced by the monthly or quarterly payments of principal provided for in the plan of liquidation.

The really shameful practice and one that will soon have to be aired, is the second and third mortgage system. It is well known that in New York State, there is a limit of six per cent allowed by law as interest for the use of money. However, credit institutions have invented many subterfuges to avoid the legal limit. It appears that as long as there is no public outcry, the supervisory agencies such as the Banking Department and the Federal Home Loan Bank will await the reaction of some judge whose sense of equity and justice will revolt against the system and an explosion will occur. If a serious political issue can be raised, the Legislature or Congress will step in and perhaps act. As it stands at present, a prospective purchaser with limited funds as a rule can count on securing a first mortgage. By agreeing to pay a highly inflated purchase price, a second mortgage and sometimes a third will be arranged for him. It is contemplated by the seller that these mortgages will be resold to money dealers at a discount of from twenty to thirty-five per cent in the case of the second and from twenty-five to forty per cent in the case of the third mortgage. The installments are necessarily arranged so that these second and third mortgage loans are repaid quickly, in from three to five years.

The burden of debt is staggering and the pressure of the installments on the homeowner is often unbearable. It is difficult to avoid the conclusion that there is an expectancy on the part of those who deal in this type of financing looking towards the time when the mortgage payments will fall in arrears and the property be taken away from the purchaser with the substantial investment, sometimes also improvements, completely wiped out. This is a result that is all too common with colored buyers especially where they fail to consult with lawyers in whom they have confidence. Too frequently are they persuaded to "save the expense of a lawyer" by having the seller's lawyer "make up the papers."

Nevertheless, this is the way the colored family has come to acquire some interest in realty in New York. The sacrifices, the exploitation, the wholesale larceny that have been involved in the efforts of blacks to own real property—the excessively high purchase prices, the bonuses in mortgage financing—all represent millions and millions of dollars of wealth unjustly syphoned away from the non-white community. They have left deep wounds of resentment, hostility and flaming hate to be added to the scars of four centuries of degradation and planned dehumanization, unmatched by any experience in human history save, to some slight degree, by the actions of the German people under Hitler against the Jews.

As with the purchase of realty, so it is with the acquisition of personal property. It is generally well known that automobiles are purchased on the credit installment plan but what is not as fully appreciated is that children's clothing, women's dresses and coats, men's suits and shoes as well as the household furniture, radio, television, watches and jewelry are all acquired on the hire-purchase system to a considerable degree. Under the stimulus of newspaper advertising, television and radio announcements, people will agree to buy what they want, not merely what they need. The automobiles that line the streets of Harlem are chiefly used to drive the owners a few blocks after work each day, from home to 125th Street or to visit someone a short distance across town. The automobile has become important to blacks as it is to whites, as a status symbol. The difference is that the average earnings of the white auto purchaser are so much higher than his colored counterpart who has to stay in debt so much longer to complete the purchase while many important needs of the family remain unfilled.

The whole system of credit purchasing is loaded with abuses. In a community in which the reading level of the inhabitants is low, a written contract has little significance to the purchaser. As a rule, he signs "here" without reading anything. He frequently neglects to demand a copy of the agreement. He seldom preserves receipts or money order stubs. The result is that payments in excess of the amount owed are constantly made and ascend to staggering sums annually for the entire community.

high rentals in Harlem

The conditions relating to apartment rentals are too well known to require elaboration. Colored New Yorkers pay more for less in rented apartments than any other people in our city. Luxury rentals of fifteen to twenty-five dollars per week for a single room, with or without private bath and utilities are about average for rooming house accommodations. This is an area in which supply and demand determine price and the orthodox American economy is preserved. To lawyers who frequent the inferior criminal courts where the complaints against landlords are processed, it is a matter of constant wonder that the filthy backyards and area ways and the dark, rat-infested tenements in which so many of our working people live, seem to continue unchanged in their condition, year after year. Rumors of understaffed agencies and widespread corruption in the form of payoffs to inspectors continue to circulate with no one ever being willing to come forward with the facts. The control of rentals has undoubtedly operated to protect the tenants, but the failure to achieve reasonable adjustments in the face of rising costs has also made for the constant deterioration of housing in Harlem and similar areas, bringing to the tenant less value for his rental dollar than ever before.

How then does the Harlem dweller eat? In this era of frozen and refrigerated foods, the people of Harlem have comparatively easy access to average food supplies. The nationally known food chains have not neglected to take advantage of the concentrated purchasing power of black New Yorkers. The outlets are everywhere. The small shopkeeper is rapidly being eliminated by the competition of the chains. He can exist only as an after-hour parasite, charging thirty cents for a quart of milk at 8 p.m. which the housewife could have purchased for twenty-five cents at 6:30 p.m. and similarly for other staples. He earns the ill favor of his customers and when finally, under the pressure of competition he is eliminated, no one mourns his passing. The small shopkeeper has become a casualty to the economic change that has given the shopping center to the American community.

But on wages of fifty to seventy-five dollars per week, how much can the Harlemite in the lower income brackets spend for food? Rent comes first, then food. Balanced diets are expensive. The great irony of the American civilization is here illustrated—excess food production—meats and vegetables in embarrassing surplus—while the cost to the low income consumer of such staples as milk, eggs, flour and meat places them beyond his reach.

Where, then, does the money come from to keep the bars and grills busy with customers, the liquor stores thriving, and the drug pushers active? There is no simple answer to these questions. It is naive to be glib in suggesting that the people have too much money to spend. The fact is that the money that is withheld or diverted for liquor is often, though not always, that which should be reserved for the landlord, the furniture salesman or the insurance collector. The proliferation of drug addiction is concomitant with the spread of crime. The drug addict cannot earn enough to meet the cost of the indulgence. Theft eventually is the only means by which he can supply his daily needs. The cost of drug addiction to the Harlem community is becoming ever more burdensome and the end is not in sight. Both city and state officials have been extremely unrealistic in not assessing the clear and present danger of the proportions of this vice. Yet it must come up for a reckoning and when it does, heads will undoubtedly roll. The tendency though, is still to brush all reference to the drug traffic under the social and political carpet and pretend that it has disappeared.

It has been asked whether drug or policy rackets could thrive without the permission or protection of the police. Both seem to flourish in Harlem. Clearly, the police are handicapped in law enforcement without the cooperation of the average citizen. Mr. Average Citizen in Harlem is convinced that the police cannot or will not protect him against organized crime, so there is little or no assistance that the police can expect or will receive from the colored citizen whether he is a victim or an informed observer. The examples of reprisals against loyal citizens who have aided the police are too many and too vivid not to be remembered and no one wants to be that patriotic.

For many years, there has existed a belief that Harlem provided a ready market for stolen goods. The truth appears to be that the once thriving "hot" market in Harlem has long ceased to have any real meaning. However, there is a class of shrewd peddlers who have learned that carefully selected bargains secured in "close outs" or from jobbers, purchased at auction prices, can be resold in Harlem, through the beauty parlors, nursing homes, restaurants, under the "hot goods" label much more readily than through normal channels, and for cash. Sometimes stolen goods also flow along this route, but the bulk of the furtively displayed, once-in-a-lifetime bargains, that so readily appeal to the cupidity of the respectable housewife or career woman are entirely legitimate offerings.

power of the church in community

It has been said, perhaps with a high degree of truth, that the largest business in Harlem is done by the churches. The colored ministers are alleged to collect more money, net, than those in any other enterprise or profession. Questions are being raised with greater insistence as to what the ministers and the churches are giving in return. "Sister Mary" says "amen" much more generously when the minister talks about some "pie here and now," than at his unctious references to "pie in the sky." The promise of a life in the hereafter with abundance of "milk and honey" recently caused one skeptical street corner critic to call to his hearers' attention the cathartic properties of both these foods when taken in excess.

Some churches have instituted thrift programs by forming and operating Credit Unions. Others have developed Community Centers in which various forms of social action for youth and adults are carried forward. But the potential of the churches, through their ministers, for influencing the economic life of the Harlem community is far from being organized or released. The possible conflict between the church's interest in money and the diversion of the churchgoer's finances to other areas of interest, is one for which the churchmen do not as a group intend to be responsible. It is inevitable that a revolt will set in against this general situation—indeed, it may have already begun. The Muslims are preaching a doctrine of self-help. They consistently refer to the lack of ownership of any of the means of production. Their program provides for the organization and operation by blacks of restaurants, factories, chain stores, and canneries that will create jobs. They scoff at the efforts of the Urban League and the NAACP to seek jobs in the white man's enterprises. The logic of their arguments is strong, appealing, effective and persuasive. And the fact is, that except for their demand for a separate state for blacks, their enunciated program and statement have achieved general acceptance by a majority of colored Americans. The blacks in Harlem, like those in the west and south, understand more and more clearly the relationship between their economic exploitation and deprivation, and the denial of rights and liberties. They are discerning that the segregated living imposed on them, confers economic advantages—with profits—on whites. Racial discrimination is looming as an economic factor in their minds. It is no longer a question of "social equality" but rather one of "economic justice." This is the ship, all else is the sea.

Proportionately, colored New Yorkers feel the weight of the tax burden most heavily because so many fall into the low income brackets. The indirect taxes which contribute to the inflationary high prices of goods and services have their impact. But black workers are actually called upon to subsidize those who are better off economically by providing services in institutions and in industry at prices that are below the true value of their labor. The recent hospital strike demonstrated that hospital workers—chiefly colored and Puerto Rican—were furnishing labor at wage levels that were recognized to be below the poverty level of subsistence. The voluntary hospitals did not hesitate to use such labor at low wages in order to remain competitive in respect to their paying patients. And so it is in those industries and trades where unskilled labor is used. In the semi-skilled and skilled crafts which have organized to protect their wage levels, the practice of racial discrimination has long been firmly fastened. Blacks have not been permitted to work as bricklayer's, carpenter's, and electrician's helpers over the years. Thus, Negro workers have not become skilled in these trades.

It was recently pointed out to the present Governor of the State of New York that a minimum wage of one dollar and a quarter per hour was wholly inadequate to meet the needs of any family in New York no matter how small. When it was noted that the minimum subsistence budget of the Department of Welfare was much higher than the minimum wage, he indicated that he was fully aware of this. However, on being asked to commit himself to support a minimum wage of one dollar and a half per hour, he declined on the ground that he wanted to be sure that such an increase would not drive industry from the state. The Governor was admitting to a policy of expediency that legalized sweatshop wages in the state. The moral weight of the argument did not touch the Governor's conscience. It seemed clear that his economic theory provided for the existence of a class of workers whose labor would be priced below the subsistence level and that it was now the turn of the blacks and Puerto Ricans in New York to fulfill that role. Other national and ethnic groups in past years had done so and moved on to more favored brackets. In the light of the great wealth that our state and nation have developed and our economy of abundance, the Governor's thinking was unimpressive. It was difficult to refrain from associating the apparent absence of moral conscience with the vast inherited fortune of which this man is a principal administrator. Political ambition requires that concepts of right and justice be balanced with Machiavellian calculation and sense of timing. It seems clear, however, that it would have been wiser politically to support a minimum wage more in keeping with the needs of decency and self-respect.

schools fail to meet needs

The system of public instruction has long been geared to depress the level of education of colored children. For many years the attitude of educational planners as well as teachers was that it didn't matter too much whether pupils in Harlem schools learned or did not learn.

They were thought to be biologically inferior anyway and what was the point in expending energy to make them learn when the work that would be available to them would be in unskilled categories where minimum education would be adequate.

Generation after generation of colored pupils were processed through Harlem schools, promoted from one grade to the next and turned out as graduates, unprepared, unable to read at the level established by the curriculum and ill-equipped to compete in the world of labor and industry with their white opposite numbers. There have been protests and much agitation, with considerable attention focused on the problem for many years, but the segregated schools stemming from segregated housing continued to repeat the process. Now at last there appears to be some appreciation on the part of the school authorities that "where there has been no learning, there has been no teaching." Confronted with the problems of "dropouts," drug addiction among teenagers, the mounting number of pregnancies among girls of school age, and continued street gang activities, the community is finally taking a closer look at the schools. The understanding is beginning to get through to more and more parents and community leaders, that Johnny's low reading level will be a barrier to his earning capacity in the years ahead just as it is to his father today, and bears directly on the economic potential of the group.

Statistics show that a disproportionate percentage of the colored population of Harlem receives assistance from the Department of Welfare compared with white families in the city as a whole. There should be nothing surprising in this fact. The family budget established by the Department of Welfare is even well above the income of many families that do not and would not accept aid from that agency.

Chickens will come home to roost. There have been so much time, energy and money invested in these United States in planned programs to retard the progress of black citizens, to create barriers in their path, to humiliate and discourage them, that it is to their eternal credit that there are as few criminals, derelicts and habitual drunkards as there are. The injustice, denial of due process, police brutality, gratuitous humiliation, cowardly assault by many against the few or one, are ways in which the white majority has sown the wind down through the years. Can the whirlwind be harnessed? Deflected? Prevented? Only time will tell and time appears to be running out.

The future? The ferment that has gripped our country in the area of race relations will continue to seethe until a healthy change occurs. The young people of the Harlem communities of the nation will continue to challenge and defy the customs, practices and methods that operate to deny them the right to work, the right to equal pay and equal opportunity. They have actually accepted the proposition that they are born in and belong to a democracy—that they are created equal to all others in this democracy and that they cannot be deprived of life, liberty and property without due process of law. They believe that the denial, because of color, of the opportunity to qualify for a job is deprivation, without due process, of a property right having economic value. They are determined to play their part to defend and uphold this democracy for their own benefit and the benefit of all, until those who are legally charged with the responsibility to uphold it, come forth to its defense. By the strong irony of fate, the centennial of the Emancipation Proclamation finds the grandchildren and great grandchildren of the bondsmen in the forefront of the battle to save the nation and to fulfill the American dream.

The healthy impatience of the black American in Harlem, the refusal to tolerate bigotry and injustice, the emerging unity of purpose to force a common front against racialism, are heightened by the knowledge that black, brown and yellow brothers, in all sections of the world, have their eyes focused on this, our homeland. There is one tie that binds them all—one alone—their common hatred of racist oppression that, in varying forms, they have all experienced, as the blacks in America continue to experience, always from the whites. We must expect a tightening of the sinews of opposition as those who are irredentist in their attitudes resort to desperate measures, until sanity arises in this bewildered and floundering land of ours.

The blacks are the only Americans who did not ask to be admitted and did not volunteer to come. Their right to stay and to inherit the land in indefeasible and they know it now.

The achievement of the right to work—a property right—untrammelled by racialist exclusionary practices— will remove the primary obstacles to the equality of people, regardless of their race and color. The purchasing power of the people of Harlem is now estimated to total several billions of dollars annually—a factor that is proving to be extremely consequential to the industrial and business community.

It would therefore seem to be logical and factual to conclude that there is no special economic theory applicable to the Harlem Community. Colored people who were once limited to Harlem for their living space by the social pattern evolved for them by the whites, have, by and large, elected to continue to live in Harlem now that they are freer to live wherever they are able to purchase or rent homes.

This freedom is of course highly relative in that the majority of the colored population simply cannot afford to move into more desirable housing.

The gap in family income between whites and blacks is the primary determinant of the social distance that exists and will continue to exist between the two ethnic groups until the gap is narrowed.

Removal of educational inequality in the public school system, whatever the reasons for its existence, will work a major change in the income potential of the black family. With improved participation in remunerative employment, some significant capital accumulation may be anticipated. This will lead more rapidly to integration of non-white persons into business, trade and financial operations. Penetration of the power structure will mean inclusion in broad policy-making. It will be simpler then for black representatives in business and finance to drive home the truths, now mere postulates, to the majority, that it is costly and unprofitable to support a segregated industrial society and that non-discriminatory patterns of living avoid waste, improve business and increase profits.

There are many hopeful signs that suggest that the Harlem community can leap forward economically; not the least important of these is that the controllers of business in Harlem are anxious to find ways of changing old images and creating new ones, fresher and more realistic and there are also those in the ranks of the blacks who feel that this is good and are working to see what can be done about it, quickly.

REVOLT OF THE ANGELS

JOHN HENRIK CLARKE

THE TWO Harlem piano movers who had taken the negative side of the argument were quiet now, waiting for the defender of the affirmative to gather his thoughts. He was a big man; seemingly bigger than his two friendly opponents put together. Because of this, it did not seem unfair that he had no one to assist him in imparting his point of view.

For more than an hour the three men had been standing by their large red truck, waiting between assignments. It was their custom on these occasions to test each other's knowledge of the great subjects and issues that influence the destiny of mankind. The fact that their formal knowledge of these subjects was extremely limited did not deter their discussions in the slightest.

The two small men waited and stole quick glances at their large companion. Their faces were aglow with the signs of assured victory. Finally one turned to the other and said: "We've got 'im at las', Leroy. We've taken King Solomon off of his throne. We've made another wise man bit th' dust."

The speaker's dark face looked as if age had been baked into it. He kept watching the large man who was collecting his thoughts in preparation for stating his side of the argument.

"I knew we'd tame this wise man some day," the other small man said. The note of triumph and mock haughtiness in his voice gave it a distinct play acting tone. "We got 'im up a creek without a paddle," he went on, laughing a little. "Now, Hawkshaw, lemme see you talk your way out of this trap."

"Don't count your eggs before you buy your chickens," the big man said, straightening up as his loosely hanging stomach spilled over the rim of his belt. "Th' thing to be resolved is whether a man who has been a drunkard most of his life can straighten himself out and become a pillar of respectability an' a credit to his community. You fellas have said this can not be done an' I disagree . . . I know just th' case to prove my point." He exhaled audibly with some of the pompousness of a political orator preparing for a long discourse. Then he spoke again, slowly, measuring his words very carefully at first.

"During th' last part of th' depression years there was a fella here in Harlem named Luther Jackson who had been drunk so long nobody could remember how he looked when he was sober. Luther wasn't a violent man; he didn't bother nobody unless he wanted some likker and they wouldn't give it to him.

"One day when Luther was near th' end of a three week stupor, he wandered into one of Father Divine's restaurants and sat down at th' bes' table. He thought th' restaurant was a bar and th' bes' table in th' house meant nothing to him. Now, fellas, when I say this was the bes' table in th' house, I mean it was th' bes' table you'd see anywhere. In those days most of Father Divine's restaurants set up a special table for Father just in case he came in an' wanted to dine in style. This special table had snow white linin, th' bes' of silverware, crystal glasses, th' kind you only see in the homes of millionaires, and a fresh bowl of flowers. A picture of Father Divine was in front of th' flowers with a message under it sayin', 'Thank you

tom feelings

Father.' It was some kind of deadly sin for anybody but Father Divine and his invited guests to set at this table.

"A big fat angel saw Luther at th' table an' strutted out of th' kitchen blowin' like a mad bull.

" 'Peace, brother,' she said real loud, 'This is Father Divine's table, get up an' get out of here.'

" 'I want some likker,' Luther says, 'an' I want some more t' wash it down.'

" 'Peace, brother,' th' angel says, puffin' an' trying to keep her temper from explodin'. 'This is Father Divine's table, get up an' get out of here.'

" 'I won't go 'till you give me some likker' Luther says 'an I don't care who's table this is.'

"Th' angel threw her hands in th' air and looked at th' ceilin' like she expected something over her head to come down an' help her. 'Peace, Father,' she says, 'remove this evil man from your premises.'

" 'I want some likker!' Luther shouted at her an' slammed his hand on th' table, knockin' down some of th' fine silverware. 'A drinkin' man is in th' house. Go away old woman an' send me a bartender.'

"This made th' angel madder than ever. She went back to th' kitchen holdin' her head like she was scared it was goin' t' fly off.

" 'Where's th' bartender in this place?' Luther asked an' stood up lookin' 'round like he was just fixin' to mop up th' place with his madness.

"Th' big angel was standing in th' kitchen door, shoutin', 'Father Divine don't allow no alcohol drinkers in here. No obscenities! No adulteries!'

"Luther slammed his hand on th' table again an' knocked down some more of th' fine silverware. This made th' angel so angry she couldn't speak. She just stood in th' door of th' kitchen swellin' up like a big toad frog.

" 'Gimme some likker and let me get outa here,' Luther says.

"Then th' angel hollered out all of a sudden and frightened Luther so much he almost jumped over the table.

" 'Peace Father!' th' angel was sayin'. 'Give me console, Father, you are wonderful.'

"Father or someone else must have given her console an' some new strength to go with it, because she threw a pot at Luther's head like he was a long lost husband who deserted her with a house full of hungry young'uns.

"The pot bounced off of Luther's head an' he hollered like a wild bull. 'What's goin' on in this place?' Luther was sayin'. 'Where's th' bartender?'

" 'Father Divine don't 'low no alcohol drinkers in here,' th' angel was sayin' again, 'No obscenities! No adulteries.' Before she finished sayin' this she threw another pot at Luther's head.

"Luther ducked and stood up in a chair as a skillet missed his head by an inch. Then he stepped into the middle of th' table. He had knocked down th' flowers and some of th' fine silverware. Now th' angel was hollerin' like judgment day was at hand. You see, fellas, Luther was standin' on Father Divine's picture. She ran out of pots an' began t' throw big spoons an ladles.

" 'Peace Father, give me strength,' she hollered, 'give me th' strength to move this satan from your premises.'

"Then she jumped toward Luther like a tiger an' knocked 'im off th' table with a rollin' pin. As Luther fell, he turned th' table over. All of th' snow white table linen was on th' floor. Th' silverware was scattered around th' table and some of it was in Luther's pockets. Most of th' millionaire crystal glasses were broken.

"The fat angel kept screamin', 'Peace! Peace! Peace!' until some more angels joined up with her. They came at Luther with fire in their eyes. They beat him until he got up, then they beat him down again. Still more angels came and joined the war on Luther—black ones, white ones, lean ones, fat ones, an' all th' sizes in between. They kicked him, they scratched him an' spit on him. While all of this was happenin', an angel came up an' started whackin' at Luther with a cleaver.

"Now Luther was screamin' for his life an' tryin' to get to th' door. Th' angels knocked him down gain an' he crawled out of th' door hollerin' for a police to save him. He saw a red box on th' side of a building an' opened it, thinkin' it was a police telephone. He pulled down a lever an' let it stay down. Th' angels had followed him into th' streets. Soon, fire trucks started comin' from every direction—patrol wagons from th' riot squads an' th' emergency squads came. Policemen in cars an' on foot came to th' scene like they were being

rained down from th' sky. Still th' angry angels kept chargin' at Luther. The commotion tied up traffic for ten blocks.

"It took more than one hundred policemen to rescue Luther from them angry angels. They had hit him every place including under his feet. The policemen had to take him to th' hospital before they could take him to jail. When he was well enough for his trial, th' judge threw th' book at him an' said he was sorry that he did not have a much bigger book. Life in jail changed Luther. He was, indeed, a new man when he came out. He was upright, law abidin' and he refused to drink anything stronger than coffee.

"So, fellas, I give you the case of Luther Jackson as my proof that a man who has been a drunkard most of his life can straighten himself out and become a pillar of respectability an' a credit to his community.

"Now Luther is a foreman of a stevedore group down on th' docks an' he's also an officer in th' union. He sent down south for his wife an' children an' he made a good home from them right here in Harlem. He is a church goin' man too an' a senior deacon. Nowhere in this land would you find a more peaceful an' law abidin' citizen than Luther Jackson. Since th' day of that fracas with those angry angels to this day, he never again touched another drop of likker."

The opposition had conceded defeat long before the fat man finished the story. A rebuttal was unnecessary.

A CONVERSATION WITH JAMES BALDWIN

INTERVIEWED BY KENNETH B. CLARK

Taped by WGBH-TV Friday May 24 immediately following Mr. Baldwin's now celebrated meeting with Attorney General Robert Kennedy and with other Negro leaders on the strategy of integration. Interviewed by Kenneth Clark, Professor of Psychology at the City College of New York.

CLARK: One of the significant things of the present revolution of the Negro people in America is maybe the fact, that for the first time, there's genuine communication between Negroes and whites. Negroes are saying out loud now things which they have long said only to themselves. Probably one of the most articulate, passionate and clear communicators to the American conscience is my guest, James Baldwin. James Baldwin's name is known throughout America for saying so passionately and so clearly and with such grace and style what every Negro has long known and has long felt. Welcome James—it's good to have this opportunity to talk with you and have you share with us some of your present feelings about our country, America, but before we get into the issues of the day, I'd like to know a little more about you. I've read practically everything that you have written, but I still would like to know something about you, the young man growing up in Harlem, what schools you went to, maybe a little about some of the teachers that you might have come in contact with in Harlem.

BALDWIN: What a funny question! My mind is some place else, really, but to think back on it—I was born in Harlem, Harlem Hospital, and we grew up—first house I remember was on Park Avenue—not the American Park Avenue, or maybe it is the American uptown Park Avenue where the railroad tracks are. We used to play on the roof and in the—I can't call it an alley—but near the river—it was a kind of garbage dump. Those were the first scenes I remember. My father had trouble keeping us alive—there were nine of us. I was the oldest so I took care of the kids and dealt with Daddy. I understand him much better now. Part of his problem was he couldn't feed his kids, but I was a kid and I didn't know that. He was very religious and very rigid. He kept us together, I must say, and when I look back on it—that was over 40 years ago that I was born—when I think back on my growing up and walk that same block today because it's still there, and think of the kids on that block now, I'm aware that something terrible has happened which is very hard to describe. I am, in all but in technical legal fact, a Southerner. My father was born in the South—my mother was born in the South, and if they had waited two more seconds I might have been born in the South. But that means I was raised by families whose roots were essentially southern rural and whose relationship to the church was very direct because it was the only means they had of expressing their pain and their despair. But 20 years later the moral authority which was present in the Negro northern community when I was growing up has vanished, and people talk about progress, and I look at Harlem which I really know—I know it like I know my hand—and it is much worse there today than it was when I was growing up.

CLARK: Would you say this is true of the schools too?

BALDWIN: It is much worse in the schools.

CLARK: What school did you go to?

BALDWIN: I went to P.S. 24 and I went to P.S. 139.

CLARK: We are fellow alumni. I went to 139.

BALDWIN: I didn't like a lot of my teachers, but I had a couple of teachers who were very nice to me—one was a Negro teacher. You ask me these questions and I'm trying to answer you. I remember coming home from school—you can guess how young I must have been—and my mother asked me if my teacher was colored or white, and I said she was a little bit colored and a little bit white, but she was about your color. As a matter of fact I was right. That's part of the dilemma of being an American Negro; that one is a little bit colored and a little bit white, and not only in physical terms but in the head and in the heart, and there are days when you wonder what your role is in this country and what your future is in it. How precisely are you going to reconcile yourself to your situation here and how are you going to communicate to the vast headless, unthinking, cruel white majority; that you are here, and to be here means that you can't be anywhere else. I could, my own person, leave this country and go to

Africa, I could go to China, I could go to Russia, I could go to Cuba, but I'm an American and that is a fact.

CLARK: Yes, Jim.

BALDWIN: Am I going ahead?

CLARK: These are certainly some of the things that we are after, but as I read your writings and know that you came out of P.S. 24 and my alma mater—Junior High School 139—I see that no one could write with the feeling and with the skill with which you write if you did not get—in P.S. 24 and 139—a certain type of education. Now I'd like to go back to the point that you made that the Harlem you knew when you were growing up is not the Harlem now and see if we can relate this also even to the school.

BALDWIN: Let's see if we can. It was probably very important for me—I haven't thought of it this way for a long time—at the point I was going to P.S. 24 the only Negro school principal as far as I know in the entire history of New York was a principal named Mrs. Ayer, and she liked me. In a way I guess she proved to me that I didn't have to be entirely defined by my circumstances, because you know that every Negro child knows what his circumstances are but he cannot articulate them, because he is born into a republic which assures him in as many ways as it knows how, and has got great force, that he has a certain place and he can never rise above it. What has happened in Harlem since is that that generation has passed away.

CLARK: Mrs. Ayer was a sort of a model in a sense.

BALDWIN: Proof. She was a living proof that I was not necessarily what the country said I was.

CLARK: Then it is significant Jim, that we do not have a single Negro principal in the New York public school system today.

* * *

BALDWIN: The great victims in this country of the institution called segregation, which is not solely a southern custom but has been for a hundred years a national way of life—the great victims are the white people, and the white man's children. Lorraine Hansberry said this afternoon when we were talking about the problem of being a Negro male in this society. Lorraine said that she wasn't too concerned really about Negro manhood since they had managed to endure and to even transcend fantastic things, but she was very worried about a civilization which could produce those 5 policemen standing on the Negro woman's neck in Birmingham or wherever it was, and I am too. I'm terrified at the moral apathy—the death of the heart which is happening in my country. These people have deluded themselves so long, that they really don't think I'm human. I base this on their conduct and not on what they say, and this means that they have become in themselves moral monsters. It's a terrible indictment—I mean every word I say.

CLARK: Yes, well, we are confronted with the racial confrontation in America today. I think the pictures of dogs in the hands of human beings attacking other human beings——

BALDWIN: In a free country—in the middle of the 20th century.

CLARK: In a free country. This Birmingham is clearly not restricted to Birmingham as you so eloquently pointed out. What do you think can be done to change—to use your term—the moral fibre of America?

BALDWIN: I think that one has got to find some way of putting the present administration of this country on the spot. One has got to force somehow, from Washington, a moral commitment, not to the Negro people, but to the life of this country. It doesn't matter any longer, and I'm speaking for myself, James Baldwin, and I think I'm speaking for a great many other Negroes too. It doesn't matter any longer what you do to me; you can put me in jail, you can kill me. By the time I was 17, you had done everything that you can to me. The problem now is, how are you going to save yourselves. It was a great shock to me—I want to say this on the air—that the Attorney General did not know——

CLARK: You mean the Attorney General of the U.S.?

BALDWIN: Mr. Robert Kennedy—that I would have trouble convincing my nephew to go to Cuba, for example, to liberate the Cubans in the name of a government which now says it is doing everything it can do but cannot liberate me. Now, there are 20 million Negro people in this country, and you can't put them all in jail. I know how my nephew feels, I know how I feel, I know how the cats in the barbershop feel. A boy last week, he was sixteen, in San Francisco, told me on television—thank God we got him to talk, maybe somebody thought to listen. He said, "I got no country. I got no flag." Now, he's only 16 years old, and I couldn't say, "you do." I don't have any evidence to prove that he does. They were tearing down his house, because San Francisco is engaging . . . most cities are engaged in . . . something called urban renewal, which means moving Negroes out; it means Negro removal, that is what it means. The federal government is an accomplice to this fact. Now, we are talking about human beings, there's no such a thing as a monolithic wall or some abstraction called the Negro problem. These are Negro boys and girls, who at 16 and 17 don't believe the country means anything it says and don't feel they have any place here on the basis of the performance of the entire country. Am I exaggerating?

CLARK: No, I certainly cannot say that you are exaggerating, but there is this picture of a group of young Negro college students in the south coming from colleges where the whole system seems to conspire to keep them from having courage, integrity, clarity and the willingness to take the risks which they have been taking for these last three or four years. Could you react to the student non-violent movement which has made such an impact on America, which has affected both Negroes and whites, and seems to have jolted them out of the lethargy of tokenism and moderation. How do you account for this?

BALDWIN: Well, one of the things I think has happened, Ken, is that the Negro has never been as docile as white Americans wanted to believe. That was a myth. We were not singing and dancing down on the levee—we were trying to keep alive; we were trying to survive. It was a very brutal system. The Negro has never been happy in his place. What those kids first of all proved—first of all they proved that —they come from a long line of fighters and what they also prove is not that the Negro has changed but that the country has arrived at a place where he can no longer contain the revolt. Let's say I was a Negro college president, and I needed a new chemistry lab, I was a Negro leader, I was a Negro leader because the white man said I was, and I came to get a new chemistry lab, please, suh, and the tacit price I paid for the chemistry lab was to control the people I represented. And now I can't do that. We were talking to a Negro student this afternoon who had been through it all, who's half dead and only about 25, Jerome Smith. That's an awful lot to ask a person to bear. The country sat back in admiration of all those kids for three or four or five years and has not lifted a finger to help them. Now, we all knew. I know, you knew and I knew that a moment was coming when we couldn't guarantee, that no one can guarantee, that he won't reach the breaking point. You can only survive so many beatings, so much humiliation, so much despair, so many broken promises, before something gives. Human beings are not by nature non-violent. Those children had to pay a terrible price in discipline, moral discipline, an interior effort of courage which the country cannot imagine.

CLARK: You said something—that you cannot expect them to remain constantly non-violent.

BALDWIN: No, you can't! And, furthermore, they were always, these students that we are talking about, a minority. The students we are talking about were not in Tallahassee. They were some students protesting, but there were many, many, many, many more students who had given up, who were desperate and who Malcolm X can reach, for example, much more easily than I can.

CLARK: What do you mean?

BALDWIN: What Malcolm tells them in effect, is that they should be proud of being black, and God knows that they should be. That is a very important thing to hear in a country which assures you that you should be ashamed of it. Of course, in order to do this, what he does is destroy a truth and invent a history. What he does is say "you're better because you're black." Well, of course that isn't true. That's the trouble.

CLARK: Do you think this is an appealing approach and that the Black Muslims in preaching black supremacy seek to exploit the frustration of the Negro?

BALDWIN: When Malcolm talks or one of the Muslims talks, they articulate for all the Negro people who hear them; who listen to them. They articulate their suffering, the suffering which has been in this country so long denied. That's Malcolm's great authority over any of his audiences. He corroborates their reality; he tells them that they really exist.

CLARK: Jim, do you think that this is a more effective appeal than the appeal of Martin Luther King?

BALDWIN: It is much more sinister because it is much more effective. It is much more effective, because it is, after all, comparatively easy to invest a population with false morale by giving them a false sense of superiority, and it will always break down in a crisis. That is the history of Europe simply—it's one of the reasons that we are in this terrible place. It is one of the reasons that we have five cops standing on the back of a woman's neck in Birmingham, because at some point they were taught and they believed that they were better than other people because they were white. It leads to moral bankruptcy. It is inevitable, it cannot but lead there. But my point here is, that the country is for the first time worried about the Muslim movement. It shouldn't be worried about the Muslim movement, that's not the problem. The problem is to eliminate the conditions which breed the Muslim movement.

CLARK: I'd like to come back to—get some of your thoughts about the relationship between Martin Luther King's appeal—that is, the effect of non-violence and his philosophy of disciplined love for the

CONVERSATION WITH JAMES BALDWIN

oppressor. What is the relationship between this and the reality of the Negro masses?

BALDWIN: Well, to leave Martin out of it for a moment. Martin's a very rare, a very great man; Martin's rare for two reasons; probably just because he is and because he's a real Christian. He really believes in non-violence. He has arrived at something in himself which allows him to do it, and he still has great moral authority in the south. He has none whatever in the north. Poor Martin has gone through God knows what kind of hell to awaken the American conscience, but Martin has reached the end of his rope. There are some things Martin can't do—Martin's only one man. Martin can't solve the nation's central problem by himself. There are lots of people, lots of black people I mean, now, who don't go to church no more and don't listen to Martin, you know, and who are themselves produced by a civilization which has always glorified violence unless the Negro had the gun, so that Martin is undercut by the performance of the country. The country is only concerned about non-violence if it seems as if I'm going to get violent, because I worry about non-violence if it's some Alabama sheriff.

CLARK: Jim, what do you see deep in the recesses of your own mind as the future of our nation, and I ask that question in that way because I think that the future of the Negro and the future of the nation are linked.

BALDWIN: They're insoluble.

CLARK: What do you see? Are you essentially optimistic or pessimistic, and I don't really want to put words in your mouth, because I want to find out what you really believe.

BALDWIN: I'm both glad and sorry you asked me that question, but I'll do my best to answer it. I can't be a pessimist because I'm alive. To be a pessimist means that you have agreed that human life is an academic matter, so I'm forced to be an optimist; I'm forced to believe that we can survive whatever we must survive, but the future of the Negro in this country is precisely as bright or as dark as the future of the country. It is entirely up to the American people and our representatives, it is entirely up to the American people whether or not they are going to face and deal with and embrace the stranger whom they maligned so long. What white people have to do, is to try to find out in their own hearts why it was necessary to have a nigger in the first place, because I'm not a nigger, I'm a man, but if you think I'm a nigger, it means you need it. Why? That's the question you have got to ask yourself—the white population has got to ask itself—north and south, because it's one country for a Negro. There's no difference between the north and south. There's just a difference in the way they castrate you, but the fact of the castration is the American fact. If I'm not a nigger here and you, the white people invented him, then you've got to find out why. And the future of the country depends on that. Whether or not it's able to ask that question.

CLARK: As a Negro and an American, I can only hope that America has the strength and the capacity to ask and answer that question in an affirmative and constructive way. Thank you very much.

'ASHES, ASHES, WE ALL FALL DOWN'

(Note: For that community with segregated air raid facilities.)

Helter skelter
Head for shelter
They done dropped a bomb.

Hurry scurry
In a flurry
Get the kids and Mom.

Goodness gracious
Sure is spacious
In our little site.

But out he shout
And don'tcha pout
This is just for white!

W. HAYWOOD BURNS

PARTIES AND
POLITICS IN HARLEM

PAUL B. ZUBER

I HAVE found the subject of this article much more complex than I expected. After much investigation and reflection I discovered that the subject was as elusive as trying to catch an eel with your bare hands. There are political clubs in Harlem and political leaders in Harlem, but I feel that this is where the similarity with any political organization ends. In other words, we have a political frosting but no political cake.

The question now must be answered as to how the aforementioned situation came about. There is a historical background to the development of the alleged Negro political community and what observation I am making about Harlem would be true of any Negro community in any large city or small town located in the northern part of this country. In slavery days the plantation owner, when he did permit the slaves to participate in any form of religion, would usually select the minister. Needless to say, the slaveowner had a sinister motive—namely, means of control over the slave. After the Civil War the Negro intellectual took the reins of leadership in the south and was moving towards a sound political structure .This type of leadership never manifested itself north of the Mason-Dixon line. The Negro intellectual was quickly displaced during the Reconstruction and the white power structure reverted to the plantation system. The Negro minister was therefore projected to being the political as well as the spiritual leader of the Negro community. It was the rule, therefore, rather than the exception for a Negro in Harlem to go to his minister if he wanted a political job. If a person was arrested and the family needed help, they would seek out the religious leaders who in turn would contact the political boss downtown. On the other hand, if the political boss wanted something done, he would contact the minister who in turn would deliver the message to his congregation. There are many who will refute these observations, particularly the ministers, but I submit that this system is as strong as ever and also that the most powerful political figures in Harlem are not J. Raymond Jones and the district leaders but a group of ministers whom the white political power structure honestly believe control the thinking and actions of the Negroes in Harlem.

political structure of Harlem

Unfortunately, the complex described above has had an adverse effect upon the creation of a sound political structure in Harlem. As Harlem shifted to a black ghetto, the white power structure gave up the leadership of the political clubs to Negroes. I doubt if the white political boss ever really become concerned with the power of the political clubs because he continued his alliance with the Negro clergy. The Negro political boss, therefore, never became strong enough to balk at distasteful tasks ordered from downtown because he feared open conflict with the Negro clergy. He never criticized the Negro clergy for interfering in politics because he knew that he would never get the support of his challenge from downtown. The political boss in Harlem could only settle for whatever jobs "downtown" wanted to give. He could only run those candidates who were acceptable to downtown. He was and still is a jockey without a horse to ride.

The division of the political complex in Harlem has been further complicated by another interesting fact which warrants consideration. Harlem and other Negro communities in New York City suffer politically because of the presence of the national offices of our civil rights organizations in the City of New York. You can rest assured that the leaders in these offices have more to say about political appointments in New York City and New York State than most of the Negro politicians and elected officials. The more the "white power structure" can keep the top separated and at each other's throats, the less the black man in the street gets. It is well known that one Negro leader of a civil rights group has as much to say about federal appointments as the members of the House of Representatives elected by the Negro voter. It is obvious, therefore, that as long as the division exists, the vote of the Negro in Harlem has the value of a lead slug. It is amazing to note the political power of the Negro clergy and leaders of civil rights organizations, and at the same time observe the absence of their presence and participation in the regular political organization. You can count the number of ministers on one hand who are active participating members of a Harlem political club of either party. If the leading civil rights leaders showed up at a regular meeting of a Harlem political club of either party, the members would probably have heart attacks. What has been said thus far is that at the present moment the political power in Harlem is not feared in City Hall, Albany or Washington. As long as the clergy, civil rights leaders and politicians vie for position, the top of the power role of politics will never be reached.

Congressman Powell in Harlem

There are many who will automatically ask about the power of Congressman Adam Clayton Powell. First, let us look at the facts. Mr. Powell inherited a politico-religious structure from his father. The late Reverend Powell, Sr. can be credited with getting more Negroes jobs with the city than any other man alive or dead. If a man wanted to get on the police force before civil service, he usually went to see Reverend Powell, Sr. Secondly, Congressman Powell heads a Protestant church with the largest membership in this country. Thirdly, many ministers who have taken pastorates at other churches received their training under Reverend Powell, Sr., or Reverend Powell, Jr., and the fraternal bond of teacher and pupil has never been broken. Finally, at the time Congressman Powell ascended to power, civil rights organizations did not have the status they now enjoy. Powell, therefore, represents a serious threat to one and all. To the white politicians who developed the plantation system, Powell can expose the alliance at any time. He has never been reluctant to label a black foe as an "Uncle Tom" or a tool of the white man. He will, with great flamboyance expose the clandestine meetings of the white and black power structure and imply sinister motives to this interracial political love affair with the ease of a man stepping on a fly. Powell can chastise other ministers for hiding behind a collar and a robe. He can cite himself as a minister who can service God and politics with equal fervor for the benefit of all. Powell rides at the head of the posse and none of the deputies dare to get ahead of the sheriff. I believe that Powell's recent blasts at various civil rights organizations clearly indicate that Mr. Roy Wilkins and company have made too deep an invasion into what Mr. Powell considers his private political domain. It is believed that Powell has openly resented what some believe is Wilkins' influence in the selection of federal, state and local appointments. It is not so much the power of Mr. Wilkins which has resulted in the appointments being made as it seems to be the tacit support of Mr. Wilkins' choices by powerful white members of the National Board who represent the white political structure and the white power bloc in American labor. It is doubtful that President Kennedy, or Mayor Wagner would reject Mr. Wilkins' choice, particularly if the choice was supported by the late Mrs. Roosevelt, ex-Governor Lehman and Walter Reuther. I believe that this is Mr. Powell's resentment and Adam Powell is not one to tolerate anyone stealing his marbles. I anticipate the Powell-Wilkins feud to continue. To the loser, I suggest that he remember the old adage, "That's politics."

what road for politics in Harlem?

The question now remains as to where does Harlem politics go from here. At the time the new leadership team ascended to the throne, with Powell as King and J. Raymond Jones as Prime Minister, the political leaders agreed to the man that a district leader had too big a job developing the political community to also function as an elected representative. Today, district leader Powell is a Congressman; district leader J. Raymond Jones a City Councilman; district leaders Lloyd Dickens and Mark Southall are members of the State Legislature. Only district leader Hulan Jack is not functioning in a dual role. The membership in the political clubs has dropped sharply. Young people have begun to avoid the clubs like the plague because the opportunities for advancement are either extremely limited or non-existent.

I have excluded any discussion of the political structure of the Republican Party in Harlem because if the Democratic Party structure is limited, then the machinations of the Republican Party in Harlem is a mirage.

From this article one would assume that I feel that all is lost. That is my position unless that apathetic John and Jane Doe awaken and begin to play their roles as responsible citizens. First, the roles of the leaders must be clearly defined and these leaders compelled to function in that role. If a civil rights leader wants to play politics, let him test his strength at the polls and stop hiding behind the banner of civil rights. If a minister wants to play politics, let him do it from the political platform and not the pulpit. Next, there must be an honest attempt to increase voter registration in Harlem. If a minister can preach hellfire and damnation to his congregation for drinking or adultery, it shouldn't be hard for him to issue the same admonition to those of his pastorate who are not registered to vote. A sharp increase in voter registration in Harlem will cause the decline of the white power structure. After the registration is increased, the Negro in Harlem must learn to pay his own way. As long as candidates go downtown to get money for their campaigns, as long as the bills are paid by someone else, our elected officials may pay homage to two masters. The man who passed out the money will always win. Candidates for each office must have formidable opposition. If the Republicans don't wake up, then a fusion ticket must be formed to run against the Democrats. Competition is the only sure way to guarantee the best man will be elected. I have been in Harlem for ten years now and have yet to hear more than two candidates discuss *issues*.

youth participation vital

Finally, I believe that the present political organization has to be completely overhauled. A program must be developed to stimulate the interest and participation of our young people. The young, aspiring politician must be encouraged, not squelched. The political clubs must build their program around the community and its needs rather than jobs for the party faithful. There are so few civil service exempt jobs left that too much energy in the direction of the latter is hardly worthwhile. If, on the other hand, the community responds to the efforts of the political organization, the message will be received in Washington, Albany and City Hall. This activity must go on throughout the year and not just during the two months preceding election day. Last, but not least, there must be more coordination of activity and less competition for superficial power between the politician, the minister and the civil rights leader.

If that great day arrives when the black powers that are in Harlem ever move with a singleness of purpose, everybody, no matter what his station in life, will be able to cut into that beautiful frosting and find the proverbial cake.

Gertrude Elise Ayer

NOTES ON MY NATIVE SONS
—Education in Harlem

GERTRUDE ELISE AYER

A T THE ANNUAL CONVENTION of the Association for Supervision and Curriculum Development, held recently at Lake Placid, N.Y., several revealing statements were made that warrant special consideration by Harlem citizens. The group meeting comprised more than a thousand curriculum workers, administrators and teachers. This supposedly is an influential body of policy makers. A newspaper reporter selected excerpts that had sensational news value but unwittingly disclosed what harm a thoughtless speaker can do. Instead of making a contribution, he spread alarm. At this crucial time in race relations, this serious disservice was done by the speaker, Dr. Charles M. Schapp, who is presently the superintendent of three school districts in heavily populated Harlem. He is quoted as saying: every city of any size "... has begun to face the problem of educating underprivileged children" and, "all indications are that this problem is to grow in the years ahead."

Dr. Schapp has been in charge in Harlem for some half dozen years or more. He, particularly, should not be "just beginning" to face the problems of the disadvantaged child. Rather, he should have many ideas to contribute, culled from work in this field whose records are surely available to him. One, nearly thirty years ago, was an experiment tried in Harlem as well as other schools. It involved special teaching methods and administration. It was scientifically controlled and finally evaluated by the State Education Department of New York, and approved for use officially in all the city schools. Superintendents Dr. John P. Conroy and Miss Ellen A. G. Phillips were in charge in their successive assignments. Because John P. Conroy had practiced medicine before being an educator, he knew there is more in common than in differences between races. Children were children to him, and their needs, whatever they might be, had to be met. He was not restless with a desire to leave Harlem. He served many years until his death. His legacy was a district with well-run, stable schools. Miss

Phillips, who succeeded him, built well on that foundation. Her task was to meet the administrative challenges posed by the new experiment, known as the "Unit Activity Method." It was not easy for her to accept new ways. She was, however, dedicated to whatever would prepare the children for their life ahead. She asked the same of her principals and teachers. She insisted also that the Three R's be mastered and they were. She, too, left a good heritage well worth noting today. She is remembered with respect and appreciation in Harlem.

shifting of teachers creates problems

Dr. Schapp did not ease the tension felt at the convention and in educational circles throughout the country. He emphasized the idea that where there are underprivileged children, they, *ipso facto,* are the cause of the teachers' problems. As a matter of fact there is the practice of shifting superintendents and teachers in and out of such schools before any real understanding and skill can be acquired. That is one reason they are always "just beginning" and make little contribution to the children's achievement.

According to the reporter, Dr. Schapp went on to say, ". . . between the middle class teacher and the disadvantaged child, yawn chasms of language, cultural patterns and of values." Of course, most of this is his opinion. It takes many thousands of teachers to man the hundreds of schools in New York City. Surely, he did not mean to convey the idea that all of them come from what is known as the middle class. Perhaps this was more nearly true generations ago when job opportunities were scarce and "well-brought-up young ladies" were expected to enter the teaching profession.

On the other hand, business men have become aware that there is now a sizeable middle class of Negro Americans and that they wield power as consumers. Dr. Schapp should also know that children from this class are a leaven in the schools where the underprivileged child outnumbers them. If it were true that "chasms yawn between teachers and children," the teacher is trained in ways to span that difference and build rapport, that is, if there is a will to do so.

As to the language barrier between teacher and pupil, what has been done to remove it? Very little. In fact, the Board responsible for testing and licensing teachers, has prevented progress being made. It has rejected highly-trained graduates of the University of Puerto Rico from teaching positions, because of even the slightest trace of Spanish accent. At least, that is the reason given. Fortunately, Dr. Gross, New York City's present head of its school system has spoken forthrightly on this question. He favors teaching the curriculum to Spanish-speaking children in their own language, until they learn English as a special subject. The Puerto Rican teacher could aid greatly in this setup knowing as she does the customs, the celebrations and ways of life of the children. The American teachers and children could learn much from this exchange in languages. Through no fault of his own, the Negro American child is often a total stranger to many teachers. Many of them cling to preconceived notions they have acquired about Negroes. There has been improper or inadequate briefings for teachers before assignment to minority neighborhoods.

Teachers can cause serious neighborhood disturbances by careless words, harsh and peremptory conduct and general condescension and lack of inate respect for the dignity of pupils and parents.

Dr. Schapp included what he termed "differences in values" held by the disadvantaged child and the teacher. Can it be that values no longer evolve partly from precept and example of the teacher? Are not the Harlem parents native Americans for the most part, who perhaps more than others cherish the value of dignity for their personality, the value of opportunity for advancement for themselves and their children, and the values inherent in equal protection under the law. From the days of the Pilgrims, the values have been established, not only in the minds of the white American but in the bonded and the enslaved. The idea is preposterous that teachers should contrast their values with those of the immature pupil. It is serious that Dr. Schapp has, in this quote, so misunderstood one of the main purposes of education—to instill worthwhile values.

Most disturbing of all, Dr. Schapp disseminated defeatist views that augur ill for progress in Harlem schools under his administration. I quote again: "The consequent failure to meet the challenge has caused consternation and frustration in educational quarters." I cannot believe that there exists any wide basis for this emotional statement. I do know there are many who seek to enhance their personal importance by magnifying the difficulties of any job they hold. Not much can ever be expected from such persons.

The tragic aftermath of this speech is that all of its derogatory implications of racial inferiority are being commented about in Harlem. The enlightened parents are duly concerned. Yet the speaker seemed not to grasp the full meaning of what he was saying. Added to this, the tragedy is further deepened when shortly after, Dr. Schapp was given the first Annual Educators' Award by the Afro Arts Cultural Center. There is a cynical resignation to the fact that there are members in every race who, for personal favors accept the role of "trusties" to carry out the adverse will of those in power. This is never to be forgotten.

needed: capable teachers in Harlem

Harlem desperately needs, in key leadership positions, educators who are cultured, capable, and humanitarian. I recently saw an excerpt from the writings of Jacob Burckhardt, the great historian of the Renaissance. As he put it, in describing the leader: "Without him the world would be incomplete. He appears complete in every situation but every situation seems to cramp him. He beholds the true situation and the means at his command. He knows what can be the foundations of his future power. Confronted with.... public opinion, he knows at any moment how far it is real or only imaginary. He will curb his impatience and know no flinching . . . there is no study too toilsome for him." Harlem needs just such leaders.

Fortunately, because of pressure stemming from the survey of New York City schools made by the State Educational Department, and by the revelation of untoward conditions in many of the schools, a whole new Board of Education has come into being. Leaders from other cities are now at the school helm.

A few years ago, there was a revival in one school, on the edge of Harlem, of a program, many of whose features have long been in use. Under the attractive name of "Higher Horizons," it concentrates on motivation to inspire youngsters to acquire more learning and culture for a better future life. The schools where it has been revived are in underprivileged sections and in real need of such a program. Many more schools, some in Harlem, are now taking part in the experiment. Additional funds are alloted for special guidance, social work and remedial teacher personnel. It is really history repeating itself, intensified to meet the more serious situation facing the youth of today. A principal has been selected to head this project who is held in high regard by his co-workers. He evidences the warm personality and enthusiasm so necessary for this kind of assignment. He has been prudent in admitting that he is learning much that he did not know about Negro Americans, their problems, their history and their achievements. Above all he is not a defeatist, which means he is determined to accomplish the task he has been set to do. Harlem can hope that the impetus will be be maintained and not allowed to wither away at the end of the experiment. It should stay an integral part of education.

The forerunner of "Higher Horizons" in experimental educational methods was undertaken some thirty years ago. Culture being a necessary part of the better life, it had its place in that experiment known by the esoteric title of the "Unit Activity Program." It was the brain child of two outstanding superintendents who believed that the prevailing school procedures were too artificial for children. They decided they would have school work done in situations approximating real life.

program was worthwhile

The Superintendent in charge of all elementary schools, Dr. Stephen Bayne, convinced his fellows on the Board of Superintendents that his theories were worth trying. He got the approval of the State Department of Education. The latter agreed to have the method observed by trained teams in the classrooms. Their reports were checked by the State officials. To further validate the results, control schools were assigned and their results in academic achievement and the intangibles, were weighed against those in the "activity" schools. It fell to Dr. John Loftus, the other moving spirit of the plan, to be the administrator of the program as a whole. His leadership was of the highest order: resourceful, imaginative, creative and kindly. He was patient and optimistic. He kept in close contact with the teachers, observed for himself and brimmed with helpful suggestions. It was a rare experience to work with him.

A call went out from headquarters for principals to volunteer to participate. Seventy-one responded, among them this author, then principal of Public School 24, on East 128th Street, Manhattan. Her student body was at that time 98% Negro Americans and West Indians, with a few Finnish children not yet withdrawn from the neighborhood.

It was first necessary to give special attention to improving the intangibles. As class work proceeded, attitudes toward fellow students and ability to work well with them improved. They came to understand the role the teacher must play in guiding pupils in learning, how to respond to courtesy and kindness rather than to force. This was the constant concern of the teacher. Improvement in these regards were recorded on each child's progress sheet. Habits and skills were practiced in situations created and planned by pupils and teachers together to approximate those in real life. Conferences and discussions were chaired by the more gifted youngsters. Others came to like arithmetic through learning how things were bought, sold or exchanged.

Some learned through managing the class individual savings accounts. Those with a flair had plenty of opportunity to write anything from reports of committees to slogans, lyrics and even some creative prose and poetry.

One very gifted and mature teacher created a pupil-run "School City." Its model was the government of the City of New York. It was a tremendous job especially since this teacher carried a full classroom load of instruction, and no special allotment was given this experiment. Qualifications for any office or position in the "School City" were high. Self-control and high effort in class work were demanded. Candidates for school judge, head of patrol and sanitation squads, election inspectors and other posts had to win nomination and election by superior presentation of their plans at the school assembly. The judges learned under the teacher in charge how to hold simplified hearings; squads learned how to bring charges and others to defend themselves. The value of truth, of justice tempered with mercy (hard for the young to learn, we found them to be strict task masters) and the necessity for laws in a society were all learned from this splendid teacher, Mrs. Kathleen Travers, and others.

fascinating program

An interesting opportunity was presented to teach children to understand others who differed from them. Friction was noticed between children of West Indian background and those born in the United States. A social studies unit was planned on life in the Caribbean Islands. Even the parents were involved, proudly bringing precious mementoes to illustrate what was being studied. After weeks of study, the program culminated in a School Fair. Every class contributed songs, dances or little plays to the evening's entertainment. Pupil artists decorated the walls of the halls with vivid murals of lush scenes from descriptions they had heard. Childrens' arts and native crafts were offered for sale. After that cooperative venture, there was no more friction due to ignorance. The undertaking yielded considerable reward to parents, teachers and of course, to the children for whom it was designed.

The experiment in methods lasted six full years. Finally the State Education Committee submitted its evaluation. The expectation that the "Three R's" would suffer was not born out. Results showed achievements were in most instances better than those achieved in the traditional control school. In attitudes, habits, ability to work well with others, the experimenters were far in advance. Consequently, the teaching method was approved and recommended for city-wide use. Unfortunately, teachers opposed the method, largely because they did not have the ability to use the skills demanded of them. When overtones of religious controversy entered the picture, the method fell into disuse. And, so, history repeated itself.

Coming out of the happy milieu of this "progressive" school are many boys who have since distinguished themselves in manhood. Among them are Judge Kenneth Phipps, a graduate of Lincoln University, now presiding in the highly important Criminal Court of New York City. Also, David Means, now manager of the main branch of the Bowery Savings Bank in New York City. Another, Dr. Earle Manson, is a prominent dentist practicing in New York City. There was Harcourt Dodds, graduate of Dartmouth College, now holding a diplomatic post in Algeria. James Greer went into business and is now credit manager for the 125th Street Jewelry Store. James Barker is an attorney connected with a Wall Street firm and Calvin Pressley is pastoring a church in Brooklyn.

remembering James Baldwin

Public School 24 basks in the reflected glow of the eminence of James Baldwin as a consequence of the small part it had in shaping his career. The author was his principal during his fifth and sixth years at school. I vividly remember his haunted eyes and his slim physique. He was active in school affairs but never intrusive. I remember too, his mother above all other mothers. She had the gift of using language beautifully. Her notes and letters, written to explain her sons' absences etc. were admired by the teachers and me. This talent transmitted through her is surely the basis of James' success. It is said that he too writes as an angel, albeit an avenging one. But his mother expressed only calm devotion to her family. Today, with three novels, two books of essays, the best seller *The Fire Next Time* and a play in the making, James has reached permanent stature as an outstanding author. Recently, he has come to mean more to the Negro American whom he so brilliantly interprets to the white American. He has caused the white American to seek, rather than, as in the past, avoid communication of ideas with the Negro. As an expert in his craft, he has become a sought-after lecturer on television and platform. Fate seems to have created turbulence in race relations just before James returned to his country. He is using his great talent to convey the sufferings of the Negro Americans and to exhort the white American to examine what his thoughts and acts have made of him. We like to think that the study his class made of the lives of the great Negro heroes in American history inspired him to take active personal part in the present struggle.

We must not overlook the other boys who grew to be uncommon men. I meet them straightening out traffic snarls and continuing to use their school patrol skills at street crossings. Many hold civil service jobs in Post Office and social welfare work. Once, I hailed a taxi and to my pleasure found the driver to be "one of my boys." He hastened to tell me he still remembered a talk I gave in assembly, urging boys never to desert their children. He was pleased that I remembered his name, Majesta. Of these, and hundreds more, I am proud.

another native son

George Barner is another alumnus who stands out in my memory. This, for his fine reporting as feature writer for Harlem's largest weekly, the Amsterdam News. He was recently assigned to cover the atrocities being perpetrated on the Negro American in Birmingham, Alabama.

I like to remember George as the son of a wonderful mother. Not only was she doing a fine job with George but she found time and energy to give help to the sons of others. This she did by taking on the difficult position of the president of the Parent-Teacher Association of the school. The parents had not had much help in learning new ways of meeting problems of children in and after school. Mrs. Barner led the group in examining themselves as mothers and fathers. To ask themselves the questions: was the home atmosphere conducive to study or was there not even a quiet corner provided? Was the home run with democratic procedures where each opportunity meant a responsibility? Were the children respected enough to be listened to when they expressed themselves, or were they silenced even though they were polite?

Families found fun and instruction exploring the city on Sundays and holidays. These trips supplemented the already large number of excursions which were part of the cultural program of the experiment. Parents and children became familiar with the sights and sounds of the city outside of the block where they lived. The teachers already knew that reading would be improved by such activities. The parents were pleased that their cooperation had helped.

Mrs. Barner was one parent who must have seen a vision of the coming school crises in which we find ourselves today. Preventive work must start in the elementary school. The child should be motivated in his most impressionable years. The need is even greater today.

Several generations back, Negro Americans had a hunger for education which was denied them. They were determined that their children would not suffer as they had. A respect for learning was instilled in the young. They came north seeking its advantages. New York, then with a much smaller population, was benefited by their arrival.

Today New York is faced with serious problems. Our dropouts from schools are the most numerous; our achievement in schools is the lowest; our Negro labor supply the most unskilled and the possibilities of obtaining work grow steadily worse. Our parents, as well as our workers with the young must not flinch from the challenge it poses. It was inspiring to hear James Meredith announce that he will devote himself to preparing Negro youth to be ready for the opportunities they fight for. There must be real zeal shown for that too.

New York school officials are only now in the experimental stage of zoning, open enrollment and other devices. Now, instead of ready acceptance by parents and community, there is discontent and resentment when elementary pupils are transported out of their neighborhoods. They go where there are empty seats and strange faces. The policy so long adhered to in New York of hopping from one crisis to the next, playing it by ear, has caused distress and ill-feeling among teachers and citizens and especially the parents of New York City. The boast that New York is the first city in the north to integrate falls on cynical ears. So far it is only token integration. It cannot be denied that New York has allowed *de facto* segregation to exist for many years.

Belatedly the nation is aroused to the dangers in having a semi-literate citizenry with an insufficient number of professional personnel and trained skilled workers to meet the demands of survival in a tensely competitive world. The Negro American has contributed admirably to the life of our country in the past. On the campuses of the country's colleges, today's youth are more serious scholars deeply concerned with the questions of the day. The Negro student is no exception, as he knocks at the school door and pleads to add his contribution to his country.

THE NEGRO THEATRE
AND THE HARLEM COMMUNITY

LOFTEN MITCHELL

The majority of the history contained herein was originally the subject of two articles prepared for European publications—the Encyclopedia Della Spetta Colo in Rome and the Oxford Companion to the Theatre.

A SCENE IN THE PLAY, *Star of the Morning,* describes the disbanding of the Williams and Walker Company in 1909. Bert Williams asks Jesse Shipp, the company director: "Jesse, where'll you go?" Jesse answers: "Uptown. 100,000 Negroes in New York now. Lots of them moving to Harlem. I'll go there. Maybe they'll be needing a theatre."

Fifty-three years after Jesse Shipp's statement, Ed Cambridge, the director of *Star of the Morning,* read these lines at an audition. The shoulders of a number of theatre people sagged as the lines left Cambridge's lips. A sharp pain stabbed me. I wished the lines had not been written.

Later that night Gertrude Jeanette, Esther Rolle, Lynn Hamilton, Louis Gossett, Rick Ferrell and Irving Burgie sat in the home of Michael Allen, rector of St. Marks-in-the-Bouwerie, discussing the fact that there was a theatre in Harlem when there were only 100,000 Negroes in the city and not one at present when the population totalled approximately one and a half million black people. Our trembling fingers spilled coffee into overflowing saucers and onto Priscilla Allen's tablecloth. Ed Cambridge shuddered, banged his cup into the saucer, and growled: "It's a good thing Jesse Shipp didn't go up there this year looking to work in theatre. He'd have been hungry as hell!"

The Harlem to which Jesse Shipp went—like the Harlem of today —was peculiarly a part of this society—this society created by an impoverished, decaying Europe reaching out, searching for a new route to India and finding instead a new Eldorado in the west. The European underprivileged raced to these shores, staked claims, then warred with the red man and with rival European groups. Other Europeans found the rich African continent, enslaved its people, then attempted to justify these atrocities. "The image of Africa," says John Henrik Clarke in his essay, *Reclaiming the Lost African Heritage,* "was deliberately distorted by Europeans who needed a moral justification for the rape, pillage and destruction of African cultural patterns and ways of life."

The image of the African was also distorted in America where a ruling aristocracy sought to break its ties to the old world. Grandiloquent phrases declared equality of all—with the exception of those who were black or those who were white and owned no property. Patrick Henry demanded liberty or death, but he ignored the twenty-three slaves in his possession.

America was, for the African, a strange, hostile land. Everywhere people spoke of freedom, yet he was not free. Everywhere he heard others speak of their glorious ancestry, yet he was told his Africa was a huge jungle, inhabited by cannibals. Sometimes the Negro believed these distortions and saw himself as others saw him—as something sub-human, deserving a cruel fate. Yet, somehow he dared to dream that someday he would be free.

His dreams were not idle ones. He fought the nation's wars. His hands built the economy. His cultural gifts were either stolen or ignored by white historians who interpreted the nation's history in biased terms. In his essay, *Negritude and Its Relevance to the American Negro Writer,* Samuel Allen describes the Negro's subjection to the cultural imprint of a powerful, dominant majority in an unfriendly land. Mr. Allen tells us that the American Negro group became—if not the only—one of the few black minorities in world history. Despite colonialism, those in Africa had the sheer weight of numbers for allies, plus the realization that the land was rightfully theirs. The West Indian Negro also had the advantage of numerical strength, plus an infrequency of contacts with the ruling group.

The American Negro, however, underwent a physical and spiritual alienation without parallel in modern history. He was overwhelmed militarily and economically, transplanted from his native soil, then subjected not only to a dominant elite, but to what the poet Claude McKay called a cultural hell—a hell created by a powerful, materialistic, brutal frontier society that was uncertain of its own identity, yet seeking to assure itself of status by denying status to its victims.

after the Civil War

The slave system crumbled. The Reconstruction Era followed, but this was sabotaged by those who sold the Negro back to his former owners.

Jimcrow legislation further oppressed him. The southern slaveholding oligarchy remain unchallenged and now, more than one hundred years later, as the Negro struggles to complete the first American Revolution, it seems remarkable indeed that he ever owned a house, let alone a theatre.

Despite hostility, the Negro was part of the drama long before the United States became a nation. John Leacock's *The Fall of British Tyranny* (1776) described recalcitrant slaves who promised to kill their masters upon attaining freedom. *Yorker's Stratagem* (1795) dealt with a New Yorker's marriage to a West Indian mulatto. Murdock's *The Triumph of Love* (1795) featured the cackling, comic servant, despite the fact that black Crispus Attucks was not comic when he shed the first blood in the American Revolution and black Phoebe Fraunces did not cackle when she saved the life of George Washington.

In the early part of the nineteenth century a group of free New York Negroes, spearheaded by James Hewlett, organized the African Company at Bleecker and Grove Streets. In 1821 this group performed Shakespearean plays before mixed audiences. Disorderly whites forced the management to segregate them and also to lament that whites did not know how to behave at entertainment designed for ladies and gentlemen of color. This theatre, eventually destroyed by white hoodlums, is reported to have influenced the great Ira Aldridge who went abroad where he was acclaimed by European royalty.

origin of minstrel tradition

In the middle of the nineteenth century a number of plays attempted to deal with the Negro as subject matter. J. T. Trowbridge's *Neighbor Jackwood* (1857) and Stowe's *Uncle Tom's Cabin* were notable efforts. Dion Bouccault's *The Octoroons* reflected many of the traditional attitudes towards the Negro—that he was either a happy-go-lucky creature or a person with "unclean blood." The nineteenth century was, however, chiefly the era of the minstrel tradition—*the tradition originally created by slaves to satirize their masters.* White performers copied this pattern, popularized it, and spread the concept of the shuffling, chicken-stealing Negro to a society willing to embrace any representation of the Negro that denied his humanity. Following the Civil War, Negroes themselves joined the minstrel tradition, blackened their faces and imitated whites imitating them.

The wave of minstrelsy overflowed into the latter part of the nineteenth century. A group of showmen objected to it. Sam T. Jack's

The Creole Show (1890) broke with the minstrel pattern. Later came *The Octoroons*, then Bob Cole's *A Trip to Coontown* (1898), the first show to be written, directed and produced by Negroes. In 1898 Will Marion Cook and Paul Laurence Dunbar offered *Clorindy—the Origin of the Cakewalk*. Bert Williams, George Walker, Ernest Hogan, Alex Rogers, Jesse Shipp, S. H. Dudley and J. Rosamond Johnson saw to it that the break with minstrelsy was complete. They produced a series of musicals with plot, characterization and meaning.

But, Thomas Dixon's *The Clansman*, later filmed as *The Birth of a Nation*, echoed existing attitudes towards the Negro. Race riots flared. The robber barons built their empires and the Theatrical Trust Syndicate brought the big business concept to the American theatre. This Syndicate controlled the theatre and, because Mrs. Fiske and Sarah Bernhardt incurred their disfavor, the former was compelled to play in second rate theatres and the latter in a tent. The Negro artist found himself unable to get inside the Broadway theatre as performer or patron. Only Bert Williams worked on the Broadway stage. In 1910 the Negro performer had to go to Harlem.

He went because the fabric of theatre life excluded him. Some Negro actors welcomed the exile to Harlem. There they could perform roles previously denied them. They could play love scenes—something that was "taboo" while performing before whites. There, too, they could escape the raging hostility rampant in downtown areas. Many remembered too well the 1900 race riot when the mob yelled: "Get Williams and Walker!" Many knew, too, that comedian Ernest Hogan had to lock himself in a theatre overnight to escape from a lynch mob.

Harlem, therefore, offered the new Negro resident a haven from an unfriendly world despite the fact that he often had to fight neighboring whites in hand to hand battles. Many classes of Negroes poured into Harlem. Although a large number came from the south, this group had either heard about the theatre or seen Negro touring companies. In America at the turn of the century there existed approximately five thousand theatres as well as tent shows and civic auditoriums. To these came the Williams and Walker Company, Black Patti's Troubadors, and others. The movie industry had not yet challenged the economics of theatre. Despite the rise of the Syndicate, theatre was then a primary form of entertainment. It had not yet become a totally middle class luxury.

The Negro who moved to Harlem, therefore, was receptive to the theatre movement that grew around him. For one thing, he could not go into any other theatre. Had he been able to go, he would have witnessed vapid Cinderella stories unrelated to his daily life. Therefore, he flocked readily to the Crescent Theatre, opened by Eddie Hunter on 135th Street. Lester Walton leased the Lafayette Theatre and later stock companies appeared at the Lincoln and Alhambra Theatres. These groups presented Negro versions of Broadway plays, originals, dance-dramas, classics and musicals. The carriage trade often journeyed uptown to openings. Florenz Ziegfeld bought the finale of *Darktown Follies* for his own production. Another show, *Darkydom*, saw many of its sketches sold to Broadway producers.

On April 5, 1917 the Negro drama again moved towards downtown circles. Ridgely Torrence's *Three Plays for a Negro Theatre,* directed by Robert Edmond Jones, opened at the Old Garden Theatre. Charles Gilpin appeared in John Drinkwater's *Abraham Lincoln* and in Eugene O'Neill's *The Emperor Jones* (1920) at the Provincetown Theatre. Later, O'Neill's *All God's Chillun Got Wings* fanned flaming headlines because the play dealt with miscegenation. The Negro theatre artist had returned to the downtown area, doing what he felt whites would pay to see, or performing plays that reflected a white point of view.

The Negro Renaissance flowered. *Shuffle Along, Goat Alley* (1921), *Strut Miss Lizzie* (1922), *The Plantation Revue* (1922), *How Come?* (1923), *The Chipwoman's Fortune* (1923), *Chocolate Dandies* (1924), *Dixie to Broadway* (1924), *Topsy and Eva,* and Paul Robeson in a revival of *The Emperor Jones* (1925) were major downtown offerings during the 1920's. 1925 ushered in the first Negro-written Broadway drama, Garland Anderson's *Appearances.* Also seen were such offerings as *Lucky Sambo, My Magnolias, Deep River, In Abraham's Bosom, Show Boat,* and Wallace Thurman's *Harlem.* Later, too, came *Porgy,* then *The Green Pastures.*

effect of movies on theatre

Theatrical activity continued in Harlem. Night clubs flourished. This was the period when the Negro was in vogue. Commercialism flooded the community. Stage presentations gave way to vaudeville sketches as the commercial-minded sought to sell to whites what they wanted to see and hear about Negroes. And then the movie industry reared its head. Where there had been approximately five thousand American theatres in 1900, the arrival of talking pictures reduced this amount drastically. By 1940 there were only 200 in the nation. The moving picture replaced the stage and, in addition to the novel form, the prices were considerably cheaper. And many Negroes frankly sought this type of entertainment because at least it was honest. It did not attempt to represent them in any light.

One of the ventures that suffered as the movies rose to power was the Theatrical Owners and Bookers Association. This group, known as "Toby" was organized, owned and managed by Negroes who controlled a nation-wide circuit. Negro performers were assured of continued work.

The depression, the movies and the extended influences of white managers destroyed Toby. Veterans Sidney Easton and Elsworth Wright have declared that Negro actors did not know unemployment until Toby went out of business.

The depression of 1929 temporarily halted the Harlem theatre movement. Negroes appeared in a number of professional shows: *Hot Rhythm, Brown Buddies, Lew Leslie's Blackbirds, Sweet Chariot, Fast and Furious, Swinging the Blues, The House of Connelly, Sugar Hill, Savage Rhythm, Never No More, Bloodstream, Black Souls* and *Blackberries of 1932.* Negroes were in a sober mood during the depression years. Hall Johnson's *Run, Little Children,* Langston Hughes' *Mulatto,* John Wexley's *They Shall Not Die* and the Paul Peters'-George Sklar's *Stevedore,* were serious works. This era ushered in, too, such vehicles as *Four Saints in Three Acts, Mamba's Daughters, Roll Sweet Chariot, Porgy and Bess, The Swing Mikado* and *The Hot Mikado.*

The nineteen-thirties brought professional attempts to the Harlem area. Rose McClendon and Dick Campbell organized the Negro People's Theatre. The Harlem Players, a stock company, presented Negro versions of *Sailor, Beware* and *The Front Page* at the Lafayette Theatre. This group tried to speak to a community that concerned itself with eating regularly, with being dispossessed, and with relatives being lynched in the southland. The troubles of a sailor and the problems of a newspaperman hardly interested Harlem. The Harlem Players soon went out of business. Another group, the Harlem Experimental Players, produced Regina Andrews' plays, directed by Harold Jackman. The Harlem Suitcase Theatre presented Langston Hughes' *Don't You Want To Be Free?* and Dick Campbell and Muriel Rahn organized the Rose McClendon Players. Housed at the 124th Street Library Auditorium, this group produced George Norford's *Joy Exceeding Glory* and Abram Hill's *On Strivers Row.*

Best known of the uptown groups, however, was the Negro Unit of the Federal Theatre. It presented at the Lafayette such plays as George McEntee's *The Case of Philip Lawrence,* J. Augustus Smith's *Turpen-*

tine (written with Peter Morrell), Frank Wilson's *Walk Together, Chillun,* Rudolph Fisher's *Conjure Man Dies,* Shaw's *Androcles and the Lion,* William Du Bois' *Haiti* and George Kelly's *The Show Off.* Its most highly acclaimed production was the Orson Welles—John Houseman offering, *Macbeth* on April 14, 1936. Canada Lee was a member of the cast. This Federal Unit was a solvent, skillful group that attracted theatregoers of all incomes. When an act of Congress ended the Works Progress Administration, it left Harlem without a low-priced professional theatre.

The Negro Playwrights Company, organized towards the end of the nineteen-thirties, attempted to supply the community with professional theatre. Theodore Ward's *The Big White Fog,* directed by Powell Lindsay, opened at the Lincoln Theatre and introduced Frank Silvera to New York audiences. Financial difficulties brought this organization to an untimely end.

During the 1940's the Negro was involved on Broadway as well as in Harlem. The Richard Wright-Paul Green play, *Native Son,* starring Canada Lee, and Paul Robeson's *Othello* were significant achievements. *Cabin in the Sky* enjoyed a successful run. In Harlem, Abram Hill, Frederick O'Neill, Austin Briggs-Hall, and a number of talented theatre people formed the American Negro Theatre, and housed it in the auditorium of the 135th Street Library. In addition to Hill's two plays, *On Striver's Row* and *Walk Hard,* such worthwhile ventures as Theodore Brown's *Natural Man* and Owen Dodson's *Garden of Time* were shown. But, it was the Abram Hill-Harry Wagstaff Gribble adaptation of *Anna Lucasta* that created a sensation and later moved to Broadway. That sensation also brought the Americn Negro Theatre into commercial focus—a move not welcomed by the group's founders. Despite its continued efforts to build a community theatre, the group found that, because of its success with *Anna Lucasta,* it was judged in terms of Broadway fare.

With the end of World War II a number of dramatists turned to the post-war adjustment of the Negro. *Deep Are the Roots, Jeb, Strange Fruit* and *On Whitman Avenue* appeared. *St. Louis Woman, Carib Song, Lysistrata, Mr. Pebbles and Mr. Hooker, Bal Negre, Beggar's Holiday, Finian's Rainbow, Street Scene, Our Lan',* and *Set My People Free* all involved Negro artists.

American attitudes towards the Negro underwent a change in the post-war world, a change reflected in many avenues of the nation's life. Nationalism roared from colonial lands. American Negroes echoed this roar. Some whites found it easier to accept this roar as the voice of the "New Negro." To some extent this concept alleviated numerous guilt complexes and permitted the ruling group to believe it had only subjugated the "old, non-protesting Negro." What was not faced was the truth that Negroes had been protesting, agitating and fighting for human rights since 1619. But, now, after World War II, sharper lines of communication brought the revolts in Asia and Africa into the lives of Americans. The revolt of suppressed peoples became a reality that had to be met.

A number of barriers relaxed. Negroes now found they could purchase seats to Broadway houses—seats that were not on the aisle. Prior to 1945 only three Broadway houses sold seats to Negroes that were not on the aisle. This practice was based on the belief that whites did not want Negroes climbing over them. The Playwrights Company's declaration of principles in 1945 had much to do with this shift in policy. In addition, the company also declared its members would deal specifically with Negroes in dramatic terms. Interesting examples of the integration of the Negro in "white shows" followed. *Detective Story* (1948) and *The Shrike* (1951-52) featured Negro actors in roles that were not specifically Negroid. Actors Equity Association launched repeated drives, urging the continuation of this pattern. The Greenwich Mews Theatre, a professional Off-Broadway company, followed this pattern in productions of *Widower's Houses, Major Barbara, Time of Storm* and *Monday's Heroes*. Broadway, however, continued to use the Negro actor in specified roles, and in roles the Negro himself did not always find to his liking. *The Member of the Wedding, Lost in the Stars, The Wisteria Trees, The Autumn Garden, The Climate of Eden* and *The Crucible* are plays involving Negroes.

In November, 1950 a group of Negro playwrights met in Harlem with representatives of four community theatre groups: the Harlem Showcase, the Committee for the Negro in the Arts, Ed Cambridge and the "Y" drama group, and the Elks Community Theatre. The American Negro Theatre had disbanded and many of its charter members wandered into the aforementioned groups. At the meeting a Council on the Harlem Theatre was formed. A resolution noted that the use of Negro actors in non-Negro roles offered limited employment to a large group of actors. In addition, it neither encouraged nor assisted in disseminating the cultural values of the Negro people. The Council noted, too, that the commercial failure of Theodore Ward's *Our Lan'* (1947) —after its initial Off-Broadway success— suggested that the commercial theatre wanted to tolerate the Negro, but it did not want to deal with him in strong, truthful, dramatic terms.

The Council members declared that the serious play of Negro life met repeated commercial failure because it was often written from a "white point of view." Generally, plays involving Negroes had a "good" white character helping the black people out of trouble. The obvious implication, the Council noted, was that white theatregoers faced psychological barriers and could not identify with central, sympathetic Negro characters.

The Council urged the representative groups to produce plays by Negro writers and to mutually assist one another in casting, producing and promoting. The target was the Off-Broadway area. A number of Negro-written plays appeared in library basements, in community auditoriums and lodge halls, financed quite often because the group collected money from its members and launched a production. Some of the plays shown were: Harold Holifield's *Cow in the Apartment* and *J. Toth,* this writer's *The Bancroft Dynasty* and *The Cellar,* Gertrude Jeanette's *This Way Forward* and *Bolt From the Blue,* Julian Mayfield's *The Other Foot,* Ossie Davis' *Alice in Wonder* and Alice Childress' *Just A Little Simple.* These plays, written, directed and produced by Negroes, appeared primarily during the 1950-51 period.

In the midst of what Harlemites considered a Renaissance, the Apollo Theatre sponsored two shabby productions of "white" plays with Negro actors: *Detective Story* and *Rain.* Both productions were artistically and commercially unsuccessful. The Apollo's management stated publicly that Harlemites did not care for serious drama. The Council on the Harlem Theatre issued a statement declaring: "The owner of the Apollo has insulted the Negro people by bringing to this community two inferior pieces with little meaning to our lives. Ridiculous prices were charged and, when we exercised the buyer's right [of withholding patronage] we were accused of lacking taste."

The Apollo management's charge, however, served as a catalytic agent for productions by Negro authors. On October 15, 1951 William Branch's *A Medal for Willie* was presented by the Committee for the Negro in the Arts at the Club Baron on Lenox Avenue. The critics hailed the play which posed in strong dramatic terms the question: should the Negro soldier fight and die abroad or should he take arms against the prejudiced southland. In September, 1952, Ossie Davis' *Alice in Wonder* opened at the Elks Community Theatre and it, too, roared the truth about the Negro's plight in America.

The early nineteen fifties witnessed another significant event. Large numbers of Negroes moved from Harlem to Long Island, Brooklyn, the Bronx and Westchester. Many theatre workers and playgoers moved, too. Apartment houses became rooming houses, occupied by those who fled the south in terror. There was a shift, too, in methods of producing plays. Community theatres all over the city broke down. The Yiddish Theatre saw an era approaching when it would no longer profit on Second Avenue. Producers were no longer anxious to own theatres, but rather to rent them, produce a play there and let some-one else worry about maintaining the property. Those Negroes who had sought so valiantly to build a theatre in the Harlem area now turned towards Broadway and Greenwich Village.

Most of the professional theatre work since that time has been per-formed in those areas. On September 24, 1953 Louis Peterson's *Take A Giant Step* opened on Broadway. The Charles Sebree-Greer Johnston play, *Mrs. Patterson,* also appeared on Broadway. On October 24, 1954 William Branch's *In Splendid Error* excited audiences at the Green-wich Mews Theatre. In 1955 Alice Childress' satire, *Trouble in Mind,* delighted audiences at the same theatre. Luther James produced an all-Negro version of *Of Mice and Men* in the Greenwich Village area and, on March 29, 1956 Earl Hyman appeared as *Mr. Johnson* on Broadway. Despite Mr. Hyman's remarkable performance, the play failed.

The 1956-57 season brought three Negro-written plays to Off-Broadway stages: Louis Peterson's *Take A Giant Step,* revived at the Jan Hus House, this writer's *A Land Beyond the River* at the Green-wich Mews, and the Langston Hughes-David Martin folk musical, *Simply Heavenly* at the 84th Street Theatre. These plays should have ended the bromide that Negro audiences do not support theatre. Negro theatregoers were directly responsible for the financial success of these plays.

On March 11, 1959 Lorraine Hansberry's *A Raisin in the Sun* opened on Broadway to acclaim and later won the Critics Circle Award. It enjoyed a long and successful run, then later toured. Dur-ing the 1961-62 season Errol John's *The Moon on A Rainbow Shawl* was shown on the Lower East Side and in May, 1961 Jean Genet's *The Blacks* settled down at the St. Mark's Playhouse for a long run. *Fly Blackbirds,* a revue, won critical acclaim Off-Broadway while the Ossie Davis satire, *Purlie Victorious* was hailed by Broadway theatre-goers during the 1961-62 season.

In reviewing this brief—and, of necessity, superficial—survey, it seems amazing that Negro theatre workers have managed such a considerable output. It should be remembered that many of the ventures discussed here were written, directed and produced under harrowing circumstances. The artists generally worked full time at other jobs. They had no well-to-do relatives who could maintain them. They performed at night while working or struggling during the day to pay their rents. And, too, these plays were supported by people whose incomes were, at most, uncertain.

Whether it is possible to build a Harlem community theatre in an era when community theatres are almost non-existent remains a tantalizing question. However, people like Maxwell Glanville, Jay Brooks and other tireless workers continue their efforts in Harlem. They fight eternally rising costs, the omnipotence of Broadway, cheap movie and television fare and a changing community.

For the theatre worker outside Harlem, we can only foresee an occasional successful production. One cannot resist noting, however, that the produced plays will be written by whites dealing with the strings attached to an interracial love affair or some other area of Negro life receptive to white audiences. We may even have the Birmingham story brought to the stage, but it will probably be written by a white author who will deal with the problem of a "good" white caught in the throes of an uprising. Theatre in America remains a middle class luxury wherein the playwright speaks, cajoles, seduces, and lies to an expense-account audience. Until it becomes once again an art form willing to attract all people, we see no change in the type of play being produced.

Yet, a courageous producer has before him a rich opportunity. Negro playwrights are numerous and they wait eagerly for a producer who has not been "brainwashed." One of the most needed theatre workers at present is the Negro producer. He could utilize the rich dramatic history of these times, the wonderful artists and the splendid audiences that can be attracted if the theatre speaks to them in terms of the truth of their daily lives.

THE NEED
FOR A HARLEM THEATRE

JIM WILLIAMS

I N THE SPRING, 1962 issue of FREEDOMWAYS I read a stimulating article by the author-actor Ossie Davis. In *Purlie Told Me!* Davis points out that the white world emasculates him and all Negro men; that the term Negro and man are mutually exclusive; that we will never be able to define our manhood by asking the white man to define it for us; and that no matter how many white middle class standards we adopt or how mildly we petition for our rights we will never be integrated into American society one at a time.

He also mentions that *Purlie Victorious* was kept alive mainly because of the yeoman work of Sylvester Leaks and John H. Clarke in "bringing the Negro people to Broadway." As a result of this salutary and unprecedented experience (Negroes keeping a Negro play going on Broadway) Ossie Davis urged Negro artists, scholars and thinkers to rejoin the people and to turn homeward again. He adds that if we can "create for our own people ... we will no longer be forced into *artistic prostitution and self-betrayal* in the mad scramble imposed upon us far too long, to belong to some other people" (italics mine). To this I can only add a hearty "Amen!"

Ossie's urgent "turn homeward again" however is a healthy but vague plea unless accompanied by an answer to the questions: where is home and how do we turn there?

We read many articles on the Negro in the theatre, follow avidly the hearings on discrimination conducted by Rep. Adam Powell and his Congressional Committee, and join in spirit the picketing on the part of Negro actors to force their natural inclusion in theatre productions, but nowhere do we read the obvious (to us) conclusion to be drawn from all the foregoing. The only realistic way for theatre workers and buffs to turn home is to build a Negro Community Theatre now! "Only then," to quote Mr. Davis further, "can we begin to take a truly independent position within the confines of American

157

culture, a black position. And from that position, walk, talk, think, fight, and create, like men. Respectful of all, sharing with any, but beholden to none save our own."

We believe fervently in the truth of an oft quoted dictum that "art is not an end in itself, but a means of addressing humanity." But who is humanity—and where is our home?

If we take the Broadway theatre as a guide, then for the most part the Negro people are not a part of humanity, nor do we reside in the U.S.A. If we use the flickering pictures of Hollywood as our image, then the Negro people exist, with the possible exception of Sidney Poitier, solely as servants or ciphers or grotesques—and where is their home? If we believe that the attitude of white southern politicos and educators reflects our reality, then we are dehumanized tools to be worked and then returned to the shed until called for further use. If we accept the nothern liberal attitude as expressed in his prayers, platitudes and pleas, then we will remain quarantined for another 100 years in the big city ghettos with all the hopelessly inferior health standards, half-education and demoralizing joblessness attendant hereto.

Television, the infant medium of communication, is playing follow-the-leader despite the so-called twenty billion dollar Negro market which consumes enormous chunks of the products beamed at us every day by the advertisers. Book publishers are a little better. They're beginning "to find a Negro writer" and also have begun to have a Negro work on their list each year. Magazines and newspapers have begun to vie with each other for a market hungry with curiosity and a world filled with concern for these "dark citizens" who have been enjoying the "fruits of the free world and the benefits of democracy for so many generations." Oh, what wonders the liberation movement has wrought!

But what of Harlem, the Negro community geographically closest to the Broadway theatre?

earlier theatre groups

Harlem is the largest black community in the world where about 400,000 people live, play and die. At one time or another Harlem has been home to over seventeen theatre groups of more or less significance. Some of these come readily to mind—the Lafayette Players, Harlem Suitcase Theatre, The Negro Playwrights, American Negro Theatre, Rose McClendon Players, Federal Theatres and the Committee for the Negro in the Arts, to name but a few. Their careers were all too brief but they have bequeathed to us a body of experience from which we can draw guidelines. Many reasons have been advanced to explain the failure of these groups to endure: the pervasive influence of Broadway; too much dependence on intellectuals, professionals and dilettantes who were far removed from the community; admission prices which were too high; assorted coteries or cliques trying to meet their own narrow, short-sighted, selfish needs while ignoring both the needs of the community and their own long term needs as well. We know that all these reasons are valid and can be expanded greatly with strict adherence to truth. While we may disagree as to emphasis, one thing is certain; we are today without a serious cultural center speaking for and in the name of Harlem citizens. As Langston Hughes says, "They done took our blues and gone."

Is it presumptous to say flatly that home for Negro actors and playwrights is Harlem? Is it presumptuous to add that the Negro actor and creative author can achieve true stature only by addressing themselves directly to their own people? Unfortunately, while having many things in common, man today cannot be addressed as humanity. The differences are many and deep. National differences, class differences, caste differences and ethnic differences are only a part of the welter. The classic anthropologists and ethnologists Boas, Mead, Montagu, Finot, have firmly established the biologic oneness and the potential likenesses of all mankind. It seems to us however that if mankind is ever to achieve the equality of opportunity about which the American founding fathers wrote and spoke so eloquently, we must proceed from a clear recognition of the sociological and psychological differences. Indeed, we American Negro theatre people will fail ourselves and our people by our continued neglect and by our persistent refusal to turn home fully.

Stanislavsky, the father of the great Moscow Art Theatre, often told his pupils that the theatre was the most powerful instrument of education for modern man, more powerful than the school or the pulpit could ever be. Even people who are illiterate still enjoy looking at plays, movies, TV and listening to music. Perhaps this is the reason we have not been able to sustain a theatre tradition, for if there are forces that would deny us our freedom, would they not deny us such a powerful weapon?

Theatre people, like all other sections of the population, can find their correct path only by proceeding from objective facts, from their concrete experiences in life. W. E. B. Du Bois said that the twentieth century was the century of the color question. Well, the twentieth century is still with us and so is the color question. Our decade, the decade of the sixties, serves only to emphasize the correctness of Dr. Du Bois' observation. Spurred by the freedom struggles of the African colonies and their leaders' articulate participation in United Nations debates, encouraged by the 1954 Supreme Court Decision making segregated schooling unconstitutional, the Negro people have leaped forward with ever deepening national consciousness.

role of the artists

In a speech delivered at a rally to abolish the House Un-American Activities Committee, Lorraine Hansberry, the author of *A Raisin in the Sun,* urged artists to leave the studios and to participate in protests and rallies, to become committed in the struggles that surround us. As if to answer her *A Challenge to Artists,* Al Hibbler, Ray Charles and Dick Gregory hit the headlines with their participation in the Mississippi movement.

We hope that the ranks of the artists who are identifying themselves with the mass movements of our time and people will continue to swell. The formation of a militant national liberation movement is the prime consideration of the decade of the sixties. The civil rights and liberties taken for granted by the population as a whole can no longer remain dead letters to the Negro people. Every Negro in the United States should become a part in some way of these political and economic struggles for the rights to unsegregated education, to worship wherever we please, to spend our money wherever we please, to vote for candidates of our choice, etc. The mood of our people today is such that they will settle for no less. It is inevitable that this movement soon will take on, in addition, a struggle for jobs, job training and upgrading. With unemployment two and one-half times higher among Negroes, with the introduction of automation by industry making higher skills necessary and the concomitant elimination of the traditional unskilled Negro jobs, we cannot ignore for long the job question nor can the white labor movement continue to rest on its already rusty laurels as fighters for economic rights for Negro workers. According to the 1960 census figures there has been no change since 1950 in the earning gap between white and non-white workers. The Negro wage worker's earnings are three-fifths of the average white worker's and lately even this has been slipping backward.

While the victories are few and by no means far-reaching and the sacrifices great in our sociological struggles, the freedom movement continues unabated. In *Crisis* (March 1963), Carl T. Rowan's article *The Travesty of Integration* (reprinted from *Saturday Evening Post,* Jan. 19, 1963), has this to say: "It bothers me—and it should bother lawyers, judges and all who treasure a society based on justice under law—that in the current school year only 901 of North Carolina's 339,840 Negro school children have secured relief from a practice that, according to our highest tribunal, 'generates a feeling of inferiority ... that may affect their hearts and minds in a way unlikely ever to be undone.'" And further, "In Texas they may boast about 'the peaceful transition' to 'integration' in Dallas or Houston, but the meaningful thing to me is that a 'whopping' 2.16% of the Negro children in that state attended integrated schools last year ... Alabama, South Carolina and Mississippi have yet to free a single Negro child from this stigma of state-imposed racial isolation." Certainly this is tokenism with a vengeance. The Negro people's answer to this has been simply to step up their struggles, increasing the numbers of demonstrations and increasing the number of lily-white institutions assailed.

One could ask how it is that, in an article which purports to deal with the need for a community theatre, so much time and space is being devoted to politics, economics and sociology. Well, I'm of the school of thought that believes that politics and economics are the basis and foundation of our lives and that art and literature are the superstructure; that the superstructure reflects the base—that the base is specific and concrete. However once the superstructure comes into being it does not play merely a supine role or remain indifferent to the base. Exactly the opposite obtains; the superstructure plays a vital and dynamic role, aiding and buttressing the old base or helping to destroy an old moribund base in preparation for new conditions and new social forces. No longer can Negro writers and artists continue to rely on spontaneity or simple willy-nilly expediency. The special conditions inherited from the incomplete character of our Civil War have blunted the development of class consciousness and the sharp distinctions of classes among our people. Our struggle to complete the tasks of the second American Revolution (against chattel slavery) takes on an all-class character. This struggle is being led at the moment by the preachers and students of the South and cries out for the active engagement of our creative writers and actors as participants à la Hansberry, Gregory, Hibbler and Charles but also and perhaps more importantly as craftsmen.

Ernest Kaiser, in his article *The Literature of Negro Revolt* (FREEDOMWAYS, Winter 1963), notes that until a year and a half ago there was very little writing in depth on the five and a half year southern

Negro revolt. He also quotes a SCLC *Newsletter* (August 1961) calling attention to the participation of teachers, preachers, and students in the struggles but lamenting the paucity of poems, essays, pamphlets and books appearing from their pens. He encouragingly lists the increase in books, record albums and articles that since have made their appearance. Nowhere, however, has a play made its reluctant debut.

We know that there is a lag between the construction of a foundation and the fashioning of the superstructure but certainly now is the time to close the gap. It seems to us that it would be naive in the extreme to expect the white people in any sizeable numbers, who control the finances of theatre, to allow any honest dramatizations of the lives of Negro people to be placed on the boards at this time. On the contrary, the decisive forces of the power elite seem to be committed to maintaining the status quo at all costs. On the other hand the Negro revolt against the continuing restrictive shackles of second-class citizenship begs for artistic creations in the new image.

How can our creative writers ignore the freedom movements and the police, fire hoses, dogs, bombs, jailings, etc., used to oppose them?

In the qualitative worldwide change represented by the dissolution of classic colonialism and the concomitant national liberation struggles of our own people, lies the richest of mines awaiting the creative Negro writers' golden touch. If only our writers will base themselves on the firm foundations being laid down by our people, self-pity and the pathetic tendency to imitate the white middle class intellectuals' sterile absurdities will vanish like fog in the bright sunlight.

Culturally, is it too much to hope that a theatre caucus can be achieved in Harlem from which we can probe the no man's lands of Broadway, Hollywood and Madison Avenue? I think that this paradox conforms to the reality of Negro experience. We are a part of and yet separate from white people in every walk of life. To expect Negro acting and play writing to flourish without a Negro theatre is like asking a farmer to grow vegetables without roots in the soil. You may get the vegetables but, man, they sure will be stunted.

Lionel Abel in *Theatre of Politics and the Negro* (*Nation*, April 27, 1963) says that "the lack of political movements in recent times of the kind we witnessed during the thirties" has been the reason, as he puts it, for the absence of "political plays." He goes on: "However, there have of late been political events that give promise of future effects—political and theatrical. For if there is no labor movement or Socialist movement on the march in this country, there are two new political developments: (1) the peace movement and (2) the movement for Negro liberation ... My claim is that the existing movement for Negro liberation has again made political plays possible ... What is new in the present situation, as a result of what Negroes have achieved in the North and in the South, is that the individual Negro, representing his fellows has become a historical figure."

By contrast, Esther Merle Jackson in *The American Negro and the Image of the Absurd* (*Phylon*, Winter 1962) says, "The modern arts, in particular, the art of literature, have dramatized the fact that an ever larger segment of humanity seems to share the kind of existence which has been the lot of the Negro for some three centuries or more. The shape of human suffering defined by Dostoevski, Proust, Gide, Malraux, Mann, Sartre and others mirrors the actual condition of the Negro; his alienation from the larger community, his isolation within abstract walls, his loss of freedom, and his legacy of despair. Although many modern writers trace their vision of the human dilemma to developments in European intellectual history, it is quite clear that one of the perceptions profoundly affecting the modern mind has been the image of the Negro. Indeed, it may be said that he has served as a prototype of that contemporary, philosophic species, the absurd."

Isn't it interesting that though the American Negro may very well be an objective prototype for the absurd having lived in a world from which he is alien, estranged, unsheltered, threatened, opaque; a world that has been really desolate and bleak for over three hundred years, we have not succumbed subjectively to it nor have we in any numbers embraced the white man's currently popular nihilistic philosophy. Perhaps the reason is that the capitalist world is not ours nor of our making and therefore its dissolution is not of such grave concern to us. On the contrary, if we Negroes are ever going to be able to share in the fruits, real and potential, of mass production, industrial society, it is my belief that the capitalist system will have to be so modified as to be almost unrecognizable.

It is also my belief that our creative people must find another way to create artistically the sinew, sense and soul of the Negro. In an article by John Mason Brown, *What's Right with the Theatre* (*Saturday Review*, May 11, 1963), some of the answers may be found. He said, "Fortunately, there have been exceptions [to the Absurd Playwrights], such as Jean Anouilh, Archibald MacLeish and Robert Bolt, who even in a darkening world have not been embarrassed by a larger vision. They have seen man and seen him plain, and therefore seen him whole, recognizing the strengths that exist within him, side by side with weaknesses. They have not been blind to what Dostoevski called 'the fury and the mire of human veins.' But, in the interest of the total rather than the fractional truth, they have acknowledged what it is that man can rise to in spite of his mortal frailties.

"Prudery, piety and copybook morality have nothing to do with their attitude toward life as *Becket, J. B.* and *A Man for All Seasons* have proved. Anouilh, MacLeish and Bolt have been as unafraid of evil as they have been prepared to admit virtue. They have sensed that people are what they prove to be in the moments of being most cruelly tested . . . Their characters have risen to the testing and sought for the reasons that have caused it, rather than submitted to the sheer senselessness of things."

We have cited these examples of the current political, sociological and artistic ferment not to come to any firm conclusions at the moment, but to underscore our deep belief in the need for a Harlem Community Theatre. This Harlem Theatre not to be viewed as "Little" theatre or institutional theatre but a theatre embracing the highest off-Broadway technical standards; a theatre free to experiment; a theatre free from the stench of commerce; a Negro theatre dedicated to "telling it like it is." By a Negro theatre we do not mean a theatre that will exclude the white world as audience, patrons, technical advisors, teachers or actors, for this would be almost as false and phony as the unreal, commercial, white theatre world. Nor am I concerned at this time with whether the plays that will be performed are expressionistic, realistic, poetic, absurd, political, Freudian or what have you, as long as they do me and do me right.

The theatre I envision needs the active support of every Negro actor, writer and creative person with five minutes to spare from his present work whatever it may be. A Harlem Theatre cannot be looked upon as a contradiction to the understandable ambitions of our theatre workers to emerge on Broadway, Hollywood or TV. If I learned one thing from seeing Jean Genet's black un-merry-go-round, it was that with a fine stage manager such as Edmund Cambridge, a play can remain tight though the original cast moves in and out of it like kids seeking a brass ring. Cicely Tyson, Godfrey Cambridge, Helen Martin and many other members of the cast were able to leave *The Blacks* to try more ambitious productions only to return after the closing of the other plays.

home to Harlem

I think it's high time we turned all the way home, home to Harlem.

Only such an indigenous theatre can take the initiative to distill the essence of our people; can give deeper consciousness to our actors; can give direction to our muted writers. Combining as its does so many arts and crafts, such a theatre can become a small but dynamic voice in the cultural life of our country. With the winds of change blowing up a storm I have deep faith that this theatre would find a healthy direction and in a short time become a jewel in the cultural crown of a new, more rational America.

To continue my temerity just a little further, if one play, *The Blacks,* can run for three years with its song of futility, its message of hopelessness, and cynical nihilism, then certainly a clutch of such fine plays as Loften Mitchell's *A Land Beyond the River,* Langston Hughes' *The Emperor of Haiti,* and William Branch's *In Splendid Error,* if properly housed, cast, directed and promoted, should be able to play in the aggregate for three years to a Negro audience that has never seen them.

In 1958 an attempt was made by twenty actors to establish a Harlem community theatre called Manhattan Art Theatre. Two of them, Godfrey Cambridge and Beah Richards, appeared in *Purlie Victorious.* Despite many minor differences of opinion it appeared that we might succeed, especially when Langston Hughes gave us his play *The Emperor of Haiti* for our first production. But the then promising Broadway Negro family drama *A Raisin in the Sun* sent out its call and our actors were off and running. Diana Sands, Douglas Turner, Lincoln Kilpatrick, Frances Foster, Louis Gossett, all erstwhile Manhattan Art Theatre members, were to enjoy long runs in the justly successful Lorraine Hansberry play. Abandoned by so many of its creators, Manhattan Art Theatre became a victim of infant mortality. We were able to mount *Emperor* in the fine St. Martin's Episcopal Church Theatre for four weeks and in the Joseph P. Kennedy, Jr. Memorial Community Center Theatre another four weeks. We Manhattan Art Theatre members had pledged ourselves to:

1. Immediately acquire a base of operations (a loft suitable for a small, 199-seat or less, theatre and office).
2. Acquire a number of plays, musicals, etc., to insure the continuity and proper level of work of the group and project.
3. Spell out a constitution which will provide a guide, rules and regulations for the orderly and business-like conduct of this project.
4. Elect a responsible slate of officers to administer the project.

5. Acquire sufficient funds and the proper type of fund-raising to insure the financing of this project.
6. Form a school and staff same with teachers capable of stimulating the development and growth of the many crafts involved.
7. Acquire the best legal advice possible to insure the protection of our project.
8. Secure the best public relations and publicity possible to guarantee the foregoing.

Let's bring theatre *to* the Negro. When we find the key to open Harlem to a sustained, stable, artistic theatre we will have solved our craft problem of theatrical form and meaningful content, and inevitably some of us will have achieved universality as playwrights and greatness as actors.

We must break through the sound barrier surrounding a Negro people's theatre.

WHAT IS THE PURPOSE OF JIVE?

Basic Jive has two main purposes:

1. To serve as an auxiliary language, one that is easily and quickly learned, in which the rules of grammar and sentence construction are so simple they are practically non-existent. This "second" language can be picked up with very little effort for use in general communication and social intercourse.

2. As a means of providing a rational—or irrational if you prefer—introduction to basic American slang for those who because of lack of time or money, find it impossible to concentrate on learning the routine principles of grammar, verb conjugation, sentence construction, etc. Jive requires very little concentration but serves to develop clarity of thought and expression for English speaking people at any stage of proficiency in the mother tongue.

from DAN BURLEY's *Original Book of Harlem Jive*

HARLEM NIGHTCLUB

JOHN A. WILLIAMS

DESPITE RACE RIOTS and intergroup tensions, two things persist in restless, teeming Harlem, black capital of the world. One is the rumor that the city fathers secretly plan to turn 125th Street into an east-west artery linking the Triboro Bridge with the West Side Highway and the George Washington Bridge approaches. The other, more tangible, more concrete-and-glass, of infinitely more distinction, is Big Wilt's Smalls Paradise.

After a succession of owners, the internationally known night spot, now in its thirty-eighth year, has passed into the hamlike hands of Big Wilt Chamberlain, greatest basketball player ever. Smalls Paradise squares its lettuce green front between Taylor's Luncheonette and Wimples's, a diner just a few paces south of 135th Street. One cannot pass the club without noticing it, for a long, brown-gold marquee, reaching from door to curb, shades the passerby for a second or two from the hot sun, the pelting rain, the driving snow. Smalls is on the ground floor of an office building which in addition to attorneys' quarters also houses the Apex Beauty School. The long, rectangular windows of the restaurant give a view of the hustling Seventh Avenue traffic, the Trailways, Greyhound and Fifth Avenue busses, the sleek cars and, at night, the scurrying, dome-lit taxis.

More than a quarter of a million people have visited Smalls since its latest boom began early in 1962. Sixty per cent of the annual visitors are white. Where Smalls, after its opening in 1925 titilated the fancies of Cafe Society Downtown and the trans-Atlantic steamer set, today the average kicks-digging couple—if they can find a New York cabdriver who will take them to Harlem—goes without the black tie and gown and mixes with the brown-skinned foxes and their perfectly tailored men, the thinning Jet Set and celebrities in every field from all over the world.

The Club, the last remnant of all the famous old Harlem clubs, has survived the last half of the Roaring Twenties, Prohibition, the Crash, Depression, Wars, Recessions and even the Peace; it will probably outlast the African Nationalists and the Black Muslims as well. Playgrounds have a way of surviving—and Smalls is one of the best known in the world.

Perhaps its location has helped it to survive. The rawness of 125th Street, the noise, the kaleidoscoping color, is not here. Businessmen and professionals seem less tense as they stroll down the street to lunch at the Y.M.C.A. or at Wimple's, where the food (at great, low prices) is next to fabulous. The executives from the New York Urban League on 136th Street are pleasant and in good humor as they saunter up the street a couple of blocks to Jock's or the Red Rooster, whose chitterling nights are Wednesdays. (Chitterlings came to America from medieval France and were first popular in the South.) These clubs are small, intimate, and comparable to any downtown luncheon or dinner spot. Except in rare cases the two- or three-drinks-for-one bars lie south of Smalls. The whole area seethes with a taut, new kind of prosperity: the Riverton, Lenox Terrace Apartments and other sleek buildings rise above the shabby Lenox Avenue skyline. A new school is around the corner from the Club; the Schomburg Collection, one of the most famous in America on Negro life and art is only one block east of Smalls. To the west (right around the corner from the nightclub) is the 32nd Precinct and, rising abruptly from Manhattan Avenue, Morningside Heights, which forms a natural barrier between Harlem and the properties of Columbia University.

(To reach Smalls from downtown take (1) the No. 2 Fifth Avenue bus and get off at 135th Street and Seventh Avenue; (2) the Seventh Avenue IRT to 135th Street and Lenox Avenue, get off and walk one block west; (3) the IND express to 125th Street, change to the local and get off at 135th Street. Walk two blocks east.)

For all its notoriety as an international playground, Smalls has always been calmly accepted by Negroes who live in Harlem. From time to time—not often—Smalls has had good music. It's a good place to meet someone because you have window space for watching. Harlem is an area jam-packed with neighborhood bars, and one gets used to the proximity of the Lenox Lounge, the Shalimar, or Sugar Ray's. What has calmed them further are the prices, which go zooming on weekends. The help at Smalls generally agrees, with frigid righteousness, that it is the white customers who pay the freight, leave the best tips, not the Negroes. And in the scheme of dollar-discrimination, the most attentive courtesies are extended to the white visitor from downtown, or Europe, and to some Negro celebrities. Dollar or not, Harlem Negroes, for the most part, refuse to be discriminated against in this fashion, especially by "their own kind." "To hell with them," one patron said, "I'd rather go to Jock's anyway."

For all this, the bar at the front of the Club is usually packed. Here the ratio is 90 per cent black and 10 per cent white, according to Big Wilt; it is in the Club itself that 60 per cent of the patrons are white. The bar is a place where one could die of thirst, for the hustling, jolly bartenders and barmaids don't push; they wait with admirable restraint until they are summoned. If one is short of money, it is a remarkable bar; a beer could be nursed until it was boiling hot. Here gather the hard-drinkers, the waiters-for-action; here are the fine brown frames and the impeccable, sunglassed males. From one of the many sides of the bar one might hear the boyish tones of Met pitcher Al Jackson on a night off, or the eager, skipping laughter of Willie Mays. From another, precise, curving French from a group of Paris businessmen nursing gin and tonic; from still another, Portuguese or Swedish or Spanish. But above all one hears shreds of stories and jokes and conversations from the Negroes; rocketing laughter assures the visitor that the place, no matter who comes or goes, is solidly Negro at the core. This is just what the visitor wants.

The bandstand separates the bar and the Club. Beginning Thursday nights the traffic between the bar and the Club is curtailed and a swing-gate let into the place. There is but one entrance to the nightclub and one becomes two dollars lighter using it. At the time *Cavalier* was covering the nightclub, the Willis Jackson Quintet was providing the music, music that was less special than it should have been. It was designed to please dancers and listeners, and even though its quality was pedestrian the rhythm-and-blues line approached a neat groove.

R & B roots are far deeper than those of rock 'n' roll. After World War II singers like Wynonie ("Blues") Harris got R & B off to a rollicking start; true R & B gives itself over to solid rhythms, while rock 'n' roll with its light lyrics, its pedestrian cleverness, is weak, its rhythms superficial and always overreaching.

Jackson likes to tune up with his breathy tenor a la Coleman Hawkins; he runs up and down the scales, tackles a bar of "Body and Soul." Behind him sit Joe Hedrick, drums; Bill Jones, guitar; Frank Robinson, trumpet; and Carl Wilson, organ. In the Prestige Records stable, Jackson has pressed "Bossa Nova Plus" and "San Francisco," albums which he says are moving well.

Past the crowded little bandstand is the Club itself, long, shadowed, some of its walls touched with surrealistic landscapes. Here are the white-topped tables, the stage which thrusts out into the audience so that the performers are surrounded on three sides by patrons.

On one of the walls there is a montage of warping pictures. The ones with Big Wilt and Floyd Patterson are prominently displayed; here, too, is Congressman Adam Clayton Powell, Jr., and candid shots of tables filled with happy customers. There are many views of the twisters who, early in the spring of 1962, launched Smalls Paradise into world-wide fame once again.

Before the twist craze seized New York fully, Smalls had been limping along with third-rate floor shows and some good jazz. Giving up on jazz, the management moved closer to the guttiness of rhythm and blues; this seemed to attract more people. Perhaps this move was due to the judgment of Big Wilt, who will not be pinned down to the exact kind of music he likes. ("Like jazz?" "No, no, I won't say that. I like music— R & B, not rock 'n' roll—no, I like music.")

A Tuesday Night Twist contest was started. After all, the twisters in Harlem had to be the best in the city, including those who worked out at the Peppermint Lounge downtown. Hadn't Harlem given the world trucking, boogie-woogie, pecking and the Lindy hop? Challenges flew from Smalls downtown, probably at the suggestion of Major Robinson, sometime publicist for the Club and *Jet* gossip alumnus. White people began arriving in droves, not only for the Tuesday night hip-tossing affairs, but for every night. The stage is also used for dancing and there was a lot of twisting going on. The Peppermint Lounge never did accept the challenge, but it didn't matter; Smalls had been rediscovered. Twist combos worked down the night; the best twisting chicks, black and white, ordered twist dresses. Here came Patrick O'Higgins, Diahann Carrol, Baron Paolo Tallarico, Harry Belafonte, Duarte Pinto-Coelho, Mrs. Gustave Ajo, Sidney Poitier, Marianne Greenwood, Countess Nicoletta Attolico, Phil Silvers, Anthony Quinn, Van Johnson, Keely Smith, the great athletes from incoming professional teams, and hundreds more—all to "Twist Again."

The publication-day party for James Baldwin's novel, *Another Country,* further spurred business by introducing New York's literary set to the nightclub. It had been a good twenty years since the Book Set had really invaded Harlem, probably made aware of it by Carl Van Vechten. Baldwin, who likes to twist, had invited almost two hundred people: writers, critics, literary agents, editors and others from related fields.

Director Robert Rossen was there, and such other celebrities as Kay Boyle, Sidney Poitier, Phillip Roth, Ralph Ellison, Cecil Hemley, Ruby Dee and Ossie Davis, Brian Glanville (in from London), Godfrey Cambridge, Gerald Walker and Maurice Dolbier. Millions of dollars worth of talent turned up their rear ends and twisted. One literary agent said, viewing the crowded dance floor: "You can see all the nasty, mean, vicious personalities coming out when they dance; and you can see the ones who think they're damned sexy and the ones who're shy but come on like they're real tough. This party's been a revelation!"

Outside, the cabs kept coming; they double-and triple-parked to discharge their literary passengers. Residents in the area with nothing to do drifted close to peer in the windows or listen to the music or watch the girls coming and going. What an invasion!

Baldwin's party was held at the height of the twist craze, a fad that has since gone steadily downhill. There no longer is a Tuesday Night Twist contest at Smalls, although Tuesday night still brings up small crowds from downtown. The bossa-nova, the wobble and the pony are in many quarters replacing the twist, a dance which followed the Madison and the mashed potato.

The forty-odd people who help run the night spot, which costs half a million dollars a year to operate, say that white people dance better today than they did in the past when they came to Harlem. Jackson says, "It's the younger people; they catch on fast."

A nearby waiter sneered. "It's the goddamn twist. It's easy to do—easiest dance in the world—that's why they're still doing it instead of moving to the bossa-nova or the wobble. Look! Look up there."

Upon the stage a white couple was doing the twist. The girl was very good, very graceful; there was a certain poignance in her movements. But her partner was twisting like the Little Old Winemaker.

"Are the white women better twisters than the men?"

"Baby, you'd better know it," the waiter said, and sped off to take care of a party of smiling Germans.

Saturday and Sunday afternoons are quiet at Smalls. The big showroom is empty. The dancers and singers and musicians who make up the show are home and still sleeping. The Seventh Avenue strollers pause at the bar. "Throw me a little taste, baby." The sun sends lazy rays through the windows; the jukebox plays. Glasses tinkle and there is the blurble of warm water as they are washed out. There is the continual hissing of beer bottles being opened, and there is

171

laughter and a steady flow of soft voices. Outside, standing in the doorway of Taylor's Luncheonette, is a cop. If it is Saturday he will undoubtedly be sent down to "Harlem Square"—Seventh Avenue and 125th Street where the African Nationalists, the Black Muslims and other groups hold their rallies. He will be sent with a hundred other uniformed cops, a couple of police lieutenants and a few plainclothes-men—to see that order is maintained.

No matter. There is little action at Smalls or anywhere else on a mild spring day early in the afternoon. It is the Saturday and Sunday afternoons in winter that cause trouble, for then "Hawk"—biting cold weather and hard times—sends the homeless, the desperate, scurrying into the warmth of the Club. The cop knows that these are the people, very often, who cause the most trouble anywhere.

But Smalls is well equipped to handle trouble itself. Including Big Wilt's partner, Pete Douglas, there are four "floor managers"—the term bouncers is passé, and indeed, only one of the four gives the raw impression of being, in spite of the innocuous title, a bouncer. He is George Austin. He goes about 240 pounds and stands about six-four. Even next to Wilt he looks more than formidable. Austin stands guard at the swing-gate that separates the bar from the Club. He can look very pleasant when he wants to, but he can also look as evil as hell. "Trouble," he says, "can start anywhere in here, at the bar or in the back or downstairs. There's just no telling. It's kind of catching. One rumble breaks out and for a few days other little rumbles break out." Mr. Austin smiles. "But we can handle them."

When the music tilts over and gets into a groove, Mr. Austin, light on his feet for all his weight, stands at his post and does the twist. Pete Douglas, who usually guards the other entrance, where the cover charge is paid, also dances when the mood hits him, but in the hall to the approving smiles of the two hatcheck girls—and when business is slow. One night a wino turned up at this entrance. Mr. Douglas took one look at his casual attire—shirttail out, battered straw hat pulled rakishly down over one eye—and reminded the visitor that there was a cover charge of two dollars.

"Two dollars!" the wino yelled. "What the hell you *get* f' two dollars?"

"Man, that's just to get *in*," Mr. Douglas said, "and after that, Jack, it's up to you. You can spend all you want."

The wino stumbled away, muttering, "Two dollars! *Two* dollars!"

Floor Manager Tyler doesn't look as though he could handle

trouble. He wears glasses, and suits darker than any of the other managers. He walks around crowds instead of through them, and he speaks softly, but firmly. He's probably the most dangerous; he doesn't dance.

Most remarkable of all is Odell Boyd, a 73-year-old gentleman who once managed the old Cotton Club. Mr. Boyd has a counterpart in every Harlem in America. Plump, cigar-smoking, he has been in the nightclub business for fifty years. He believes that had he been white he could have owned half of Las Vegas. "Even now I could go out there and run a li'l ol' casino," he says, "but who inna hell wants to be bothered with li'l ol' women and their damned nickles and dimes playin' the bandits?" There is no numbers banker, nightclub owner, gangster, cop or celebrity he doesn't know. An example of this was one night a young Negro couple came in and as Mr. Boyd was showing them to a table he overheard the man mention the name of his home town. "You know ——?" Mr. Boyd asked.

The young man turned. "Sure I do. He bought me my first Boy Scout uniform. You know him?"

"Yeah," Mr. Boyd said, puffing his cigar. "We're old friends." The man who was the topic of this brief conversation is an old-time, still operating numbers man in a city of 500,000 people.

Boyd has the quick eye and twinkling feet of a practiced maître d'; he guides the customers to their tables and summons the waiters. He loves the nightclub business; even on his night off, he shows up at the Club to look over the bar and back room.

To Mr. Boyd, it seems, has fallen the task of keeping a delicate kind of order in the Club. His old, glassless eyes sweeping from wall to wall, he sits at the rear on a raised platform and paternally watches out for the white couples. He, too, knows the smell of trouble; he knows that the pomaded and marcelled Negro, watching like a hawk, has received some kind of sign from the white woman sitting with her white male companion. The woman may not even be aware that she has tapped the sharp one's wavelength and found the reception good until he is there at her table, smiling down, confident that she will be easy to have. He has paid little or no attention to her companion, who, trying to be civil, smiles, laughs stiffly, suffers through a dance or two, bites his lip. By now the woman has come to her senses; the scales have fallen from her eyes and she tries to refuse further invitations to dance. But the sharp one insists; he reeks with confidence. He holds her hand and looks longingly into her eyes. But Mr. Boyd has sized up the situation. With a flick of his finger he signals the nearest floor manager; the white-jacketed waiters have all moved a step closer. The floor manager moves in at the precise moment when people at other tables, embarrassed for the three involved, have turned their heads. "Mr. Boyd wants to see you, boy," the floor manager says. Reluctantly, the sharp one precedes him to where Mr. Boyd has raised his globular form from a chair to address him. His voice is harsh; he waves his cigar. "Got a table? Where's your table? Why don't you leave that couple alone? What's the matter with you? How you get in here, anyway? I say, how did you get in here? Put this boy out." The last is disdainfully said and before it has time to echo, the marcelled one, the lover, the sharp one, is being escorted firmly (unless he should recklessly try to pass for bad) to the sidewalk.

The white trade, even with the cover and the minimum (the cover charge is as much to keep out the "rabble" as it is to sock it to the pleasure seekers) goes for the mixed drinks—the Martinis, Gibsons, whiskey sours and champagne demis. A white party seated at one of the ringside tables brings down the wrath of the house when it orders beer all around. Mr. Boyd doesn't often make that mistake. But when it does happen, the whites are given the same kind of "snip service" usually reserved for Negroes who also drink beer, but whose tables are seldom at ringside. By and large the white couples are man and wife, a sure sign that Smalls has gained a certain measure of respectability. What brings them to Harlem? Just the aura of Smalls? One waiter insisted that "white folks come to Harlem to do what they can't do downtown." But surely no one would go that far out of their way just to do the twist. During the Cavalier's stay, there were no signs of any outlandish behavior on the part of any of the customers.

White women, like Negro women, seldom come alone. Occasionally they come in twos or threes or fours, a good nucleus from which to operate. White men are in the minority of lone men at the bar. Like the Negro man, he is looking for action, and if he is lucky he may then move into the Club. One weekend night a middle-aged white man and a Negro woman of about the same age sat down at a table. The first show, featuring the dancing Tommy Johnson Trio, with Arlene and Sandy, a bowlegged "song stylist" named Moondog, and singer Carl Bell, had just ended. The couple drank Martinis, a terrific expense on a weekend night when both cover and minimum are in effect. It was obvious that the man was waiting for the woman to drink herself out and give herself over. Unfortunately, he didn't

dance and when the dancers took the floor she found herself a
partner from a neighboring table. After the dance the lady returned
to her seat and had another Martini. Then she pulled her wrap
around her and, patting her companion on the cheek, told him she was
going to the washroom and would return in a moment. She never
returned. Although he looked high and low for the "action" into
which he had poured perhaps a gallon of Martinis, the man never
found her.

The other mixed couples observed at Smalls appear less casual in
their relationships. Largely Negro men and white women (although
one may here see more white men and Negro women than downtown),
they mount the stage to dance without the self-consciousness that one
sees in other parts of New York City. For the most part they are young
and have taken up the slack the Jet Set is leaving. Unless these
interracial couples are well known, they will be given an intermediate
table. The Negro man with his white date will almost certainly be
placed in some middle area; the white man with his Negro date will
get a table closer to the stage. All of this would be of some immediate
concern were it not for the fact that the position of the stage makes
it possible for a patron to see from almost any location.

Of course, many patrons like to be close to shaking bodies of the
dancers. In this case they are the vigorous, saucy Tommy Johnson
and his partners, the tall and handsome Arlene and Sandy. Johnson
is a muscular, writhing young man with a whole bag of fearsome
movements. Obviously, his oiled, half-naked body, his fantastic con-
tortions, the fake diamond in his nose, are all intended to titillate
the hosts of white women in the weekend audiences. (Arlene and
Sandy, almost as skimpily clothed as Johnson, elicit from the white
males equally evocative emotions.) In a highlight number, Johnson,
clothed only in a loincloth, runs upon the stage with a torch clutched
in either hand, and, during a series of highly suggestive steps, coupled
with intermittent yelps which can hardly be heard above the quintet,
he draws the flame slowly across his body, around his back, under his
armpits and finally, head held dramatically back, thrusts one of the
torches into his mouth.

Each girl has her special number too; each has that fixed, white
smile, the fine brown frames with the long, tantalizingly curved legs;
each has the belly and buttock moves calculated to drive weak men
out of their minds. In the audience, black and white agreed completely that these were dancers. "Pretty goddamn good, if you like
interpretive dancing," Willis Jackson remarks.

Moondog, who follows the dancers, is a stubby fellow whose disk jockey father was involved in a suit over *his* use of the name, but won out over the original Moondog. (The original Moondog, a white man, was famed as the Nature Boy of the fifties. A gigantic man, the impresarios hailed his hand-drumming as the latest thing in jazz. He was exploited quickly and to the full. Disgusted, Moondog returned to the world he had left, a lonely world of standing on corners holding out a tray for the coins of passersby. His great size and posture, the stern expression on his face, belied the fact that he was a beggar in the common meaning of the term. His most recent post was at the southwest corner of Bryant Park in the heart of Manhattan.) If the original Moondog was all concrete and poise, this one is a jiggling, bent-legged, raucous shouter. A smile splits his face from ear to ear. It is quite plain that he thinks a great deal of himself and his work. At his finale, he flings himself out of a black-and-white plaid jacket and, clutching the lobolier mike, shouts down the clamor of the quintet.

It is Carl Bell, who also acts as M.C., who grabs Moondog's coat and stands, a tight smile on his face, hands poised to lead the applause. Then he comes forward to sing. One of his favorites is "What Kind of Fool Am I?" in which he imitates Sammy Davis, Jr., Al Hibbler, Billy Eckstine and "Anthony Newley after he met Joan Collins." His pièce de résistance is "This Land is Mine," complete with cantorial wailings at the finish.

No part of this show attracts so much attention as the appearance of Big Wilt, table-hopping. His arrogance is said by many to be exceeded only by his height. He is an impatient-seeming man, with his mind on other matters; his managers, for example, seem to know more about the functioning of his Club than he does. Perhaps that is why he pays them top salaries. To talk standing up to Wilt is rather like talking to a belt buckle—his. It seems to be, mockingly, on a level with one's eyes. To talk to him is also to be made aware of the fact that he makes in the neighborhood of $65,000 a year, is an internationally known athlete and, finally, that he is a supernatural being. It would be difficult to mute these points; Big Wilt doesn't try.

But now that the members of the floor show have together completed their finale, it is time for the dancers to take the floor. The best dancers quite knowingly pick spots at the front of the stage; the worst retire from the critical eyes of the nondancers to a spot at the rear. One can see a mixed couple at the front, a handsome white man and an attractive Negro woman, working out of a galloping twist; a hefty Negro man who could pass as a double for George Austin, at least in bulk, wobbles with the concentration of a laboratory technician; an older couple hang on to each other for dear life.

From the fast-paced music, Jackson will move his quintet into a series of ballads or standards, take each through the fox trot, rhumba, waltz—"A little something for everyone, y'know," he explains with a smile. Among the numbers he most frequently plays are "After Hours," "Tenderly," "What Kind of Fool Am I?" and "As Long As She Needs Me."

The patrons keep coming despite the less than top-notch shows; it is Smalls that is the attraction—*Smalls*. A young Danish girl explained: "Often we have heard about it in Copenhagen. So many people mention it and other Europeans who have been here talk about it; quite naturally I wanted to see it." Was she disappointed at all? Diplomatically she said, "I think I expected more." She paused. "But this *is* Harlem, isn't it?"

Fifty Frenchmen who had heard about the Club in Paris called when they were in New York last month to reserve tables; before the night was over more than 250 Frenchmen on a Franco-American exchange program were in the Club watching the floor show.

Jean Benoit, Kesse Kesse and Kopa K. Bernard, journalists and television commentators from the Ivory Coast in Africa, heard about Smalls in the Présence Africain book store in Paris. They sat in Smalls one night drinking beer (at a rear table) and said they were in New York for six days. This was their first night in town and they had rushed up to Smalls, clutching the address in their hands. Asked if they knew M. Dadier, an Ivory Coast poet, who only two months ago had been in America, they replied, *"Oui."* M. Dadier, they advised, was in prison.

"Pourquoi?"

Shrugging they replied, *"Raisons politique."*

Their eyes drifted to a table of Chinese patrons and the conversation was ended before they could be asked whether or not they had seen footage of the Club which had been shown over Paris television last fall. (Dominique Pierre Gaiseau, director of "The Sky Above and the Mud Below," had arrived in New York during the summer of 1962 and, together with expatriate-novelist Chester Himes, prepared a documentary on Harlem for French consumption. Smalls was one of the many places included in the film.)

It is because of Himes and Gaiseau that Torun, of Biot, sits ringside taking a break from her exciting exhibit at Georg Jensen's on Fifth Avenue. Torun, a Swede of classic beauty, is married to American painter Walter Coleman. She is considered one of the best contemporary silversmiths and designers of costume jewelry. She has even made buttons for Picasso's workcoat. Torun lives with her family on the French Riviera, where Himes visits between books.

Few white patrons go downstairs at Smalls, or even know that another room, almost the size of the upstairs Club, exists. This space is used by many of the hundreds of men's and women's clubs which are rampant in Harlem. Some are geared for light-colored Negroes, others for dark; some are set up along professional lines or other lines of common interest; some are for college graduates only and some are alumni groups. In the increasing scramble for prestige, the private groups try to hire the most famous rooms or halls for their functions, which are usually black-tie affairs.

"Every week we have two or three private club affairs down here," Wilt says. "This place jumps, too, but in a quiet way." A dance floor, band and bars set this room totally apart from the transient patronage in the upper rooms. Here one may see the Negro middle class of Harlem at play. The world above them is transitory; downstairs, away from the never-ending waves of tourists, Harlem endures.

It costs a lot to endure in Harlem. Catering to mixed patronage traditionally has cost Harlem club owners a lot of "grease." The recent investigations of the State Liquor Authority and the revelation that club after club had to make the payoff to stay in business, prompted the question, "Do you have to pay off?"

"No!" snaps Wilt.

"No!" snaps Odell Boyd. "We run a good club; we close on time and take care of any trouble right away. We have nothing to do with the police."

And this is very, very probably true. Certainly no such taint could touch Wilt without courting disaster to his career. So famous a figure would make corrupt officials think more than twice before applying any pressure. Harlem and Smalls are indeed fortunate to have so invulnerable a personage as Big Wilt, although the invulnerability of any Negro in America is quite questionable.

A few weeks ago, however, the police from the 32nd Precinct did rush into Smalls, to the surprise of its patrons. But this was not a raid. Big Wilt explained: "We had a phone call. A bomb-scare. We called the cops. No, it wasn't a raid; we have had no raids. It was a bomb-scare and they had to search the place. Some nut. No, they didn't find a bomb." Wilt gave the impression that nothing would or could destroy his Club. Perhaps he is right. Smalls, the exotic playground for every kind of people, a miniature United Nations, having lasted this long may last forever. To a great many outsiders Smalls *is* Harlem, and there is thrill enough just sitting in the Club in the middle of the biggest racial tinderbox in the world—and coming away unscathed. And certainly diverse people come to find that when they get up to twist or wobble, little diversity really exists, that this couple or that have just as much rhythm, or just as little, as the next.

Despite the unexciting floor shows (they're booked for two or three weeks at a time) the calculated courtesies for the dollar, the loudness of the music, Smalls does have that barely definable quality, a sense of history.

Unfortunately, Smalls Paradise probably will not work very hard to maintain or build its prestige. It will drift with its lesser floor shows and commonplace music until the next fad or distinction comes its way. But no matter; Smalls is an international landmark and as such almost commands the forbearance of its patrons. The patrons seem willing to forbear forever.

THREE POEMS BY
STERLING A. BROWN

These poems, which have never before been published, were written over a score
of years ago, but the editor and Mr. Brown consider them timely, even prophetic.
The dean of Negro American poets, professor of English at Howard University,
Washington, D.C., author of numerous books and essays, Mr. Brown is now at work
on a new, revised edition of the Anthology, *Negro Caravan*, with co-editors, Arthur
P. Davis and Ulysses G. Lee.

THE BALLAD OF JOE MEEK

I

You cain't never tell
How far a frog will jump,
When you jes' see him planted
On his big broad rump.

Nor what a monkey's thinking
By the working of his jaws—
You jes' cain't figger;
And I knows, because

Had me a buddy,
Soft as pie
Joe Meek they called him
And they didn't lie.

The good book say
"Turn the other cheek,"
But that warn't no turning
To my boy Joe Meek.

He turned up all parts,
And baigged you to spank,
Pulled down his breeches,
And supplied the plank.

The worm that didn't turn
Was a rattlesnake to Joe:
Wasn't scary—jes' meek, suh,
Was made up so.

II

It was late in August
What dey calls dog days,
Made even beetle hounds
Git bulldog ways.

Would make a pet bunny
Chase a bad blood-hound,
Make a new-born baby
Slap his grandpa down.

The air it was muggy
And heavy with heat,
The people all sizzled
Like frying meat.

The icehouse was heaven
The pavements was heil
Even Joe didn't feel
So agreeable.

Strolling down Claiborne
In the wrong end of town
Joe saw two policemen
Knock a po' gal down.

He didn't know her at all,
Never saw her befo'
But that didn't make no difference,
To my ole boy Joe.

Walks up to the cops,
And, very polite,
Ast them ef they thought
They had done *just right*.

One cracked him with his billy
Above the left eye,
One thugged him with his pistol
And let him lie.

III

When he woke up, and knew
What the cops had done,
Went to a hockshop,
Got hisself a gun.

Felt mo' out of sorts
Than ever befo',
So he went on a rampage
My ole boy Joe.

Shot his way to the station house,
Rushed right in,
Wasn't nothing but space
Where the cops had been.

They called the reserves,
And the national guard,
Joe was in a cell
Overlooking the yard.

The machine guns sputtered,
Didn't faze Joe at all—
But evvytime *he* fired
A cop would fall.

The tear-gas made him laugh
When they let it fly,
Laughing gas made him hang
His head an' cry.

He threw the hand grenades back
With a outshoot drop,
An' evvytime he threw
They was one less cop.

The Chief of Police said
  "What kinda *man* is this?"
And held up his shirt
  For a armistice.

"Stop gunning, black boy,
And we'll let you go."
"I thank you very kindly,"
  Said my ole boy Joe.

    "We promise you safety
      If you'll leave us be—"
    Joe said: "That's agreeable
      Sir, by me. . . ."

IV

The sun had gone down
  The air it was cool,
Joe stepped out on the pavement
  A fighting fool.

    Had walked from the jail
      About half a square,
    When a cop behind a post
      Let him have it fair.

Put a bullet in his left side
  And one in his thigh,
But Joe didn't lose
  His shootin' eye.

    Drew a cool bead
      On the cop's broad head;
    "I returns you yo' favor"
      And the cop fell dead.

The next to last words
  He was heard to speak,
Was just what you would look **for**
  From my boy Joe Meek.

Spoke real polite
To de folks standing by:
"Would you please do me one kindness,
Fo' I die?"

"Won't be here much longer
To bother you so,
Would you bring me a drink of water,
Fo' I go?"

The very last words
He was heard to say,
Showed a different Joe talking
In a different way.

"Ef my bullets weren't gone,
An' my strength all spent—
I'd send the chief something
With a compliment."

"And we'd race to hell,
And I'd best him there,
Like I would of done here
Ef he'd played me fair."

V

So you cain't never tell
How fas' a dog can run
When you see him a-sleeping,
In the sun.

AN OLD WOMAN REMEMBERS*

Her eyes were gentle; her voice was for soft singing
In the stiff-backed pew, or on the porch when evening
Comes slowly over Atlanta. But she remembered.

* Atlanta riot (1906).

She said: "After they cleaned out the saloons and the dives
The drunks and the loafers, they thought that they had better
Clean out the rest of us. And it was awful.
They snatched men off of street-cars, beat up women.
Some of our men fought back, and killed too. Still
It wasn't their habit. And then the orders came
For the milishy, and the mob went home,
And dressed up in their soldiers' uniforms,
And rushed back shooting just as wild as ever.
Some leaders told us to keep faith in the law,
In the governor; some did not keep that faith,
Some never had it: he was white too, and the time
Was near eleotion, and the rebs were mad.
He wasn't stopping hornets with his head bare.
The white folks at the big houses, some of them
Kept all their servants home under protection
But that was all the trouble they could stand.
And some were put out when their cooks and yard-boys
Were thrown from cars and beaten, and came late or not at all.
And the police they helped the mob, and the milishy
They helped the police. And it got worse and worse.

"They broke into groceries, drug-stores, barber shops,
It made no difference whether white or black.
They beat a lame bootblack until he died,
They cut an old man open with jack-knives
The newspapers named us black brutes and mad dogs,
So they used a gun butt on the president
Of our seminary where a lot of folks
Had sat up praying prayers the whole night through.

"And then," she said, "our folks got sick and tired
Of being chased and beaten and shot down.
All of a sudden, one day, they all got sick and tired.
The servants they put down their mops and pans,
And brooms and hoes and rakes and coachman whips,
Bad niggers stopped their drinking Dago red,
Good Negroes figured they had prayed enough,
All came back home—they'd been too long away—
A lot of visitors had been looking for them.

"They sat on their front stoops and in their yards,
Not talking much, but ready; their welcome ready:
Their shotguns oiled and loaded on their knees.

"And then
There wasn't any riot any more."

SOUTHERN COP

Let us forgive Ty Kendricks
The place was Darktown. He was young.
His nerves were jittery. The day was hot.
The Negro ran out of the alley.
And so Ty shot.

Let us understand Ty Kendricks
The Negro must have been dangerous,
Because he ran;
And here was a rookie with a chance
To prove himself man.

Let us condone Ty Kendricks
If we cannot decorate.
When he found what the Negro was running for.
It was all too late;
And all we can say for the Negro is
It was unfortunate.

Let us pity Ty Kendricks
He has been through enough,
Standing there, his big gun smoking,
Rabbit-scared, alone,
Having to hear the wenches wail
And the dying Negro moan.

BEDFORD-STUYVESANT
—LAND OF SUPERLATIVES

DR. MILTON A. GALAMISON

BROOKLYN's Bedford-Stuyvesant area is a land of superlatives. Compared with other communities of the world's largest borough it claims the most residents, the most teen-agers, the most overcrowding, the most churches, the greatest religious diversity and the highest rent per square foot of living space. The area under discussion also houses the greatest economic need, the greatest number of public assistance cases, the highest rate of infant mortality, the highest incidence of tuberculosis, a disproportionate crime and delinquency rate and more exploitation than conceivable in an area so geographically limited. In countless ways the Bedford-Stuyvesant area defies statistical norms. It is the residential area of least desirability on the totem pole of cultural status-seeking.

Most articles on "The Box," as the area is sometimes called, have been insensitive and unfair. To gratify a perverted public fancy for sensationalism, to confirm prejudices, writers have consistently projected a distorted image of an abused but heroic people. They burlesque the brokenness and ignore the creativity. They dramatize the juggled crime statistics and neglect the impressive well-spring of spiritual and religious life. They catalogue the shiftless and overlook the teeming thousands who daily crowd the transportation facilities enroute to gainful employment. While intent that non-resident readers should suffer no pangs of guilt for the plight of "The Box," those who write commentary on Bedford-Stuyvesant forget that no area could be so deprived unless there were forces outside far more evil than the forces within. In short, articles that most seek to defame and incriminate the people of the area have been the most serious indictments of the people not of this area. Efforts to present the Negro as an isolated monstrosity, however literary, do not negate the reality of the political, social, economic and historic context in which the ghetto Negro has been created. They do not absolve guilt. They confirm it.

This is not a community of slum-dwellers. It is more so a haven for corrupt, absentee landlords and real estate speculators. This is not a community of shiftless husbands. It is a world of wounded men historically deprived of the right to equal employment. This is not a vast neighborhood of negligent mothers. It is a congregation of homemakers without homes and toilers without rest. Nor are our children justly depicted by delinquency statistics. They are condemned at the outset by an unequal, ethnocentric educational structure which few survive. Feeling with all other human beings the need for success, they seek to gratify this need in less creative endeavors. They have not failed so much as they have been failed. The Bedford Stuyvesant area is not a front-page anomaly. It is a land of ghettoized human beings: men denied creative work, women denied creative living space and children denied a qualifying education. Few who write about or read of the area could manage half as well under similar circumstances.

button, button, who's got the button?

The gigantic question mark, then, does not hover over the residents of the area. The basic question is whose condition is blessed at the expense of this blightedness? In what community will we find the sinners who destroy the families of men for the sake of their ambition and the minds of children for the gratification of their greed?

As the Bedford-Stuyvesant area is a land of superlatives, it is also a land of dead-end streets. Here Dante might well have posted the sign hung over the threshold of the entrance to his Hell, "ABANDON HOPE ALL YE WHO ENTER HERE." The usual routes by which people achieve redemption are few and elusive in this community. Education would be one such avenue, politics another.

There are two school systems in New York City. One is for the whites and for the sprinkling of Negroes who manage by design or grace to matriculate. The second school system is for the ghetto children and the disparity is grotesque. Unlike the conventional school system, the racial school system functions by a one-word policy called "IFISM." In essence it is a conditioned pedagogy for, according to the philosophy of the professional participants, the children involved could learn "IF." They could learn if they were not from the South. They could learn if they had a different set of parents.

They could learn if they enjoyed higher income homes or if they just weren't on public assistance. They could learn if they didn't come from a broken home or perhaps if the home, even though broken, had a library. These are obviously conditions which the child cannot change. It is also apparent that if these kinds of conditions are set up as an obstacle to learning, conditions impossible to fulfill, they will preclude both teaching and learning. The supreme and thoroughly possible condition has yet to be stated, that the children might learn if they are properly taught.

Like the community generally, the schools have their share of superlatives: the most over-crowding, the most part-time sessions, the most inexperienced and substitute teachers, the most out-of-license instruction, the most non-resident staff members and the most teachers lowest on the salary scale. The curriculum, like the low expectation attitude, is predicated on "Ifism." Since one is never quite sure what the curriculum is, it will suffice to say that it leaves the majority of children woefully unprepared to complete academically and vocationally with success aspirants from other communities. The fruit of the system is perceptible on the high school level where the mortality rate among Negroes is frightening and in the free institutions of higher learning, such as Brooklyn College, where Negroes, who most need the free education, have long since been squeezed out by the competition and are infinitesimal in number.

Mythological efforts like "Higher Horizons" have not raised standards in the ghetto schools. Innovations such as "Open Enrollment" have not desegregated one school in the black community nor aborted the growth of additional segregated institutions. Indeed, we are manufacturing retarded children so rapidly in the ghetto schools, no conceivable appropriation of funds could balance the scales.

Meanwhile, two formidable obstacles impede efforts to improve the situation. One is a conviction on the part of some, stupid if not dishonest, that standards can be appreciably raised in the ghetto schools. The second is an illusion on the part of others that, were the standards raised, the educational system would be equal. Those who hold the second view have completely missed the psychological and sociological ramifications of the Supreme Court Decision on Segregated Education. Those who hold the first point of view, who believe that it is possible to lump together thousands of children who vary from national standards and produce standard graduating classes, are hopelessly credulous. Desegregation is the only wholesome answer to this existing educational farce. Any step short of this is speculating with the destiny of little children and the future of a great nation.

One might suppose that the same concentration of Negroes who account for so many segregated learning institutions would also produce a formidable political representation. Such, however, is not the case. It should be added to the list of area superlatives that ours is the borough community most without political representation. The 255,000 residents of "The Box," who comprise nearly ten per cent of the borough's population, have no congressional or senatorial representation. The failure to produce leadership in state-wide and national offices is due largely to the ingenious zoning of the political districts. Only a colossal and diabolical depravity could have so conceived the gerrymandering of the congressional districts. Political representation, then, which might provide an escape route to freedom, is frustrated by a circuitous scenic railway of shifting district lines.

The perennial failure of the majority of qualified voters in the area to register has become the subject of public scandal. Having never regarded politics as an institution for the investment of optimism, this writer has neither joined in the criticism nor shared the enthusiasm for voter registration. In this matter, however, I bow to those who hold the contrary opinion and aid the efforts toward greater voting strength that my pessimism or their optimism might be sooner confirmed. Apparently, you see, the quantity of political representation does not depend on the length of the voter registration list. For all its scandalous neglect of the franchise, the Bedford Stuyvesant area has managed to achieve the identical political mediocrity evident in other and more affluent areas.

When the community trumpet is sounded for the promotion of voter registration, all manner of irrepressible questions come to my mind. I wonder if by some peculiar convergence of circumstances we might get a candidate worth voting for. I wonder if the failure of the people to register is due to apathy, cynicism, disillusionment or realism. I see Harlem as an example of advanced political representation and wonder, if this is the state of affairs we have to look forward to, if the end is worth the journey. With every respect for those who disagree, I have never expected political enthusiasm in a culture where the citizenry appears resignedly doomed to perpetual choices between the lesser of two evils.

Politics is the hall where decency bows to expediency. Here the bell of morality is seldom sounded. If sounded, it is seldom heard. If heard, it is seldom heeded. If this is the avenue to freedom, I, moving doggedly in some other direction, will miss it. The political world is

Ibsen's madhouse. "It's here that men are most themselves; Themselves and nothing but themselves."

the housing "Jack" built

The housing story is almost too commonplace to recount. The community is replete with stately, statuesque brownstones that speak of an era gone by. These three and four-story dwellings once gave shelter to one white family each and were more than adequate for a middle class family with servants. The advent of Negroes, from twenty to ninety per cent of the area population between 1930 and 1957, precipitated the exodus of whites and, as the face of the community changed, a number of innovations took place which would determine the course of the future. Not the least significant of these changes occurred in the mortgage policy of the borough banks. Whereas it had been policy to grant mortgages on the value of a property—after all, real estate is real estate—obtaining a mortgage now became contingent on the borrower's character or on the applicant's knowing John Smith, the one Negro among the bank president's acquaintances.

In the course of this frustrating process, real estate combines and lawyers became the accessible middle-men for the procurement of mortgage loans. Obtaining a legitimate mortgage became a kind of underground enterprise like locating a bookmaker. Practices became increasingly conscienceless and charges boundless. In many instances what might have represented a substantial down-payment was consumed in fees, carrying charges and other baffling transactions. Houses were sold to buyers with the tacit understanding that the exorbitant mortgage payments could not be met without violating fair rent and occupancy laws. The foul deed was done! The blueprints had been drawn for the construction of a ghetto.

The ensuing and inevitable overcrowding, transciency and outrageous rents had their birth in the circumstances outlined. It is common knowledge that, were the fair rent and occupancy laws enforced, countless people would lose their homes.

For the most part the proud, orderly brownstones along the tree-lined streets do not confirm the ugly, press-created image of the area. For the most part the residents are responsible, hard-working home owners and citizens. It is principally where the absentee speculator has cast his net that the most deteriorated living conditions exist.

Government housing, conceived to provide a solution to the problem, has become more a part of the problem than its answer. It has magnified and multiplied the grievous conditions created by lending institutions and real estate interests. The policy of littering an already-deprived community with low-income housing projects is visionless and contemptible. No housing development constructed with public funds should be restricted to one economic or racial group. Such a practice lends government approval to class stratifications and social distinctions. Housing units should contain apartments for varying income groups. It is one thing for a people to resist living in proximity to those at whom they would thumb the vest. It is another matter entirely when the peoples' government appropriates public funds to make practicable the acting out of these irreligious and undemocratic attitudes.

The Negro quarter is a place of comparable splendor during the greater part of the week. An average day finds the children safely tucked away in school and the adults pursuing the necessary art of making a living and there is a magnificent serenity abroad. Like the three bowls of porridge in the vacated home of the three bears, however, there are perceptible signs which tell much about the invisible residents. Countless delivery trucks, bearing national trade names and chauffeured by white drivers, congest the shopping district. They speak of far-flung union halls where this people cannot find employment. Check cashing establishments crop up here and there bespeaking the tragic anonymity and facelessness of the people, an existence that defies the deepest human needs for identity. An incredible number of bars, taverns and retail liquor stores tell the tale of congested living quarters and life lived outside the home.

On week-ends there is a bursting at the seams. The cup of frustration runneth over and some seek visions of a better world through the bottom of an upturned whisky glass. Men and women chained through the long week to the flywheel of futility find a sense of release and power. The image of the area is often unfairly defined in terms of this temporary and concentrated escape. By Sunday the storm has spent itself, the pent-up fury has run its course, drifted out to sea and the community assumes its quiet posture with little evidence of the turbulence.

can I sell you the Brooklyn Bridge?

It should be reported that an effort was made several years ago to limit the rapidly-multiplying number of liquor stores in the Negro quarter. To this end a survey was made by two qualified experts and at the expense of eight hundred dollars. The study confirmed our wildest speculations that there existed in the Bedford-Stuyvesant area more than three times the number of liquor establishments found in a comparably-sized community. Armed with this statistical picture I appealed to the area's Neighborhood Council, an echelon group composed of the presidents of the various neighborhood block associations. The response was instant, wrathful indignation and they unanimously agreed on a three-point program. First, they would underwrite the cost of the survey; secondly, they would organize a delegation to Albany to protest the heinous condition; thirdly, they would demand a moratorium on the issuance of new liquor licenses and on the transfer of existing liquor licenses into the community. The crusade to defend the community against creeping saturation was of short duration. Not many days after the eventful meeting I received a letter from the president of the association. His type is of more importance than his name, his disease more significant than his identity. The letter said in essence that the executive council of the association had found it necessary to invalidate the action of the meeting on the grounds that to prevent the opening of new liquor establishments would be tantamount to creating a monopoly for those businesses already in existence. I was stunned! The voice was the voice of Jacob, but the hands were the hands of Esau. It was not hard for even a disillusioned clergyman to conclude what had happened here. But, then, no people could be kept in this kind of predicament were not their best efforts constantly undermined and betrayed by those in whom they place their trust.

In studying another aspect of the retail liquor store business, more recently, we estimated from available facts that more than half a million dollars is gleaned annually for sales commissions alone. Of this startling sum, less than five per cent accrues to Negro salesmen. The Dorian Gray portrait of the scarred economic soul of the community becomes ominously clearer.

idle in the market place

The same dismal and disproportionate statistics that apply to Negro unemployment through the nation would apply here. A survey was conducted in the not-too-distant past to determine the number of business establishments in the quarter that did not employ Negro help. There were few such establishments in the district studied and most of those without representative employees offered satisfactory reasons for the omission. One pharmacy, for example, had the union confirm its effort to locate an available Negro pharmacist. None could be found. Another union supported a local shoemaker's explanation that no skilled Negro was available. A third store consisted of three separate concessions operated by three different families. There was almost no evidence of a flagrant refusal to employ Negroes.

The ministers did become greatly exercised over the failure of neighborhood merchants to support non-profit community agencies, such as the YMCA, and, to rectify the situation, organized a Ministers' Movement. The merchants were operating without any sense of responsibility to the area civic and benevolent causes. They were taking everything out and giving nothing back. The Merchant's Association was practically defunct. Repeated appeals on behalf of the most deserving charitable efforts achieved no response.

In the wake of this apathy the ministers and their people picketed the merchants during April and May of 1962. The demonstrations brought an instant and enthusiastic response. A series of joint meetings followed during which machinery was set up to prevent a recrudescence of the historic neglect and, while much remains to be done, there now exists a cooperative effort in a new direction. The ministers, meanwhile, have set their sights on larger, city-wide and national industries and efforts will be made to involve the people in selective buying campaigns wherever discrimination rears its ugly head.

The most blatant violation of fair employment practices was uncovered in the local plant of a prominent dairy company by an aspiring political group. This plant, located deep in the heart of "The Box," employed less than five Negroes among its more than two hundred workers. In fact, the only black face in evidence on the site was a worker with thirty-five years seniority who had been upgraded to the grand responsibility of guiding trailer trucks to the loading platform. With the help of an advertising executive of a Negro magazine, conferences were set up with the personnel representatives of the company. Since it had never been their policy to discriminate against Negroes the request for a new policy was not in order. It was all a big mistake. But they did agree to make a deliberate effort to compensate for the oversight and to provide even on-the-job training for Negroes. Within the past month I received a call from the personnel director asking for some twenty job applicants to function as salesmen on delivery routes.

The people are not idle. The storm is ever-brewing. Any evidence of injustice can precipitate a deluge of social action. Those who listen can hear the rumbling beyond the hills.

deprivation without representation

If colonialism can be acceptably defined as "a territory distant from the people who govern it," the picture we have been painting here is that of a domestic colonialism. The delivery trucks and the merchants, the real estate speculators and the rent gougers, the business executives and the bank tellers, the school principals and the ethnomaniacal school teachers, the precinct captains and the wine merchants all come from far-away places. The hospital in which I am born, the apartment in which I live and the cemetery in which I am buried are owned and controlled by commuter circuit riders whose allegiance lies in another world which I cannot visit, not even in my dreams. The masters of my destiny are faceless foreigners who find my community a satisfactory place to make a living but not a very satisfactory place to live. If my people suffer injustice it is because it is impossible to deal justly with those we neither know nor understand.

The Bedford-Stuyvesant section has not been consumed by the fires of nationalism as have some other communities in our urban centers. There is a degree of nationalism but it has neither the fervor nor the following evident in other areas. A warm evening might find at least two speakers holding forth on diametrical corners of a major intersection. But the listeners are generally few in number and the pausing passers-by seldom remain for long and never appear quite convinced. The area has never been a Roman marketplace where people exercise their idle curiosity to hear and to do some new thing. Noisy harangues and chattering public address systems do not seduce the people from their homes.

There may be several reasons for what seems, on the surface, a state of lethargy. The reader may add his own to those suggested. The people appear to be a comparatively conservative people. The issues that have commanded community attention have, for the most part, been so counterfeit, so thoroughly shallow, only the feeble-minded afford themselves the luxury of distraction. The leadership has been so divided, so shamelessly opportunistic and the fruits of invested labor so disillusioning, the people have cultivated an innate suspicion of Pied Pipers. The most frequently-heard music is the monotonous tune of the axe grinder.

who am I, anyway?

There is no intention to imply that the dwellers here, like elsewhere, are not in search of an identity. There is a growing pride in race and the towering question seems to center in what shall be done with this. Extreme nationalism has dichotomized the Negro movement. Whereas the major battle was between the forces of action and the forces of inertia, the current warfare seems to be between the forces of integration and the forces of separation. There is, on the one hand, the proud, emotional, noisy retreat to the cubbyhole where the Negro is already physically confined anyway and there is, on the other hand, the stumbling march toward a unifying, integrated life.

The nationalistic retreat has provided many Negro leaders and politicians, who never lifted a finger on behalf of equal rights in the first instance, with a convenient veneer to mask their cowardice and duplicity. It ought to be said here, lest I forget, that I regard these existing Negro separationist movements as the biggest Uncle Tom movements in the country. Look beneath the castigation of white people and the "Let's you and him fight" kibitzing and you find the black incarnation of Governor Wallace's fondest dreams.

What amazes me is how the same Negro leaders who rant with the separationists and supremacists of the North rave also with the integra-tionists of the South. I expect it's important to be on every platform.

Even more amazing is the number of Negro leaders in the North who confine their militance to the Southern issues. Safe from fear's alarm in New York City, they are as busy as the proverbial queen bee, pardon the Freudian slip, fighting the far-away battle of Alabama while the local human wreckage and civic garbage heap high to the roof-tops. It is as if there were no battle to be fought on Browns-ville's Alabama Avenue. Like Dickens' Madame Jellybee, they suffer the kind of social presbyopia that sees so readily the problems at a dis-tance but remains blind to the duties close at hand. Obviously the best way to help the people struggling in the South is not with a bundle of old clothing. Identical struggles must be waged where we are. We have too many heroes by mail who would rather sweep below the Mason-Dixon Line than clean their own doorsteps.

Even as I write there is before me a press release from the New York City Board of Education. It proudly announces that the new superintendent of schools has invited a number of civic organiza-tions to sit with him for the purpose of discussing school desegrega-tion. Conspicuously absent from the organizations listed are the two organizations that have done more than any others to revolutionize the racial policy of the school system, The Brooklyn Congress on Ra-cial Equality and The Parents' Workshop For Equality in New York City Schools. The job of desegregation will be achieved with or without the roundtable discussions and their ensuing studies. But this release dramatizes so well what we have been trying to say here. We are caught in a sick chess game and the black people are the pawns. Wherever the militant Negro fights for an equal slice in America, he is swept under the rug by local whites and climbed on by the opportunists in his own race. The white majority continues to listen only to those Negroes, hand-picked, purchased and paid for, who say what it wants to hear. There is manifest in this an arrogant refusal to listen and an unteachableness that can only lead to destruction.

Charles Dickens raised the question why Midas in his palace should care about Tom-all-alone in his slum-infested celler. Then Dickens answered his own question. "There is not an atom of Tom's slime, not a cubic inch of any pestilential gas in which he lives, not one obscenity or degradation about him but shall work its retribution."

We have hope because we live in this kind of a universe. We have hope because this greatest darkness must be the darkness before the dawn. We dare hope because, whether or not we read the face of the clock, eternity keeps its own inscrutable timetable. We dare hope because only order can come from this chaos.

Were we to pray we would pray with one voice the prayer of Ezekiel for this Land of Superlatives: "COME FROM THE FOUR WINDS, O BREATH, AND BREATHE UPON THESE SLAIN, THAT THEY MAY LIVE."

LOVE

Who is Justice? I would like to know,
Whosoever she is, I could love her so
I could love her, though my race
So seldom looks upon her face.

JOHN HENRIK CLARKE

A HOUSE IS NOT
ALWAYS A HOME

GEORGE F. BROWN

Harlem after dark is like a huge pile of sable velvet shot through with silver and gold threads—neon lights on the main streets adding a festive glare in contrast to the dimly-lit side streets. Frequent explosions of laughter lend a note of gaiety. But with the harsh light of day great slashes of sordid slums and squalid tenements are constant reminders of one of New York's most pressing problems—housing conditions in Harlem.

Even apologists for Harlem will readily admit that the area is a housing wasteland, constricting almost 400,000 souls in a ghetto from which only a comparatively few can escape. The hydra-headed problem of housing in Harlem embraces jobs, schools, crime, dope addiction, unwed mothers and despair, brought on by high rents, low incomes, greedy landlords and official inability to grapple successfully with the dilemma.

It is not a rare sight to see an evicted family's belongings callously dumped on the sidewalks somewhere in Harlem from rat-infested firetraps that in other areas would be condemned as unfit for human habitation. If the rent is not paid, out the tenants go with short shrift.

Here and there are low-rent projects, luxury apartments and cooperative buildings but the vast majority of Harlem is nothing but tightly packed tenements, often painfully overcrowded. Many, many dwellings have the sturdy appearance of middle-class respectability but once past the street doors conditons are execrable—dimly-lit or completely dark corridors and cramped, little boxlike rooms which often rent for $16 to $28 a room per month.

A check of rental agencies and newspaper want ads shows that it is next to impossible to rent a fairly decent apartment for less than $75 a month. This is one of the reasons that mothers in low income families must work in order to help their husbands pay even modest rents. But here again it must be borne in mind that unemployment is high in Harlem. In far too many cases, as virtually all social agencies have pointed out innumerable times, children in homes where both parents work are left to their own devices. This, of course, is a strong contributor to delinquency.

There is a constant clamor from civic leaders and civil rights organizations to improve housing in Harlem. Politicians who must perforce live in Harlem to retain their power often use poor housing conditions as their battle cry.

City and state housing agencies are striving mightily to curb slums and improve housing in Harlem because they are acutely aware of this explosive problem.

Wholesale relocation is not feasible in a crash building program due to the extreme difficulty in finding homes for displaced families to move to, still the city does have a relocation director, Herman Badillo, whose job is to help relocate families displaced from areas where new housing is being constructed. As matters now stand, those families which are financially able usually flee to comparatively less congested areas as the Bronx and Long Island. In return, those families which are able to flee the cramped slums of Brooklyn often settle in Harlem. So do those families which migrate from the south and so do many thousands of Puerto Ricans. So the search for a way out of the problem of housing in Harlem is like the man who is lost in the woods and keeps walking in circles and finds himself right back where he started.

tenants associations in Harlem

Neighborhood associations and tenants councils keep up a steady drumfire of criticism of conditions and prod the city to act with more speed in alleviating this grinding problem. Singularly enough, some neighborhood groups fight each other for attention and a few "community associations" are but thinly-veiled "hustles" —the operators pocket the dues and assessments and circulate mimeographed throwaways heralding their efforts to improve housing conditions.

The Consolidated Tenants League, Inc., is a respected organization that has studied the problem in Harlem for more than 25 years. In a statement the League said: "We believe that a new approach to the housing problem of low-income families . . . must be devised to meet the needs of families of moderate income. We must attack the problem with imagination, leadership and a realistic approach. The needs of low-income families . . . are immediate and pressing. We must look to the federal, state, and city governments for the answer to this problem or can we leave it to private enterprise to do the job?

"We in Consolidated Tenants League say no. We say the government must do the job. The progress made in public housing since 1938 has benefited families only in the $3,000 annual income bracket and families earning more. Today, after 27 years of dealing with the problem we still have slum areas: dark, dingy, stuffy, odorous apartments unfit for human habitation. . . ."

One of the original organizers of the League was Donelan J. Phillips, the current president, who sparked the non-profit, non-political organization, and continues to press for rent control in the face of powerful real estate interests that obviously take a dim view of controls which curb profits. Said the League on rent control: "The acute housing problems in the area . . . have not made sufficient improvement to warrant discontinuance of the rent control program. We are yet confronted with high rents and inadequate housing in the area."

Greedy and callous slumlords act to provide needed repairs and improvements to many dwelling only when forced to do so by the City Building Department, which receives some 500 complaints a day about falling plaster, holes in walls, rats, hazardous plumbing and unsanitary facilities.

In a report in the *New York Herald-Tribune,* Martin Steadman wrote: "The commissioner (Harold Birns) said that most slum complaints involve 'sordid hygienic conditions.' In the past he has pinned the label 'horror house' on several of the worst slums encountered. 'Some are unimaginably filthy,' he said. 'Sewage sometimes collects in the basement up to a level of three feet. Stairways have gaping holes, plumbing is non-existent, and rats and vermin run rampant.' "

Housing Court levies fines against slumlords found guilty of code violations. Some of these owners merely pay the fines and continue to rake in profits from high rents for subpar accommodations. Then there are the "absentee" landlords whom no one seems to know, not even rental agents who handle the buildings that the absentees own. The absentee owner is rarely apprehended for legal action and their dwellings continue to decay.

The peril of these old buildings is fire. Fires occur so frequently in Harlem that only the most spectacular are reported in newspapers. In cold weather entire buildings up to ten stories high are emptied of families fleeing into the bitter and frightening night from fires— some persons do not make it and death blocks their path to safety. This is an old story in Harlem.

Mayor Robert F. Wagner grew so concerned about slum conditions that he recently ordered the addition of 174 housing and building inspectors to speed up the processing of complaints and to bring slumlords to heel. This immediately drew the wrath of John Lamula, a Republican leader on the Lower East Side, who complained that the mayor was ten years late in cracking down on slumlords.

Said Lamula: "Mayor Wagner's newly revealed protestations against slumlords, over conditons which he has countenanced or ignored for the past ten years, has prompted Republicans to organize a truth squad to make public reports on his pious pronouncements."

Mayor Wagner has said: "There is no excuse for the degrading conditions of deteriorated disrepair under which some landlords of jaded conscience force New Yorkers to live. In the past we have waged war against the slumlords. They are still with us; we have not won the war, even though we have been intensively engaged to the maximum of available forces. We must press the attack on the slumlord's pocketbook. In the case of some slumlords, we may get further by cutting down profits than by threatening jail sentences."

is integration possible?

The possibilities of integrating the Harlem community, no matter how many new buildings are constructed, appear remote because there is no evidence of a movement of white families to the area. Still, the city with the largest concentration of Negroes in the world can become a model community with far more opportunity to offer future generations.

One factor often forgotten in the quest for better housing in Harlem is the matter of relocation. State Commissioner of Housing and Community Renewal James Wm. Gaynor, speaking at a meeting of the Citizens' Housing and Planning Council, said, "We are not meeting the demands of families displaced by demolition, nor are we meeting the requirements of families still remaining in substandard units. In sum, we are not actually running hard enough to stand still in our approach to the goal of a slumless city."

Mr. Gaynor pressed his case by offering two proposed amendments to the Federal law consistent with the present pattern of cost sharing in the renewal program. His first proposal would require an amendment to the National Housing Act to provide payments to business and commercial firms based on three months' net income or three months' rent. This would mean a minimum of $250 and a maximum of $3,000. The law at present allows only actual moving expenses and fixtures for equipment that cannot be moved from the premises without damage. So these firms are reluctant to move and there is always the possibility that these firms cannot relocate in the same area. Mr. Gaynor pointed out that payments would "expedite the clearance of sites, maintain a higher economic output by enabling enterprises to be re-established faster, and, in some cases, provide the means of re-establishing marginal operations."

The second amendment would authorize the payment of moving expenses for business and commercial tenants who move temporarily from an urban renewal site "and exercise the preference under New York State law to return later after its redevelopment. . . . The present statute covers the cost of a one-way ticket, not a round-trip ticket to the redeveloped site."

But the commissioner warned against the hazard of having the task of "undoing or re-doing a decade or two hence that which we are doing now."

Low-rent projects in Harlem now occupied or in the process of building are the Amsterdam Houses, Grant Houses, Harlem River Houses, Johnson Houses, Lincoln Houses, St. Nicholas Houses. Rentals are from $11 to $15 a room. There are other low-rent projects on the perimeter of Harlem and also luxury apartments such as Lenox Terrace as well as the Clayton cooperative apartments but low income forbids those families most in need of better apartments from moving into the luxury developments.

Robert C. Weaver, Administrator of the Federal Housing and Home Finance Agency, recently told the Harlem Neighborhood Association that racial tensions in Harlem and other communities would be wiped out only when Negroes were given the freedom to live and work where they chose.

Mr. Weaver, himself a former resident of Harlem, is an advocate of the "open city" but he stated that the open city is still to be achieved. "Urban renewal can and should be a positive tool for de-congesting Negro ghettoes and opening up additional residential areas to Negro occupancy," he said.

new housing project debated

The Harlem Neighborhood Association is concerned about the plan to build low-rent public housing on the site of the Polo Grounds. The association made headlines in the New York *Courier* and the New York *Amsterdam News*, Harlem's two Negro weeklies, when the organization bluntly declared that such a plan would "freeze the north

Harlem area into a community for the poor, since 1,500 units of low-income housing are presently in the area surrounding the (Polo Grounds) site." The area referred to is located on West 155th Street, west of the Harlem River.

The crux of the conflict is the objection to the city plan, which calls for four, low-income, 30-story buildings with 1,600 apartments. The Harlem Neighborhood Association seeks a civic complex, including an elementary school, a theatre, an indoor sports arena, a jazz institute, a marina, a restaurant and a library and exhibit hall to house Negro and African cultural materials.

The Community Council on Housing opposes the Harlem Neighborhood Association's dream plan. Certainly such a civic complex would be a showcase for Harlem but the greater needs of the people are of paramount importance. This thought was supported by Milton Mollen, chairman of the city's Housing and Redevelopment Board. Said Mr. Mollen: "There is the consideration as to whether or not this new proposal accurately reflects the greatest needs which exist in the Harlem community at this time." In any event, the city is proceeding with the original plan to erect the low-rent projects. The Polo Grounds will not be razed until late this year so there will be many additional discussions as to what will be done on the site.

The overriding issue is that Harlem is in dire need of improved housing, especially for low-income families. There is little likelihood that the economic position of the Negro will improve immediately but a step in the right direction would be to alleviate misery with better housing, which in turn would give the Negro a greater feeling of worth and self-respect. From that soil improvement can flower on a personal basis—it has already been proved that better schools are in better neighborhoods and dropouts are far fewer and delinquency relatively lower, as is crime.

Housing is a desperate need in Harlem; too urgent for political chicanery, too vital to the entire community to ignore and too important to the future of Harlem to delay.

If blight, slumlords and crime force Harlem into an even greater wasteland, where will the people go?

Arthur A. Schomburg

THE SCHOMBURG COLLECTION

JEAN BLACKWELL HUTSON

T̲HE Sᴄʜᴏᴍʙᴜʀɢ Cᴏʟʟᴇᴄᴛɪᴏɴ, a library and archive of materials devoted to Negro life and history, is considered one of the most important centers in the world for the study of the Negro. Its literature is international in scope, comprehensive in its coverage of Negro activity wherever peoples of African descent have lived. The Collection includes books by authors of African descent, regardless of subject matter or language. This is the first principle of selection. The second basis is that the Schomburg Collection should contain all *significant* materials *about* peoples of African descent.

The basis of the present Collection was the private library of Arthur A. Schomburg, a Puerto Rican of African descent, who through years of patient devotion amassed one of the largest and most important libraries devoted to the Negro. Schomburg was born in 1874, educated in Puerto Rico and at St. Thomas College in the Virgin Islands. In 1891 he came to the United States. For a number of years he was a clerk in the Bankers Trust Company. However, the motivating force in his life seems to have been the goal of collecting all evidence he could find that the "Negro had a long and honorable past." He became a scholar and expert in this field.

Mr. Schomburg often said that his goal was generated by a statement of one of his elementary school teachers that "the Negro had no history." In later years Schomburg wrote articles on his favorite theme that the American Negro must know his past, bring it to light, in order to make his future. He wrote that "a group tradition must supply compensation for persecution, and pride of race the antidote for prejudice. History must restore what slavery took away, for it is the social damage of slavery that the present generations must repair and offset."

This point of view, Schomburg said, had an earlier history and was not original with him. In 1808, Abbé Gregoire had published a book

205

about distinguished Negroes. Compendiums of the same sort have followed at intervals ever since—many of them over-corrective and over-laudatory—but the purpose has been sound. Today scholarship in this area is better balanced and the need is for a well documented history—a history that is "less a matter of argument and more a matter of record."[1] The purpose of the Schomburg Collection is to amass, preserve and organize this record and keep it up-to-date and available. At present this record of the experience of peoples of African descent throughout the world is not limited to books but includes art objects, musical recordings, sheet music, manuscripts, newspaper files (many microfilmed for permanent preservation) and periodicals. The selection of art objects was influenced by Alain Locke, who caused about half of the Blondeau-Theatre Arts collection to be deposited here. The Eric de Kolbe collection of African arms consists of about two hundred and fifty weapons, mainly from south of the Sahara.

The Schomburg Collection also has roots in the community of Harlem. When the One Hundred and Thirty-fifth Street Branch Library was established in 1905, the neighborhood which it expected to serve was a quiet, well-to-do American Jewish section. By 1920 it had become half-Negro. Miss Ernestine Rose, a librarian with vision and perseverance, was appointed to adapt this library to the needs of the growing community of Negroes. By 1924 Harlem had become the acknowledged capital of Black America. Its population, thanks to the migrations of the preceding decade, had reached approximately 150,000. At the same time it had drawn Negro talent and leadership from all parts of the United States and Caribbean.

By this time books on the Negro were in such demand that they could not be kept on the library shelves. They were read so avidly that they were worn to shreds. Titles which continued in print could not be replaced fast enough with the available funds. Books hard to obtain deteriorated without hope of replacement. Miss Rose called together a group of influential scholars and leaders from the community, including Schomburg, James Weldon Johnson, Hubert H. Harrison and John Nail.

The first result of their consultations was the decision to withdraw from circulation books relating to the Negro which were difficult to replace. The primary aim was to preserve existing resources in this field. Immediately the community responded to this modest gesture with gifts and loans from the private libraries of people like J. E.

---

[1] Arna Bontemps, "The Schomburg Collection," *Library Quarterly*, Vol. XIV, no. 3 (July 1944).

Bruce, Louise Latimer, Hubert H. Harrison, George Young, Dr. Charles D. Martin and Schomburg. Soon the reference room became a center for students of Negro history and culture both in the neighborhood and elsewhere, and on May 8, 1925, the new Division of Negro Literature, History and Prints was officially opened.

The following year, Schomburg's library was purchased by the Carnegie Corporation at the suggestion of L. Hollingsworth Wood, Charles S. Johnson and Eugene Kinckle Jones, officials of the National Urban League. Another gift from the Carnegie Corporation in 1932 enabled the New York Public Library to retain Mr. Schomburg as curator, a position he held until his death in 1938.

Among the items in Schomburg's collection when it came to the Library were:

A copy of Juan Latino's Latin verse (Granada, Spain, 1573). Remembered as incumbent of the chair of poetry at the University of Granada during the reign of Philip V and spoken of as the "best" Latinist of Spain in his day, Latino had not been thought of as a Negro for generations. Schomburg reminded scholars that Juan Latino was a full-blooded African Negro. He offered the poet's verse on the return of the Spanish prince from the battle with the Turks at Lepanto (published twenty years before the first of Shakespeare's writings) as an exhibit of Negro accomplishment.

The work of America's first Negro poet—Jupiter Harmon's *Address to the Negroes in the State of New York* (1787).

Manuscript poems and early editions of the works of Phillis Wheatley, slave girl.

The autobiography of Gustavus Vassa, which led to Granville Sharp's attack on slavery in the British colonies.

Copies of the *Almanacs* (1792 and 1793) compiled by Benjamin Banneker, the Negro whose unusual abilities were employed by Thomas Jefferson and others.

The sermons of Lemuel Haynes, the Negro who served as pastor of a white church in Rutland, Vermont, for thirty years following the Revolutionary War.

The scrapbook of Ira Aldridge, Negro actor who won fame in Europe as a Shakespearean actor during the nineteenth century.

Clotel, or the President's Daughter: a Narrative of Slave Life in the United States, the first novel by an American Negro.

Schomburg had found Latin and Dutch treatises such as those by Capitein (1717-1747), an African educated in Holland whose writings are still admired by students of the African in Europe. The first (1600) edition of Leo Africannus, and many of the subsequent editions, were present, as was Ludolf's *History of Ethiopia* (1681-1693) in Latin, English and French. Many works which are better appreciated now than formerly, such as Rattray's works on the Ashanti and the Gold Coast, were in the original Schomburg Collection. Ibn Batuta's *Travels in Asia and Africa, 1325-1354* furnished an eyewitness account of medieval West African kingdoms at the height of their splendor. *Tarikh el-Fettach* and *Tarikh es-Soudan* were books by indigenous African writers which give not only first-hand accounts but also are histories of the royal houses and dynasties which ruled the western Sudan. The manuscripts of Alexander Crummel, and the writings of Edward Blyden, American Negroes who influenced the development of Liberia, were also acquired.

As of 1962, the Schomburg Collection has more than 36,000 bound volumes, of which about half concern people on the African continent. The largest number are in English, the next largest in French, German and Spanish. Eighty drawers of vertical file materials, such as clippings, articles taken from magazines, programs, broadsides, etc., supplement the book and periodical collection. The vertical file material is valuable because it is classified in detail, mainly on biographical but also on geographical and other lines. Files have been amassed on African personalities such as Tom Mboya, Sékou Touré, Felix Houphouet-Boigny and Abdel Nasser, and on new countries such as Ghana, Nigeria, Togoland, the French Communauté and the Mali Federation.

Men such as Nkrumah and Azikiwe have been represented in our files for at least twenty years; in fact, both these men used the Schomburg Collection during their years in America. In the past it has probably been true that African students learned more about their home lands here than they could at home, because of the lack of local facilities, but plans are now being made in West Africa to try to assemble this type of collection.

Since 1954 the Schomburg Collection, as a branch library of the New York Public Library, has been housed in a three-story building at 103 West 135th Street, New York 30, N. Y.

This Collection came into existence when some leaders like Mr. Schomburg became conscious of the need to rebuild the Negro's past. Now the earlier chapters, the stage formerly called pre-history, are being rewritten, and in the 1960's readers are as excited about the treasures Schomburg found as he once was. The Collection continues to serve the function of making information in this field available to the general public. Students, magazine writers and research assistants read side by side with housewives, nationalists and senior citizens. A great deal of information is given by telephone and correspondence from all over the world.

As the emergence of the new nations in Africa continues, this Collection has become increasingly valuable in helping Americans to understand the many aspects of Africa which made this emergence a reality. With growing awareness of the American Negro's stature, this Collection presents source material on his contributions, his roots, his struggles and victories.

THE NEW CATALOGUE

A "Dictionary Catalog of the Schomburg Collection of Negro Literature and History" has recently been published by The New York Public Library.

This nine-volume publication contains, in photographic form, the complete card catalog—more than 170,000 entries all together—now in the reading room of the Schomburg Collection.

For the first time, scholars, students, and laymen throughout the world, who are interested in Negro life and culture can, by means of the "Dictionary Catalog," become aware of the rich resources and vast range of the Schomburg Collection.

Author, title, and subject entries in the "Dictionary Catalog" are arranged in a single alphabetical listing. This makes it possible for anyone consulting the published catalog to see in a quick glance how many books an individual author has written, or how many works there are on any given subject. The "Dictionary Catalog" contains 8474 pages of entries, and each page, measuring 10" x 14", contains photographic reproductions of twenty-one catalog cards.

Individual pages from the "Dictionary Catalog" can be reproduced at reasonable cost through the Library's Photographic Service, located in the main building at Fifth Avenue and 42nd Street, New York 18, N.Y.

The nine-volume edition of the "Dictionary Catalog of the Schomburg Collection of Negro Literature and History" is priced at $605.00 within the United States, and at $665.00 elsewhere. It was published, and can be obtained through G. K. Hall & Co., 97 Oliver Street, Boston 10, Massachusetts.

The "Dictionary Catalog" can be consulted, free of charge, at the Schomburg Collection, which is open until 9 p.m. Monday through Thursday, and until 6 p.m. on Fridays and Saturdays.

Racial segregation creates conflicts in self-esteem and deep feelings of inferiority in Negro youth. It depresses their motivation, constricts their perspective and lowers their educational and vocational aspirations. A general sense of hopelessness and despair so characterize the day to day lives of Negro youth that they are required to adopt protective devices in all-too-often pathetic attempts to make their lives more tolerable. Many of these young people soon learn that they can protect themselves by withdrawal, school dropouts and developing elaborate devices for protecting themselves from any real challenge which too often they are unprepared to meet realistically. Some of them seek to maintain a positive image of themselves through hostility and aggression sometimes towards others but frequently toward members of their own group. A pattern of self-hatred, fantasy, self-serving rationalizations and exhibitionism are forms of reactions found among all human beings who are systematically humiliated and denied that minimum opportunity and dignity essential for their humanity.

Of course some Negro children and adolescents appear to escape the more negative or self-destructive consequences of racial oppression. Some of these children, by virtue of family support, the influence of significant relatives or friends and, in some cases, extraordinary talent or abilities, manage to over-compensate by extraordinary forms of academic or other types of socially acceptable achievement. It is still not clear, however, the nature of the psychic costs which even these youngsters are required to pay as they struggle with the arbitrary, confused and dehumanizing forces of racism.

These symptoms of personal pathology, emerging out of the context of societal cruelty, appear to have their corollary in the characteristics of the ghetto. In its essence, the ghetto is a compound of despair, inertia, apathy, seething frustration and turbulence and chronicly covert and, occasionally, overt violence. The essential problem that is posed for the social psychiatrist after the problem of validation of this diagnosis of the ghetto community—and the more complex and subtle problem of the diagnosis of the larger community within which it is possible to have and to perpetuate such stark pathology —is the problem of trying to understand as precisely as possible the relationship between community pathology and personal pathology. *I suspect that when this is more clearly understood, it will be strikingly clear that one cannot hope to cure the individual without dealing with the difficult problem of curing the society.*

The personal pathology point of view protects one from the risk inherent in conflict with existing vested interests and those forces which have accommodated to the status quo. This luxury is not possible within the theoretical and conceptual framework that now dominates the HARYOU operation.

In seeking to obtain its goals of developing a realistic and comprehensive program for Harlem's youth, HARYOU accepts the challenge of concerning itself with the problems of social change. It recognizes that such change cannot come about merely by wish or good intentions. Effective social change as a necessary antecedent to increasing the proportion of human beings who are able to lead more effective lives can come about only through the mobilization of that power required to change long-standing habits and practices in the social, economic and political realms.

In its planning phase, HARYOU will seek to combine the skills, the methods and techniques of value-sensitive social sciences, the social action-oriented clinicians and social services, together with a realistic identification, mobilization and use of the political, economic and social power within the community itself. It would be possible to devise an excellent research document and a brilliantly imaginative, comprehensive plan and program for youth which would have only academic significance. The HARYOU operation has no intention of producing a mere academic document. For this reason, it includes, as an integral part of its planning process, the additional responsibility of testing the reliability of the various sources of power and commitment within and outside of the community that can be relied upon to effect the necessary social change.

Realistically, one must face the possibility that the corroding effect of long standing determinants of social and personal pathology might make such sources of reliable power and commitment minimal or non-existent within the ghetto community. This is an aspect of diagnosis which cannot be avoided by wishful thinking. It must be tested and the plans must be based upon the objective findings.

In this regard, it might be relevant to state still another assumption of the present HARYOU approach; namely, that HARYOU is not now geared primarily to the saturation of services approach, to the problem of controlling delinquency or the larger problem of making the lives of youth within the Harlem community more meaningful. *Rather, HARYOU is now exploring the possibilities of developing such programs which will seek to discourage dependency through an increasing sense of pride, confidence and initiative in the youth themselves. It would seem more important for these young people to*

learn how to work for social change themselves rather than to con-
tinue to have others provide them with occasional palliatives, panaceas
or worse. This is the essence of the HARYOU therapy. It combines
in its treatment of individuals the techniques for the treatment of the
society. It assumes that as the individual sees the possibility of being
a part of meaningful social action, he not only develops a more positive
self-image, supported by the reality of his social action, but he also
contributes to the movement of the society toward greater stability
and justice.

This experiment in community mental health is not without risk.
All meaningful experiments involve the risk of failure. The HAR-
YOU experiment involves not only the risk of failure but also the risk
of confrontation and conflict between those forces which seek change
and those that resist it. A measure of the significance and the seriousness
of HARYOU paradoxically must be the sources and intensity of ob-
jections and criticism. Already a fundamental question, first asked by
one of the young people with whom HARYOU seeks to work and
since by many sophisticated social analysts, is: "How can you seriously
expect to impose the drastic therapy inherent in a design for social
change when the sources of your support come from governmental
agencies which are not ordinarily associated with significant movements for change." The only answer which can be given to this question is that the rationale, philosophy and the total commitment that
is HARYOU has not been hidden from any of our present, nor will
be from any of our future, sources of support.

HARYOU believes that if it is successful, it will be making a needed
contribution to the strengthening of American democracy. Its in-
violable theme is that minority youth are not expendable. Our nation
cannot afford the luxury of the wastage of human intellectual and
creative resources. American democracy, if it is to survive, can no longer permit countless thousands of Negro youth to be sacrificed on the
altar of racial superstition. If HARYOU succeeds in developing specific therapeutic techniques for dealing with the virulent disease of
racism, it will more than justify the money spent.

THE HARLEM RIOT—1964*

LANGSTON HUGHES

I

HARLEM IN THE LAST five years has been the subject of innumerable surveys, innumerable reports published and unpublished, innumerable official and unofficial studies, hundreds of magazine and newspaper articles, columns, radio and television documentaries, plus an unending stream of speeches from men in pulpits, at forums and learned seminars. Seemingly all that could conceivably be written or said, has been said—and Harlem is still the same old Harlem.

Yet here I am the day after James Powell's funeral saying something more—but with the feeling that words are rather useless at the moment. What is needed now is quick, effective, and immediate practical action. I suppose only municipal, state, and governmental agencies have the facilities to act on a practical level. And, as we all know, such agencies are notoriously slow.

The "all deliberate speed" of the Supreme Court is a mild way to describe their possibilities for doing anything. So, as I write these additional words, my typewriter shrugs its shoulders.

The placing of blame for the current riots goes, of course, far beyond the simple shooting in front of a public school of little Jimmy Powell by Police Lt. Gilligan. Knife or no knife, Jimmy was a little boy. I saw him lying in his coffin looking very small and dead. And I heard people wondering in front of the funeral parlor why a very big man with a pistol—who had received medals for disarming grown criminals without shooting them—felt the need to shoot and kill this kid who looked, in his coffin, small even for the age of 15.

The crowd in front of the funeral parlor felt that it was because Jimmy Powell was colored. Well, there have been billions of words written on the warp and woof of race relations in America. By now not only the cloth but the words describing its condition are moth-eaten. Do we think more mere words will do any good?

It is my feeling that it is about time to stop talking, writing, setting up committees to make reports, and listening to speeches crying, "The fire next time!" I listened to gun fire last night not a hundred yards from me on Lenox Avenue. (What fire *next* time? It's here, I thought.) I heard the cries sharper than any words speakers speak or committees formulate or typewriters take down on paper. And the next time was only a half hour later when more guns fired down the street from where I live.

So it seems to me the warnings have all been uttered. Red is the color of both blood and fire. On the Negro side, the blood extends from the average of two lynchings a week in the South a half century ago to an average of one violent and unsolved black death a week in Dixie today. But Dixie is not Harlem. Of course not. Yet the fumes of its illness, like atomic fallout, seep down on Lenox Avenue.

And somehow Jimmy Powell gets all mixed up with Medgar Evers. Harlem's feet, through no fault of its own, are mired in Dixie—Emmet Till, Mack Parker, Rev. George Lee, two headless black bodies in a Louisiana river, and the three lost boys, Negro and white, who went to help people register to vote. It has all been written about, spoken about, picturized, televised—and nothing basic done about any of it.

The prices for food in Harlem are higher than anywhere else in Manhattan. A 3-cent lemon downtown is a 5-cent lemon uptown. Why? On 125th Street's long business artery, less than half a dozen shops are owned by Negroes. So whites must know the answer to the why of prices in Harlem.

Rentals in Harlem are higher than rentals downtown for the same type of shelter. Why? The tenements in Harlem belong mostly to whites. Maybe they know the answers to this.

Graft in Harlem in relation to illegal numbers, narcotics, and prostitution's quite open operations under the very noses of New York's finest is rampant. Certainly it does nothing to enhance the prestige of our Police Department. Why such a situation? Most of the police in Harlem are white. Therefore whites must know the answer to this.

Starting from scratch a century ago with 200 years of slavery behind us and no indemnity at freedom, how can Negroes control job markets, money markets, body markets, numbers, narcotics, or any

of the sources of power and millions? But that question answers itself. Should it be repeated? My typewriter shrugs.

So—there are Harlem riots. *So*—bored and jobless kids loot stores.
So—from furnished rooms with no air-cooling on a hot night, thousands come out into the streets to scream at cops. The cops, unfortunately being white, represent visually that world below Central
Park that controls life in Harlem—from the price of a lemon to graft,
bag women, numbers, heroin, and the freedom of prostitutes to operate openly at the exit of subways and on the main streets.

To help keep the peace, they are now publishing the pleas of absentee Negro leaders who do not live in Harlem, asking that Harlem
behave itself. It is nothing against Roy Wilkins that he lives on Long
Island, or that Jackie Robinson lives in Westchester, or James Farmer
lives in downtown New York—where it is easier to behave one's self—
and most other distinguished Negro leaders live as far away as they
can get from Harlem. Adam Powell has a cool and lovely home in
Puerto Rico. But these leaders this week will probably write and
speak a billion more words about Harlem—like so many other commentators who do not live here.

If the past is any criterion, however, nothing new will happen. I
wonder if their typewriters, too, will get bored just taking down words.

II

It is not unlike petting a snarling dog to say to Harlem in a period
of riots, "Now, Harlem, be nice! Harlem, behave yourself," after
Harlem has been kicked in the behind so long by so many, including
some of its own blackamoors.

It should be clear to the world at the moment that Harlem is
really not interested in behaving itself this week with an army of
white-helmeted strangers from all the police precincts of Greater New
York in its midst. No matter what brought them there, such a display
of armed might disturbs Harlem's psyche. The very sight of so many
alien uniforms and side arms, clubs and walkie-talkies, squad cars
and riot trucks, even if ostensibly for Harlem's own protection, seems
ominous.

"Be nice, Harlem! Lie down, Harlem! Now, behave, Harlem,"
coming from voices that formerly never even said a friendly "Hello"
to Harlem, is hardly conducive to calming an emotionally upset
psyche, or downing a bristling tail and causing it to wag again. Harlem has been wagging its tail so long in thanks for the bones that

have come its way that it is time now for somebody to throw Harlem, not a bone, but some meat. And then at a time like this here comes Mr. Goldwater talking about taking away what few bones Harlem has been flung. Imagine that!

They call August the dog days, when even the decent dogs sometimes go mad. Hot weather, it seems, is likely to bring out the worst in dogs, as it sometimes does in people. It certainly would be awful were New York to wake up some hot day and find a mad dog in its backyard, especially a black dog. God forbid!

"Now, be nice, Harlem! Don't snarl at me! Are you out of your mind?"

Harlem must have gone out of its mind on the evening of July 18 when it was 90 degrees and the humidity was high and little Jimmy Powell, who probably never had a dog, was lying bullet-riddled in a hot little funeral home on Seventh Avenue. The next night at 8 o'clock, when his funeral was held, a double line of big tall white steel-helmeted policemen faced the crowd on either side from the door to the curb as the casket was borne out. With so many cops, Harlem could not see what was happening—except from the roof tops, so Harlem lifted its hind legs and kicked a few bottles down on the cops. It was a very hot night and admittedly heat may produce slight irrationalities, if not complete madness.

"Be nice, Harlem, or I'll beat your head! Cut out that stuff, dog! Stop now!"

Did you ever hear a talking dog? Such a dog must be an hallucination. Do dogs talk? And from rooftops? "Go ahead and beat my head! My head's been beat before!"

As dogs sometimes do, the hind legs continued to scratch backwards on the hot tin roof and in scratching, kicked a few more objects of debris down on the cops in the street.

The cops fire in the air. But that's where that dog was—in the air. Then without bull horns, Harlem was clearly heard to say, "Kill me! Go ahead, kill another one of me! You killed James Powell! I been killed before."

"Shut up, Harlem!" BANG! BANG-BANG! "I told you to be nice!" BANG! BANG-BANG! BANG! "That for you! Take that, Harlem!"

"How many shots to hit a dog on a roof? Silence. How many shots did it take to kill a little colored boy in front of a school in Yorkville? Silence. How many shots did it take to mow down Medgar

Evers on the steps of his home in Jackson? How many bullets did it take to blast to death Rev. George Lee in Mississippi who merely wanted to vote? How many sticks of dynamite did it take to blow up Harry T. Moore and his wife on a Christmas night in Florida because he was secretary of the NAACP? How many yards of rope did it take to lynch Mack Parker? How hot a fire for a mob to burn to death pregnant Mary Turner in Georgia? How much electric current to kill all the Negroes railroaded to the death chair by all-white juries in the South? What caliber of gun last week killed the late army officer, Lemuel A. Penn, coming back on military orders from reserve duty in Fort Benning, Georgia?

"You must be an old dog with a memory like an elephant, Harlem, to remember all that. You mangy hound," BANG! BANG-BANG! "I told you to be nice, Harlem."

But what happened after the guns fired? Could the bullets have missed? Look, there's still Harlem.

"Get down off your hind legs now, Harlem! Don't rear up at me. Be cool! Stop barking! I got news for you. The mayor has flown home from his vacation in Spain just to pacify you. Everything will be all right. Listen, Harlem! HARYOU is about to throw you a million-dollar bone. Come on, calm down. Be good, I say. Now be nice, Harlem! Be nice!"

III

Opinion in Harlem is divided as to whether or not riots do any good. Some say *yes,* they achieve concrete results in community improvements. Others say *no,* they set the Negro race back 50 years. Those who disagree say, in effect, "But Negroes are always set back 50 years by something or another, so what difference does a riot make?"

Old-timers who remember former riots in Harlem say, "White folks respect us more when they find out we mean business. When they only listen to our speeches or read our writing—if they ever do—they think we are just blowing off steam. But when rioters smash the plate glass windows of their stores, they know the steam has some force behind it. Then they say, 'Those Negroes are mad! What do they want?' And for a little while, they will try to give you a little of what you want.

"After every riot in Harlem, the whites respect you more. After that big riot in 1935, the white-owned shops all along 125th Street that would not hire Negro clerks, began to hire at least one. We got a great many jobs out of that riot that we couldn't get before in our own community because the clerks, cashiers and everything were all white."

The big riot in 1943, which grew out of a white policeman shooting a black soldier at 126th Street and 8th Avenue during a period of much police brutality in the area, produced remarkable changes in police attitudes in Harlem, and resulted in a number of additional Negro officers being added to the force.

Chocolate and vanilla teams of policemen appeared on uptown streets walking together. Squad cars became integrated. And a white policeman would often grant his Negro colleague the courtesy of making the arrest, if an arrest had to be made. And for a long time after the '43 riots, seldom did Negro or white cops beat a culprit's head in public—as they frequently did before the riots. MOP-MOP! BE-BOP! MOP! is where the musical term *be-bop* came from, so say jazz musicians——the sound of Harlem police clubs on Negro heads.

After the 1943 riots, one night on Lenox Avenue, I saw two white policemen attempting to push a young Negro into a squad car. The man refused to get in. Each time the police tried to force him, he would spread out his arms and legs or twist his body so that they could not get him through the door. With a crowd of Negroes around, the white cops seemingly did not dare hit the Negro. But, to their fortune a colored policeman on foot arrived. He simply said, "Get in that car, fellow!" The Negro got in, and the car sped away with its prisoner.

Folks in the crowd said, "You see—since the riots, they sure do arrest you politely. Now his head won't be cracked, till they get him down to the precinct house." The riots of 1943 almost ended *public* police brutality on the streets of Harlem.

Out of our 1964 riot this week I do not know what concrete results will come, but certainly its repercussions have already reached into high places. No less an authority than President Johnson has spoken from the capital saying grandiloquently, "Violence and lawlessness cannot, must not, and will not be tolerated." Some Harlemites interpret this to mean that there will be no more head-bustings on the part of the police, or shooting of adolescents, black, white, or Puerto Rican by men representing New York's Finest. "American citizens have a right to protection of life and limb," continued the President, "whether driving along a highway in Georgia, a road in Mississippi or a street in New York City."

President Johnson's commendable utterances concerning the long-standing dangers of Mississippi and Georgia plus the recent intensification of urban dangers in New York, Harlemites feel, would never have been expressed had it not been for the riots. Negroes have been asking for years that Georgia and Mississippi be made safe—and getting no results from federal or state governments. But now, after a weekend of rioting in Harlem, you see what the President says! The riots have already produced one good result.

And now that our own Mayor Wagner has flown back to Gracie Mansion, Harlem awaits what new deeds will come from his official chambers. Harlem hopes it will not have to count that day lost whose low descending sun sees from the Mayor's hands no worthy action done, since man does not live by words alone.

For me personally, the best thing that so far has come out of our current Harlem riots is that on Tuesday night I saw a Chinese cop in Harlem. Had it not been for the riots, I can hardly believe this suprising example of integration would ever have happened. I never saw a Chinese policeman in our neighborhood before. But there he was right on 125th Street in the block between the Theresa Hotel and Lenox Avenue with the 95 other cops I counted in that block from one corner to the other. Ninety-three of the cops were white, one was colored, and the other one, Chinese. In my heart I welcomed him to Harlem. I hope they let him stay here after the riots are over.

To me the Chinese have always seemed a delightful people with a warm sense of humor, quiet and friendly and courteous. I am sure that this Chinese cop would not wield a nightstick so violently or shoot off his pistol so recklessly as other policemen have done in Harlem this week. In that long block between Seventh and Lenox Avenues, his was a face that looked decent and friendly.

READIN'
'RITIN'
'RITHMETIC
RACISM

BRANDON JR
1968

"— AND IN 1954 A SUPREME COURT DECISION PUT AN END TO SEGREGATION IN ALL OUR SCHOOLS!"

"THE 250 YEARS OF NEGRO SLAVERY *IS* IN THERE...GIVE ME THAT BOOK ...HERE IT IS, THIS PARAGRAPH TELLS THE ENTIRE STORY!"

"WHEN I SAID WRITE A REPORT ABOUT A GREAT AMERICAN, I MEANT SOME-
ONE LIKE GEORGE WASHINGTON OR BEN FRANKLIN...I'VE NEVER EVEN
HEARD OF DENMARK VESEY!"

"YOU CHILDREN MUST UNDERSTAND...I REALLY LIKE YOU...
BUT I *HATE* BUSSES!"

"I SAID IF YOU DON'T HAVE A HAIRCUT BY TOMORROW MORNING, YOU'LL BE EXPELLED!"

"I CAN SEE BY YOUR BACKGROUND YOU ARE WELL SUITED FOR A TEACHING POSITION HERE. YOU SEE, SINCE INTEGRATION, WE'VE HAD A DISCIPLINE PROBLEM AT THIS SCHOOL!"

"THEN THE GOOD COWBOY, ALL DRESSED IN WHITE, BEAT UP THE BAD GUY, WHO WAS DRESSED IN BLACK, PUT ON HIS WHITE HAT, MOUNTED HIS WHITE STALLION AND RODE OFF INTO THE SUNSET!"

THE EARLY YEARS
OF ADAM POWELL

JOHN HENRIK CLARKE

THE ATMOSPHERE and the conditions that influenced the formative years of Adam Clayton Powell's political career were apparent in Harlem before he was born. To fully understand his political emergence in the world's best known ethnic ghetto, some attention must be paid to the talented and effective Harlem politicians who came before him. These politicians, collectively, were the first to show the people of Harlem how to force governmental agencies to respond to their needs. The more farsighted members of this group learned that to have any impact on government, it is necessary to know not only what is possible to get, but also how and through whom to go about getting it. This involved knowledge both of the formal political institutions, and of the groups and individuals who, for one reason or another, actually—or might potentially—determine and influence what occurs within the political structure. For Harlem this meant the discovery of its political self and how to make the most effective use of it.

While A. Clayton Powell was growing up in Harlem the politics of the community was growing up with him. Harlem became a black community early in this century. From the beginning, politics was a form of community activity. After 1900 public recognition was made of this fact. Able spokesmen arose on all levels of municipal politics and demanded greater representation for the community. Before this time the black American's almost religious devotion to the Republican Party had hampered his effectiveness in the politics of New York City. The Republican Party took the Harlem vote for granted and did not feel compelled to cater to it. At this time the Democratic Party had not decided to make a serious attempt to bring the Harlem vote into the Democratic camp. The activity of Harlem's first major politicians changed this situation and started both parties to catering to the Harlem vote.

In 1898 Edward E. Lee, a former head bellman, called the Chief, helped to establish the United Colored Democracy, as a Harlem subdivision of the New York Democratic Party. The shift in the Harlem vote toward the Democratic Party came about the time of the disastrous race riots of 1900. New York's black population instinctively felt the need of more local political protest. Many influential Harlem residents criticized the shift to the Democratic Party. To offset this the party leaders saw fit to reward Edward E. Lee and his small group by giving them a measure of political patronage. James D. Carr, a Harlem lawyer, who had graduated from Columbia University Law School in 1885, was appointed Assistant District Attorney. Edward E. Lee was made Sheriff. More and better appointments followed this early recognition of the Harlem vote as a political factor in New York City.

In welcoming the Harlem contingent into the Democratic Party, the Tammany Hall leader Richard Croker said: "Your people are a poor people. Tammany Hall is a poor man's organization. The colored man rightly belongs in Tammany Hall. I'll start off by appointing a leader, thereafter, elect your own leaders and Tammany Hall will recognize him. And although your vote is only ten per cent, I will place a colored man in every department of the city government."

Harlem's influence emerges

In the main, this promise was kept. Thus began the influence of the Harlem community in New York's Democratic politics. The chieftains of Tammany Hall adhered to the principle laid down by Richard Croker and rewarded the Harlem politicians with patronage. This situation began to change early in the twentieth century when the first Harlem black politician of great significance in the entire history of the city arose in the Republican Party. His name was Charles W. Anderson. Anderson was a self-educated and self-made man. He was born in Oxford, Ohio a year after the Civil War ended and he came to New York City at the age of twenty. He immediately became active in local Republican politics. In 1890 he was elected president of the Young Men's Colored Republican Club of New York County. As a reward he was appointed to the position of Gauger in a district office of the Internal Revenue Service. From this not too important position Charles W. Anderson became "the recognized colored Republican leader of New York." He quickly rose from Gauger to private secretary of New York State's Treasurer (1893-1895), to Chief Clerk in the State Treasury (1895-1898), to Supervisor of Accounts for the New York Racing Commission (1898-1905). In 1905 he was

appointed to what was undoubtedly the most responsible and important Federal office held by any Harlem politician in the early twentieth century, Collector of Internal Revenue for the Second New York
District—the Wall Street District. Charles W. Anderson was a friend
of both W. E. B. Du Bois and Booker T. Washington, in spite of the
conflict between these two men. More important he was an astute
and effective community politician. He had the welfare of the entire
Harlem community at heart. To Charles W. Anderson, improving the
race most often meant using his influence to find more and better-
paying jobs for New York's black community.

Charles W. Anderson was successful in finding positions for residents of Harlem as mechanical draftsmen, state examiners of auto-
mobile chauffeurs, deputy collectors, gaugers in the Internal Revenue
Service, customhouse inspectors and clerks, and deputy United States
Marshals. More than any other politician before him Charles W.
Anderson made sure that the people of Harlem got their share of what
the politicians call "the little plums"—the political appointee jobs.
Anderson was the first leader in New York City history to push open
the doors of political opportunity for Negroes. The rise of Charlie
Anderson in many ways typified the political awakening of New York's
black population. He was the most able politician to emerge from
Harlem during its formative years.

The United Colored Democracy continued its existence as a special community organization within the city's Democratic Party. Its
leader after 1915 was Harvard-educated Ferdinand Q. Morton, Chairman of the Municipal Civil Service Commission.

President Woodrow Wilson's re-election campaign of 1916 focused
the attention of powerful politicians on the potentialities of the
minority vote. In two Assembly Districts of Harlem, the 19th and
21st, the black votes were becoming preponderant and decisive. The
Marcus Garvey movement had stirred a more independent spirit
among the people of Harlem. In 1917 the first Harlem Assemblyman,
Republican Edward A. Johnson, was elected to the State Legislature.
John C. Hawkins, another Republican, was elected in 1919 and re-
elected in 1920.

During this period Harlem was still a developing community. Several forces were in motion, helping that development. Politically,
the Republican forces led by Charles W. Anderson were growing
stronger. The competing Democratic forces—the United Colored Democracy led by Ferdinand Q. Morton, were gaining influence and demanding more patronage for the community. Marcus Garvey and his

"back-to-Africa" movement were preaching a kind of black nationalism that had never before been heard in this country. These competing forces started the campaign for Negro district leadership in Harlem. When this campaign was won they raised their sights and once more aimed at making Harlem a Congressional District. The early participants in this campaign were: Fred R. Moore, editor and publisher of the *New York Age;* T. Thomas Fortune, former editor of the *Age,* then editor of the Garvey publications; Charles W. Anderson, the leading Harlem Republican; Ferdinand Q. Morton, leading Harlem Democrat; Edward A. Johnson, Harlem's first Assemblyman, and the militant Socialist, black nationalist and Garveyite, Hubert H. Harrison.

During this period the leading Harlem politicians and some just plain civic-minded Harlem citizens secured maps of all the Congressional Districts in New York City. They redrew the maps so that most of Harlem would be in one Congressional District. This map was the basis for their petition to make Harlem a Congressional District. The first petition was presented during the Governorship of Alfred E. Smith, who vetoed the bill authorizing the creation of a Congressional District in Harlem, using the excuse that he would not sign "class or race legislation."

Despite the lack of interest on the part of several New York Governors in making Harlem a Congressional District, Harlem politicians continued to put up candidates for the House of Representatives.

With A. Clayton Powell not yet on the scene the way was being cleared for him to eventually become Harlem's first Congressman.

the role of Abyssinian Baptist Church

The political career of Adam Clayton Powell is closely linked with the history and development of Abyssinian Baptist Church in Harlem, founded by his father. Adam Clayton Powell, Sr., was a religious politician who used his church to project social action programs for community improvement. Powell, Sr., saw no conflict between this activity and his role as the spiritual leader of the largest Baptist congregation in the United States. This church was Adam Clayton Powell, Jr.'s training ground. His father was his first teacher.

In his book *Marching Blacks,* Mr. Powell gives the following description of the church and the influence of his father.

No history of America's Harlem can be written without including the Abyssinian Baptist Church. Standing in gothic majesty on West 138th Street, built of solid rock, concrete and steel, its foundations penetrating as much as forty feet to rest on rock—this, the nation's largest Protestant church, has been a mighty bulwark against reaction, a citadel for the oppressed and a fortress from which emerged in ever swelling numbers black pioneers determined to make a way out of no way.

When I was six months old my father and mother brought me to New York. In 1908 my father took over the pastorate of the Abyssinian Baptist Church, celebrated in those days for little more than age, an old-time Negro aristocracy and debts. The congregation numbered sixteen hundred and the debt was $126,000. Abyssinian was the church where the members spoke only to the pastor and the pastor only to God. Just a few hundred feet away was the Metropolitan Opera House. I can still see the saints of yesterday coming down the red-carpeted aisles on a Sabbath morning. With their high lace collars kept correctly stiff with whale bone, their black rustling taffeta and cloth-top, high-buttoned shoes, they were divine aristocrats, members of the Abyssinian Church, praise God! In the midst of this decadent splendor my father, former sharecropper, self-educated son of a slave, dreamed of the day when the church would be a social gospel institution. This was radicalism of the reddest type. Religion in those days was something to be heard on Sunday and not seen the rest of the week. But he kept on dreaming long before the migration hit Harlem. He dreamed of a church standing in the midst of a community of half a million souls. My father was a radical and a prophet —I am a radical and a fighter.

I am what I am because of the Abyssinian Church. I believe that Harlem is what it is mainly because of the efforts of that institution. I know that many of the gains that have been made in Harlem would have been made with or without the support of the church, but I am sure that the time table for those gains was speeded up and many of the victories more permanently secured because underwriting every step of the way was the oldest Negro Baptist Church in the North, the largest Protestant church in America, and one of the most financially independent institutions anywhere in the Negro world.

Abyssinian Baptist Church was built in Harlem at the time when the short and colorful career of Marcus Garvey was getting its first national attention. Garvey had arrived in Harlem in 1916, with the grand design of shipping 7,000,000 black people back to Africa. He envisioned a black African Republic, a black army with black generals and black cross nurses, and a black religion with a black God. Millions of black people listened and shared his dream.

The appearance of the Garvey movement was perfectly timed. The broken promises of the post-war period had produced widespread cynicism in the black population and they had lost some of their belief in themselves as a people. Adam Powell, Sr., wrote of Garvey: "He is the only man that ever made Negroes who are not black ashamed of their color." In his book *Marching Blacks,* Adam Powell, Jr., wrote: "Marcus Garvey was one of the greatest mass leaders of all time. He was misunderstood and maligned, but he brought to the Negro people for the first time a sense of pride in being black."

The Garvey movement had a profound effect on the political development of Harlem and the lives of both Adam Powell, Jr., and Sr. The fight to make Harlem a Congressional District was started during the Garvey period.

Adam Powell joins the struggle

In 1930 Adam Powell, Jr., had finished Colgate University and was taking graduate work at Columbia University in addition to helping his father manage his large church. At this time a group of doctors who had been banned from Harlem Hospital, "because they were Negroes," asked Powell, Jr., for assistance. This was Powell, Jr.'s, first major experience in social protest and his first projection of himself in relation to the grievances of the Harlem community.

Harlem Hospital at this time had a bad reputation among the people of the community. In fact, it was called "The Butcher Shop." The administration of the hospital was behind the time medically and politically corrupt. The five doctors who had been banned from the hospital were some of the most able medical men in this country. Among them were: Dr. Peter Marshall Murray, now a diplomate of the College of Surgeons, and Dr. Sidat Singh, who still has an office in Harlem on 135th Street.

Powell, Jr., organized the committee that protested the doctors' dismissal and convinced the doctors that they should join the picket line. In the spring of 1931 Adam Powell, Jr., led a mass delegation of six thousand Harlem citizens to City Hall. The Board of Estimate was in session but had not agreed to see the delegation. As chairman, Powell, Jr., made his way to the Board room and demanded to be heard. Then Acting Mayor O'Brien barred him from the Board room until Joseph V. Kee, President of the Board of Alderman, asked that he be heard.

From this demonstration there eventually came not only the reinstatement of all the five doctors, but the establishment of an interracial staff with a Harlem resident as medical director. Powell, Jr.'s, role as a dynamic community leader was now assured.

Before the government launched the public-relief program during the Depression, the elder Powell established a relief bureau in the Abyssinian Church and appointed his son as director. This brought the younger Powell in touch with the poor people and their needs.

After seven years as assistant Pastor to his father he was appointed to succeed his father when the elder Powell retired in 1937. His career as a community leader took on its full stature now. He had followers and well-wishers far beyond the church and the Harlem community. He joined the "Jobs-for-Negroes Movement" and gave it new directions. In 1938, with Rev. William Lloyd Imes, then pastor of St. James Presbyterian Church, and A. Philip Randolph, he formed the Greater New York Coordinating Committee for the Employment of Negroes.

A young black Cuban, Arnold Johnson (who is still active in community affairs in Harlem) was Secretary of the Coordinating Committee. Other members of the group were James W. Ford, Negro Vice-Presidential candidate of the Communist Party, Captain A. L. King, the Garveyite, Ira Kemp and Arthur Reed, founders of the Harlem Labor Union, and Mrs. Elizabeth Ross Haynes. The first major target of the committee was the stores on 125th Street. For years the owners of these stores had been reluctant to hire Negro help. The weekly picket lines of the committee and the "Don't buy where you can't work" chanting of the pickets struck terror in the hearts of the store owners. The Harlem Labor Union was born and grew during this period.

Powell's political career begins

The political career of Adam Powell had its incubation in the Coordinating Committee for Negro Employment. In his book *Marching Blacks* he gives the following description of the Committee and his relationship to it:

From the time the Greater New York Coordinating Committee held its first meeting at my office until the present—the Abyssinian Baptist Church has been the great foundation upon which many people's movements were built. Office space has always been afforded free. Money was ready to underwrite expenses. Eleven thousand people were available to start things moving. The Coordinating

Committee was shunned in the beginning by quite a few of the so-called big Negroes. One great intellectual giant, however, stood by my side. Our co-chairman was the Reverend Dr. William Lloyd Imes, minister of St. James, the nation's largest Negro Presbyterian church, President of the Alumni Association of Union Theological Seminary, and now President of Knoxville College in Tennessee. William Lloyd Imes brought to the Coordinating Committee that which I did not possess. I was young and he was mature. I was a radical and so was he, but his radicalism was tempered with thoughtfulness. I was impetuous and impatient; likewise Imes, but he paused to reason. A great man, one of the greatest of the great, with the mind of a scholar, the soul of a saint, the heart of a brother, the tongue of a prophet, the hand of a militant—may his tribe increase.

The Coordinating Committee's greatest achievement was a river-to-river picket line on 125th Street. This spectacular event opened up the job market on 125th Street. Now the members of the committee moved on to other targets such as The Consolidated Edison and the New York Telephone Company. The telephone company was the most difficult target. The committee found that the company was fundamentally dishonest. A Vice-President of the company told the committee that "he would not employ Negroes and that he was not particular about the employment of Jews or Catholics." The committee took this matter to Stanley Isaacs, then Borough President, who was himself Jewish. The telephone company backed down and finally agreed to employ Negroes in some departments. The Edison Company agreed to employ some Negroes in white collar jobs.

In the meantime, the fight to make Harlem a Congressional District continued. Rev. William Lloyd Imes of Harlem's St. James Presbyterian Church ran for Congress in 1938. Governors Smith and Roosevelt before him did not favor making Harlem a Congressional District.

In addition to participating in this fight Adam Powell continued to develop in other ways. In 1939 he was a leader in the fight for the employment of Afro-Americans in jobs, other than menial, at the New York World's Fair.

In 1941 Adam Powell and the Coordinating Committee fought and won what he refers to as "the crowning victory for the marching hosts of tan Manhattan." They won the right of Afro-Americans to be employed as bus drivers in the city of New York.

Adam Powell wrote a weekly column called "The Soap Box" for

the *New York Amsterdam News* after the Harlem riot of March 1935. In these years he became increasingly the spokesman for the people of Harlem. His chairmanship of the Greater New York Coordinating Committee had been the springboard of his career. In 1941 he mounted a united front campaign for his election to the City Council of New York. This successful campaign made him the first Afro-American to hold that office. Now he had a larger arena in which to operate. This only sharpened his appetite for a higher political office. The long fight to make Harlem a Congressional District was nearer to being won.

The New York State Legislature passed a reapportionment bill creating a Congressional District in the heart of Harlem. Powell started to bid for the job of Congressman at once and had already built the community machinery that would make this possible. He was then the publisher of a newspaper, *The People's Voice,* and was now reaching a national audience. At this time he had four jobs: he was City Councilman, Baptist pastor, newspaper editor and leader of the People's Committee, a militant Harlem protest group.

Powell's role as congressman

The Harlem riot of March 1943 made the people of the community more aware of the need for more political action. Adam Powell had already announced his intention to run for Congress. He had also announced that he would support Benjamin Davis for his seat in the City Council.

In 1944, during the Governorship of Thomas E. Dewey, the legislation that officially made Harlem a Congressional District was signed. Adam Clayton Powell had no difficulty in being elected Harlem's first Congressman.

In the campaign for Congress Mr. Powell's main base of operation was Abyssinian Baptist Church. This church was his spiritual and intellectual home, and the platform for the projection of most of his ambitions. Mr. Powell's bid for Congress made political history. Since 1901 only three Afro-Americans had sat in Congress: Oscar de Priest, Arthur W. Mitchell, and William L. Dawson. All three were from the Illinois First District in Chicago. Adam Powell's campaign for Congress was more colorful than difficult. He ran unopposed and won easily. He took his seat in Congress at the same time Franklin D. Roosevelt started his fourth term in office with Harry S. Truman as Vice President.

With Adam Powell in Congress and Benjamin Davis in the City

Council, Harlem now had two effective and popular political representatives. In the years immediately following the end of World War II they were greatly needed.

Adam Powell, Sr., now retired, continued to influence his son's career. He became a Democrat during the early days of the New Deal. As a minister and as a concerned citizen of Harlem he was always a radical. It was no surprise when he said in his book *Riots and Ruins*: "The Negro's only political hope is to register with the American Labor Party that is nearest to Communism in its liberal attitude toward colored people." Then he added: "Eighty per cent of the members of Congress are incurably dishonest in their dealings with the Negro. . . ."

The first years that Adam Powell spent in Congress were eventful and hectic, full of small accomplishments and some heartbreaking disappointments. Some of the Southern senators and representatives ignored him and others openly insulted him. He had been elected to public office on the mandate of three political parties. He acted with the boldness implicit in knowing what a mandate meant. This offended some of his white colleagues who soon became part of that army of critics that made a cult out of disapproving his actions. Their criticisms only helped to endear him to the Harlem community and other black communities throughout the nation. The criticisms from his white colleagues were proof to most of his people that he was truly representing them and fighting their battles in Congress bravely and alone. When his first term of office ended, the Powell political mystique had been born and was growing fast.

As the elections of 1946 approached Powell was eager to keep his mandate intact by once again getting the endorsement of the three major political parties, though he was popular enough to win an election in Harlem without the support of these parties. This is the basis of his political strength. During his first term of office he had alienated a lot of people, including some in his own political camp.

The Republicans who had supported Powell for his first term of office now mounted a campaign against him. They had proposed Grant Reynolds as their candidate. Reynolds was a minister, former U.S. Army captain and a commissioner of the New York Department of Correction. Reynolds went into this campaign with very little support from the local Republican leaders who had said, privately, that they did not want to fight Powell. They were of the opinion that Reynolds was being forced on them by downtown political bosses. Powell did, in fact, lose the Republican primary to Reynolds by 500

votes—the only election he ever lost. He easily captured the Democratic and American Labor Party nominations. Reynolds gave Powell
his first and only real test in a general election. Reynolds took his
campaign to the streets of Harlem and fought Powell on issues affecting the community.

In June of that year (1945) Rev. Powell announced that Abyssinian
Baptist Church would be his election headquarters. Joseph E. Ford
was his campaign manager. He announced endorsements from both
Henry Wallace and Father Divine. Many of the Harlem ministers
and outstanding personalities who supported Rev. Powell for his first
term of office now supported Reynolds. Among these were Joe Louis
and Rev. George H. Sims, Jr., pastor of the Union Baptist Church.

This campaign was long, interesting and hard fought. During the
campaign a large number of people in Harlem seriously questioned
Adam Clayton Powell for the first time. It was a healthy and educational sight to see someone stand up to Rev. Powell, examine him
and demand that he explain and defend his record in Congress and
his total relationship to the Harlem community.

On election day, Powell polled 32,573 votes (22,641 Democratic and
9,932 American Labor Party) to 19,514 for Reynolds. Compared
with later campaigns, Reynolds had made the most impressing showing
against Rev. Powell. This showing was not good enough to keep Rev.
Powell from saying: "My easy victory indicates the solid support
of the people in Harlem. . . . Thousands of dollars poured into Harlem could not buy the Negro vote. We have served notice on cheap
politicians to stay out of Harlem."

The first and last real political stand against A. Clayton Powell
in the Harlem community was over. Reynolds was the last opponent to force Powell to get out on the streets of Harlem and campaign for re-election.

His weekly column "Soap Box" continued to appear in the newspaper *The People's Voice* until its demise in 1948. His troubles
in Congress continued. He had previously worked in legislative
bodies controlled by Democrats. But the general election of 1946 had
produced Republican majorities in both chambers of Congress. Powell
wasted no time in addressing himself to the new power structure: "I
have come back to Washington to insist that the Republicans keep
their campaign promises to the Negro people," he declared.

In his next bid for re-election (1948) he made only one major
speech and won over his opponent, the veteran Republican Harold
C. Burton, four to one. In Congress his legislative activity gathered

momentum in the Truman years. His was the strong and clear voice speaking out against appropriations for the House Un-American Activities Committee, job discrimination, bad housing and all the evils that plague America's minorities. He was and still is a good congressman with a bad absentee record.

political deterioration in Harlem

While Mr. Powell was making a record in national politics the political structure of the Harlem community had started to crack in many places. Benjamin J. Davis, who had been elected to the New York City Council to fill the seat vacated by Mr. Powell, was in real trouble in spite of his popularity in the community. Before his last term had expired Davis was barred from the City Council because he had been convicted under the Smith Act. In 1951, the Supreme Court upheld the Smith Act and Ben Davis and a number of his fellow Communists were sent to jail. Now with Adam Powell in Washington most of the time and Ben Davis in jail, most of Harlem's day-by-day political housekeeping went undone. A period of political deterioration had started. Mr. Powell's political stardom continued to rise nationally and internationally. In 1955 he was unofficial observer at the Bandung Conference of 29 former colonial nations of Africa and Asia. In 1956 Mr. Powell attempted, unsuccessfully, to spark enthusiasm for his candidacy for Mayor of New York City.

After the election of Earl Brown as City Councilman and Hulan Jack as Borough President the political fortunes of Harlem seemed to be on the rise. This was not true. Very few demands were being made on the elected representatives. The people were losing confidence in politicians as a breed. Mr. Powell was dutifully re-elected every two years. When he had an opponent the community rarely remembered his or her name. He was sent back to Washington to "bless out the white folks in Congress." And so long as he blessed them out loud and strong very few people cared to find out whether he was right or wrong. There was a lot of talk about his activities but very little genuine discussion and examination. In the meantime, the political deterioration of the community continued, seemingly unnoticed.

Harlem as a Congressional District has not yet reached its full potential.

After the March on Washington Congressman Powell broke off relations with his long-time friend J. Raymond Jones. This happened at a time when both of these political figures were competing

with each other over a community project idea that was to become
HARYOU-ACT.

remarkable record of Powell in congress

The early years of Adam Clayton Powell represented a political
renaissance in Harlem. Potentially he could have become one of the
most powerful politicians in the history of the United States. He,
fortunately, had a constituency that made him less dependent on the
two major political parties. In my opinion, he never made the best
use of this political advantage. Yet, his record in Congress is one of
the most remarkable that any legislator can boast of in this century.
In 1966 Adam Clayton Powell celebrated his 21st year in the House
of Representatives and the fifth year as the Chairman of the House
Committee on Education and Labor. He had successfully guided to
passage 49 major laws from his committee. He has never had a bill
defeated from his committee once it reached the House of Representatives. In these five years some of the most important legislation
in the history of the country and the United States Congress was
passed. Here are 49 laws which were passed in the first five years
of Adam Clayton Powell's chairmanship of the House Committee on
Education and Labor. This is proof, if proof is needed, that in spite
of the present controversy around him and the charges and counter-
charges, he was an able community representative and one of the most
effective politicians of this century.

LESSONS OF THE 201
COMPLEX IN HARLEM

CHARLES E. WILSON

A MERICANS, BLACK AND WHITE ALIKE, are people who do not call things by their right names. Most often they prefer to deal with the world through slogans. As a people they like to term a product or an object "new" which is just a modification of something of yesteryear. As a people they enjoy labeling and mislabeling their problems and contradictions so that they will not have to deal with those problems. Finally they are deeply pragmatic people who cannot or will not face the consequences of the breakdown of their urban systems. And because the public education system reflects the values, attitudes, goals and contradictions of a people, many American urban public school systems today face a major crisis. Intermediate School 201 in New York City is synonymous with that crisis in education. This school has been the site of repeated broken promises of integrated quality education and developing cultural heritage. All have dried up like raisins. I.S. 201, with its new architectural design (windowless), could not hide organizational chaos and teachers apathy. I.S. 201, the alleged scene of extremist action and anti-white activities. That these "rites" never took place is of small import for the charges were of "irregularities" which were enough to arouse all the latent fears and hostilities. I.S. 201—the school, the complex and the complex surrounding that "demonstration district"—is a symbol and a symptom of the kind of problem that is likely to emerge in every area where the people, most often the victims of the present order, demand a voice in affecting the lives of "their children." For in those cases, parents and their allies find themselves in conflict with an Educational Establishment which can brook no interference in its performance (or rather the bungling) of their sacred trust; nor do these educators believe in sharing power

Charles E. Wilson, New York writer and educator, is now Unit Administrator, Governing Board of the Intermediate School 201 Complex.

with the communities they purport to serve. But this same kind of conflict begins to unmask the society, for it is a deeply racist, voluntary totalitarian society clearly controlled in the area of public services and public welfare by a benevolent but all knowing bureaucracy which acts as agent for an unfeeling power order. A bureaucracy which encourages *talk* of democracy but actually limits the people's participation by the manipulation of issues, by asserting that disagreements are wholly dependent on expert judgment, to which they alone have access, and by steadfastly maintaining their own political power and leverage within the system by avoiding structural and organizational change. The attitudes whether expressed or hidden behind the clichés of the educational bureaucracies have been captured by Jonathan Kozol who wrote in *Death At An Early Age*: "This less than gentle attitude seems characteristic of a less than gentle society, in which the prevailing viewpoint of those who are moderately successful is too likely to be that they have got theirs and the others can damn well wait a while before they get the same."

While the conflict exposes the agents of the ruling order for what they are, the same efforts highlight the world of those struggling against the entrenched order. In the ranks are the knowledgeable side by side with the naive, the dedicated next to the ambitious, the progressive side by side with the paranoid, the revolutionary astride the reactionary, the hard worker shoulder to shoulder with the hustler, the liberal hand in hand with the conservative. To attempt to evaluate a whole people's effort on the basis of the actions of one segment or from one of the individual value systems is to run the risk of misunderstanding the broad scope of the effort. For each of the points of view has both added elements as well as subtracted other factors from the total success.

But whether strong or weak the efforts of the people of the 201 area have been the efforts of a community, the vanguard, the committed ones, the emerging leadership as well as the followers, to achieve a better, more just order for themselves and their children.

the system—its secret overlords—and the persistent challenges

A favorite American boast is that its education system rests on a cornerstone of a free public school system. But in an increasing number of urban centers that claim is just another idle slogan. For the systems are not free from deep seated racism; and are in fact seldom "public," that is, responsive to and/or accountable to the local communities if those communities are comprised of blacks and Spanish-speaking people. Even less frequently are these systems able to educate. The systems as they are, are largely irrelevant to or have a negative influence on the learning habits of those whom they seek to teach. More often than not the systems and the people who man them are so insensitive to the fact of their own failure that they are quick to shift the blame for their failure onto the parents. or the neighborhood, or "outside troublemakers." This shift of blame obscures the fact that urban school systems themselves are deteriorating at an accelerated pace. Teachers and administrators seem generally oblivious to the educational disaster about them. Teachers, by unusual self deception or self hypnosis, are convinced that *they* are doing a fine job. It is the *children* who are uneducable. School bureaucracies resist innovation and, to compound the problem in the areas of the so-called disadvantaged, the systems are without the capacity for regeneration. Teachers and administrators, to a great degree, are both tuned out and turned off in order that they might go on with their meaningless routines. They do worry about discipline, however, because they are supposed to "keep the natives quiet."

This is not just a picture for New York City, but more and more often the current pattern of urban school systems. In New York City however, this system has come to be dominated by a professional bureaucracy with the aid of some powerful cohorts. Together they have forged a formidable coalition which has been largely successful in protecting the status quo and in preserving the system against any serious reform of its antiquated structure.

The coalition which has performed so adequately is comprised of *management* (represented by the CSA—Council of Supervisory Associations) and *labor* (the UFT—United Federation of Teachers, which concerns itself with teacher salaries, benefits and privileges) ; *civic groups concerned with schools* (the PEA—Public Education Association and the UPA—United Parents Association) who tend to work within the structure, *and an only mildly critical press*—all the news that fits the print—which cleverly labels and mislabels all serious critics of the status quo as "extremists" and thereby preserves the system. When the whole host of contractors, book publishers, and salesmen who are dependent on the system for a living are added to the coalition, it is then complete and quite formidable.

This dominant ruling coalition has for the most part been preserved from disturbance because the citizens have been focusing their fury on the lay Board of Education which ostensibly sets school policy and on the Superintendent of Schools. The coalition and in particular the entrenched bureaucrats are free to react and carry out that policy in a way that best suits them. One of the prime objectives of this entrenched bureaucracy is to protect the system against structural reform and this the coalition has done in the face of repeated threats.

Faced with growing hostility from the black and Puerto Rican parents, the NYC Board of Education has initiated a number of policy reforms but the dominant educational coalition has worked just as hard to defeat those same policies. Shielded from political interference by their civil service status and tenure laws, the bureaucracy has been free to torpedo plans for busing to relieve overcrowding, mass removal for integration, organization and reorganization of local School Boards.

Yet the repeated failure of these token efforts at reform has not dismayed the system's insistent enemies—the people. Step by step these enemies of bureaucratic totalitarianism have unmasked the various gambits and ploys of the system and now demand community control:

1. control of budget and budget process

2. control of the process and practice of construction and major repair

3. control of personnel practices

4. control of the right to purchase or participate in the purchase of books and supplies

5. control of the right to curriculum reform

6. maintenance of physical integrity of the demonstration districts themselves to insure a fair demonstration project.

The demands have grown out of the experience of the people of the community with the Board of Education and its staff. For the past 10 years the people of the 201 community have been engaged in a running battle with the Educational Establishment and like most struggles, the struggle at 201 has not always gone smoothly.

At times the Board's strategy of ambiguity and vagueness has placed the local community at a disadvantage in the *press.* At times the racism of the current order has pushed the community's response toward paranoia. At other times the sensation-seeking press has exploited the errors of the local groups. At times individuals of the community have not been able to control the rising rage or harness the self-seeking impulses or avoid the self deprecation of their fellows. These practices tend to lower the group's morale. But change is seldom according to plan—seldom going according to Robert's Rules of Order.

The Board of Education has not wished to relinquish power, even when the relinquishing of power was imperative, possible or desirable. The struggle then is not just a struggle of black versus white or local community versus the Board of Education, it is a struggle between an educational bureaucracy versus the forces pushing for educational democracy. That the people of this city have to a large measure been spectators is a clue about the true nature of this kind of educational system. It is a society in which everybody talks about "democracy," then settles down to allow a professional bureaucracy to operate the show as long as their own children or the children of their own particular group can make their way through the maze.

the case for community control

The case for community control rests on and in the schools themselves; in the operation or rather malfunctioning of the schools. In the 201 Complex, that area is an irregular polygon hewn out of the northeast section of East Harlem and an adjacent piece of central Harlem real estate around 127th Street, east of Seventh Avenue. While the majority of the community is black, there is a sizeable Puerto Rican minority (8.1%). The median income level, at $3,700 per annum as well as the median educational achievement level, at 8.1 grades, contribute and conspire to keep the people in the same place that they have always been—at the bottom.

The Complex contains four feeder elementary schools and an intermediate school. Two of the elementary schools have classes running from Pre-K to 4; another Pre-K to 5 and the fourth Pre-K to 6. This creates nightmares for anyone attempting to plan programs for so many different groups entering at different levels. Further, the uneven pattern sets up a huge internal barrier to the achievement of the NYC Board of Education's stated "4-4-4" plan for its schools.

The older schools of the 201 Complex area possess largely antiquated or outdated facilities. Two of the schools, for all practical purposes, lack gymnasiums, real auditoriums and teachers are forced to use classrooms in one school for the teachers lunchroom. One of the older schools, with a student body of 650, reports but one bathroom for boys and one bathroom for girls. The oldest school with the most limited facilities is paradoxically the most crowded. Even the newest school, I.S. 201 itself, the four-year-old windowless showcase, has a number of major defects. Cinderblocks and red tape blocked the air conditioning ducts for most of the school's life. In the old buildings or in the new ones, a traditional pattern of building maintenance is part of the system. A new combined school has been slated to replace the two oldest structures. Yet, in the face of loud protestations about community control and community involvement, new schools have still not been planned and constructed with the involvement of the community and with little involvement of teachers of that area. If the community was not involved, or had to force its way into the process of planning, it goes without saying that active teacher unionists were also not involved. Teachers who for years have questioned how functional certain new items of construction really were, were left *outside the process of developing a new school.*

within school rooms of the I.S. 201 complex area

While adults may argue the pro and cons of community control versus community stewardship (decentralization) the children and teachers of the schools have been part of a growing educational disaster. The 201 Complex Area should show signs of classroom difficulty because at the first and second line of supervision the district has been virtually stripped of the kind of creative, able, energetic leadership that is needed. Applicants from civil service tests have proven an uninspired lot who mouth platitudes to disguise questionable attitudes or who are interested in the "children" for purposes of research subjects. For the entire District 4, (Harlem) in 1966, 4 out of 10 students (44%) were reading two or more years below grade level. Superficial observation would suggest that since no coordinated organized efforts have been attempted, remedies should not be expected.

In a community of so-called disadvantaged students and a school population of 2,900 to 3,400 students, there are no health counselors, no classes for visually handicapped children, and but one class for the intellectually gifted—on the intermediate school level. In that vast area there is but one evening adult center.

Educational experiments in progress are as scarce as hens' teeth—two classes of pre-primary, CRMD (Children with Retarded Mental Development) and the project for the Institute for Developmental Studies. The full complement of students in the five schools in the special programs number less than 400, or fewer than one pupil in seven. Thus, the very children whom all the educators claim they feel "so sorry for" are in fact the ones for whom the educators, of the old order, do so little for.

The teacher situation is just as bleak as that of their charges and their supervisors. Of the 216 teachers within the five schools, 95 are permanent substitutes. In the intermediate school, I.S. 201, there are twice the number of substitute teachers as there are regularly licensed teachers. Within the entire complex there are but ten student teachers.

The inconsistent attitude of the Board of Education toward teachers compounds the problems faced. In the case of one teacher, in one of the schools of the district, this inconsistency breeds considerable strife. After securing permission from the parents, the teacher escorted his class to the Malcolm X Memorial meeting at I.S. 201. The teacher has maintained that he did not receive notice that his class would be denied permission until after his return. After a brief hearing, the teacher lost his substitute teacher's license for six months. Yet the same rigid Board of Education procedures which revoked this individual's license for this offense did not threaten the license of several individuals who are so unfit for substitute work that schools refuse to call them for available substitute jobs. The same Board of Education which revoked this license acknowledges that it has a difficult time dealing with teachers who lack the capacity for service so long as they are not insubordinate, or do not refuse to follow specific directives.

As a result of and partly as a by-product of the long term educational chaos, bureaucratic ineptitude, non-supervision, one school of the Complex is now almost completely immobilized educationally. Torn internally by strife, confronted externally by community hostility, students and teachers struggle through each day with neither plan nor a real hope for a better day. Teachers say they want to teach, students say they want to learn, parents say they want only the best for their children. No group is gaining what it wants, and each group uses the other as a scapegoat. All groups are being literally destroyed by the same decadent system which is incapable of reform from within and resists reform from without. This is not a question of the good teacher/bad teacher mythology, or the disadvantaged-child fiction, but an accurate picture of a self-serving system which is so unworkable that it commits unnumbered murders each and every day under the heading of "public education."

an important choice—decentralization versus community control

Those of us who have lived and struggled within the so-called "decentralized demonstration districts," who have taken those first few steps under so much active harassment, recognize that decentralization alone cannot and will not produce the quality education for the children of this or any other city. Left to its own devices and the limited resources, the "decentralized district" as conceived by the present educational establishment, will show a tendency to provide the same old tired unappetizing type of education children now endure.

Decentralization is simply not enough. Not enough because the public educational system's deterioration is too widespread, its cancers and malpractices run far too deep and are too well protected by various special interest groups. Because the present order denies its diseases, it cannot be cured.

The people of the 201 Demonstration District have learned that this city's educational system must encompass what America can be—a democratic, truly representative society of the people, by the people and for the people. This city and many cities require an education system which lives what it teaches and practices what it preaches. To achieve this the system must make a 180 degree turn.

Thus community control is the next step that must be taken. It is a second step, but an important step that other parts of this city and many other cities should and must consider if public education is ever to be revitalized. It is a step towards democratizing and revolutionizing one of this society's basic institutions, the school. And if this task cannot be begun, New York City cannot make a reconnection to learning. Without a reconnection for learning, the belief that America is being transformed into an urban nightmare may be more than belief.

at the crossroads

An unfortunate consequence of the "201" events is the seeming failure of many black people to learn from the struggles. Perhaps it is too much to ask that people immediately understand the importance of those courageous individuals who seek to change a formidable anti-democratic bureaucracy. It is for this reason that in the public eye 201 is actually at the crossroads. The truth is that 201, the schools, the complex, the concept have pointed a way out of the morass in which public education finds itself. 201 should remind black professionals to go to the people—not to be their "leaders," replacing the deposed white leaders, but as helpers, servants and followers.

As a symbol of community struggle 201 stands as a proud beacon. As a symbol of hope 201 stands strong and tall. To black people, to white people, to all in favor of decent education, 201 points out one direction toward human liberation.

ABOUT THE AUTHORS

John Henrik Clarke, editor of this book and Associate Editor of *Freedomways,* has been a resident of Harlem for thirty-one years. He is a well-known poet and short story writer, and teaches African and Afro-American history at Malverne People's College. Mr. Clarke is also Director of the Heritage Program of the HARYOU-ACT Project in Harlem.

Sylvester Leaks (Talking About Harlem) is a newspaperman and fiction writer.

Gilbert Osofsky (Harlem: The Making of a Ghetto) was recently appointed Assistant Professor of History at the Chicago campus of the University of Illinois. He was formerly instructor in the History Department at Hunter College.

Ernest Kaiser (The Literature of Harlem) is on the staff of the Schomburg Collection, New York Public Library.

Eugene C. Holmes (The Legacy of Alain Locke) is Chairman of the Department of Philosophy at Howard University where he served for thirty years, twenty of these with Dr. Locke. At present, under a grant from Howard, he is completing *The Life and Times of Alain Locke.*

Glenn Carrington (The Harlem Renaissance—Personal Memoir) is a psychiatric social worker trained at Howard and Columbia Universities. His hobby is collecting books and other data about Africans and Afro-Americans.

Langston Hughes (My Early Days in Harlem) (The Harlem Riots—1964) has been the poet laureate of his people for over twenty-five years. His first poem to appear in a nationally known publication was *The Negro Speaks of Rivers* which appeared in *Crisis* magazine in 1921.

William R. Dixon (The Music of Harlem) is a musician-composer-painter recently returned from a tour of the Scandinavian countries with the quartet he formerly co-led with tenorist Archie Shepp. He made a series of seven broadcasts commissioned by FM Radio Station WBAI in New York, in which were included many of his original compositions. While in Stockholm, he was commissioned to write an hour-long composition which has since been broadcast in New York and will shortly be recorded with a twelve-piece group on the Savoy label. He is a founder of the United Nations Jazz Society and lectures on the subject of contemporary jazz.

Richard B. Moore (Africa Conscious Harlem) is a lecturer and writer in the field of Afro-American History. He is owner-manager of the Frederick Douglass Book Store in New York and founder of "The Committee to Present The Truth About the Name Negro."

E. U. Essien-Udom (The Nationalist Movements of Harlem) is the author of "Black Nationalism: The Search for An Identity in America." Early last year, he returned to his country, Nigeria, and is presently a teacher in Western Nigeria.

Hope R. Stevens (Economic Structure of the Harlem Community) has been associated with progressive efforts to improve the Harlem community for over twenty-five years. He was formerly President of the United Mutual Life Insurance Company. He is now a member of the Board, The Mortgage Facilities Corporation and President, Viaduct Realty Corporation.

James Baldwin (A Conversation with James Baldwin) is considered one of the most remarkable writers and social thinkers of our time. His latest book, "Fire Next Time" is presently a national best seller.

Paul Zuber (Parties and Politics in Harlem) is a nationally known civil rights attorney. He was educated in New York City Public Schools, Brown University and Brooklyn Law School.

Gertrude Elise Ayer (Notes On My Native Sons) is one of Harlem's most distinguished residents. She was born in 1884, long before Harlem became a Negro community. She was educated in the public schools of New York City, Columbia and New York Universities. Her father, Dr. Peter A. Johnson, was the third Negro physician to practice in New York City. Her diversity of work experience include: elementary schools, 1901-1911, guidance of Negro girls in Manhattan Trade School, organizer of Negro laundry workers with Rose Schneiderman of the Women's Trade Union League. She was an Assistant Principal for ten years and Principal for eighteen years.

Loften Mitchell (The Negro Theatre and the Harlem Community) has engaged in research relating to the History of the Negro in the American Theatre for a number of years. Of his many plays, "A Land Beyond The River" is the best known. His new play, "Star of the Morning" is about the life and career of Bert Williams.

Jim Williams (The Need for a Harlem Theatre) is a poet and actor who earns his living as a beverage salesman. He has appeared in productions of "Othello," "Land Beyond the River" and "The Emperor of Haiti."

John A. Williams (Harlem Nightclub) grew up in Syracuse in upstate New York. He attended public school in Syracuse, and after war service with the Navy continued his education under the G. I. Bill of Rights. He is a graduate of Syracuse University. He is the author of six books; the best known are his novels *Night Song* and *Sissie*.

Sterling Brown (Three Poems) is Professor of English at Howard University. His works include "Southern Road," "The Negro in American Fiction," and "The Negro in Poetry and Drama."

Dr. Milton A. Galamison (Bedford-Stuyvesant—Land of Superlatives) is Pastor of Siloam Presbyterian Church, Brooklyn. He is also President of The Parents' Workshop for Equality in the New York City Schools.

George F. Brown (A House Is Not Always a Home) is the New York Editor of the *Pittsburgh Courier.* He has also worked on other newspapers and magazines and as a free lance writer.

Jean Blackwell Hutson (The Schomburg Collection) is the Curator of the Schomburg Collection and supporter of efforts to improve the Harlem Community for many years. She is also President of the Ira Aldridge Society.

Kenneth B. Clark (HARYOU—An Experiment) is Professor of Psychology at City College, New York and has been Research Director of the Northside Center for Child Development since 1946. His book, "Prejudice in Your Child" is considered a standard work on the subject of prejudice in children.

Drawings by *Elton Fax* and *Tom Feelings,* well-known New York artists.

The photographs of Harlem scenes are by *John Taylor* and *Alvin Simon.* Mr. Taylor was an Art Education major at A.M. and N. College, Pine Bluff, Arkansas who became interested in photography while in the Army. Mr. Simon attended Queens College and studied photography with Harold Feinstein of the University of Pennsylvania and with Eugene Smith, formerly of *Life* magazine.

Charles E. Wilson (Lessons of the 201 Complex in Harlem), social worker and freelance writer, received a Masters Degree in Psychology and has studied Public Administration. His articles have appeared in *Liberator Magazine, Negro Digest, Liberation, Jewish Currents, Freedomways* and other publications. Presently he is the Unit Administrator of the I.S. 201 school complex in Harlem.

Brumsic Brandon, Jr. (Readin' 'Ritin' 'Rithmetic Racism) is currently employed as a designer and animator in a New York movie studio. His cartoons appear frequently in *Freedomways* and other publications. He is the author of the book, *Some of My Best Friends.*